VOL. 2 OIL PAINTING LESSONS with REMBRANDT and 'CALCITE SUN OIL':
Includes
The CSO WORKSHOP GUIDE BOOK

by
Louis R. Velasquez
copyright 2017 Louis R. Velasquez , all rights reserved
Published in the USA

2017 Edition

COPYRIGHT NOTICE

VOL. 2 OIL PAINTING LESSONS WITH REMBRANDT AND CALCITE SUN OIL:
Includes The CSO WORKSHOP GUIDE BOOK

Previously published in 2016 as :
SAFE OIL PAINTING WITHOUT SOLVENTS AND HAZARDOUS
MATERIALS - REMBRANDT'S MIRACLE METHOD TODAY:
Vol. 2 - 'Oil Painting Lessons with Rembrandt and 'Calcite Sun Oil'

INTRODUCTION

Welcome,

This book Vol.2, published in 2017, does NOT replace Volume 1, titled:
'Oil Painting lessons with Rembrandt and 'Calcite Sun Oil (Pub. 2012).

This book [Vol. 2] and its companion [Vol. 1],are dedicated to teaching safe non-hazardous methods, materials and procedures to today's artists. Some previously published topics from Volume One, are included but with additional clarification. I encourage artists to thoroughly read Volume One to gain a firm foundation of the CSO/ Emulsions method of oil painting.

The 'Calcite Sun Oil / Emulsions Method ' of oil painting is firmly established in many countries of the World and has proven that today's artists can achieve the marvelous paint effects we see in the Masterpieces of the greatest Old Masters.

The Old Masters, worked from the 1300's to the 1700's, and varied in their methods and materials. Many of their materials were toxic – just as are many of our modern art materials still sold today in Art stores. One must be careful to purchase only safe materials.

Modern technology has had an impact on the quality of the materials available to us. Much of this was not available to the Old Masters and there is the constant need for us to adapt and grow.
I do not know all there is to know about that 'miracle oil', used by the greatest Old Masters.
The knowledge I gained over the years was initially for my understanding - and then it became my mission to share it.

As years pass, others will expand on the knowledge I have published, and I trust my books and DVDS will guide them. It is my hope this book will be of help to those artists who also want to research further, and by sharing their knowledge, will be helping others.

Thank you,
Louis R. Velasquez
San Diego, California, USA
2017

DEDICATION
To all artists and art educators,
who use and inspire others to
use non-hazardous archival materials
and procedures in Fine Art Painting

ACKNOWLEDGEMENTS

I believe the main foundation and most important aspect of the Oil Painting Medium has always been the Superior Oil of the Old Masters, but, it must be used in conjunction with the Emulsions.
Since early 2000, my research has sought ways to produce that Superior oil easily and safely at home. I am proud to say that goal was achieved but I did not accomplish it by myself.
It was a team effort with friends in various countries.

I acknowledge the following persons as having inspired me with their intellectual support, their own oil tests, and ideas that allow us all to benefit.

Francisco Pacheco (1649), The teacher of Spain's great painter Diego Velazquez
Maurice Gerson of the USA, For his support over the years
Rene Benvenutti of Puerto Rico, For his dedication to Safe oil painting
Skyla and Michael Tennyson of Canada, for their undying support and intellectual stimulation
Mary J. Brewster of the USA, for her brilliant mind and intuitive gift of painting
Daniel Tavenier of The Netherlands, for his creative ideas and teaching of CSO in the Land of Rembrandt
Frederic Taubes [1900 Poland-1981 USA] my Oil Painting guide since 1957
Peter Lankas, for enthusiastically teaching CSO in Australia
Mohamed Tawfik of Egypt, for his innovative ideas

SPECIAL APPRECIATION

Leandro Cassiano is my Internet friend, who over many years continued to inspire me with his dedication to learning all he could about the Superior Oil of the Old Masters. An emigrant from Brazil to Norway, he is a Fine artist and Teacher besides being a capable dedicated researcher. In 2015 the Norwegian Government granted him special recognition for Cultural enrichment, for the work he has done to advance the knowledge of the Superior Oil of the Old Masters for today's artists and for future generations.

Ernst Van De Wetering
This highly honored scholar is the current head of the famous REMBRANDT RESEARCH PROJECT of The Netherlands. I met him in person after a lecture he gave on Rembrandt, at the Los Angeles Getty Museum on October 27, 2011.
I walked up to him and said, *"MY NAME is Louis Velasquez, I'd like to shake your hand."*
He instantly smiled broadly and his face lit up as he said,
"OHHH, THE MAN OF THE BINDING MEDIUM!" We shook hands briskly and briefly spoke.
It was an honor to have met him and I am happy he knows about 'CALCITE SUN OIL".

I am grateful for the assistance and support of all my friends.
 Thank you,

- Louis R. Velasquez
San Diego, California USA, 2017

TABLE OF CONTENTS

CHAPTER ONE : LETTERS FROM ARTISTS
Questions and answers to artist's letters from around the globe.

CHAPTER TWO: ESSAYS ON OLD AND MODERN MASTERS
The working methods of some Old Masters are an inspiration for contemporary artists.

CHAPTER THREE: NEW UPDATES, DEVELOPMENTS AND DISCOVERIES
Important advancements and developments, to the CSO Method.

CHAPTER FOUR: ESSAYS ON VARIOUS TOPICS
Various topics that may inspire today's artists.

CHAPTER FIVE: REVIEW OF FREQUENT PROCEDURES
Repeating certain procedures that are important to observe

CHAPTER SIX: WEBSITE DATA FOR FUTURE ARTISTS
A summary of information from my website

SPECIAL ADDITION: The CSO WORKSHOP GUIDE BOOK

TABLE OF CONTENTS [DETAILED]

CHAPTER ONE: Letters from artists -p.10
The three CSO methods of removing the mucilage -p.10
The discovery of Psyllium husk p.11
Modern boiled oil vs the Old Masters Superior oil -p.12
Thixotropy p.15
Canadian Balsam p.16
Did Rubens use Mastic? P.18
Difficulty in rubbing the Emulsion p.20
The CSO Emulsions p.22
CSO Espeso p.23
Glair and Emulsions p.24
Liquidity of Oil Paint p.25
Modern Drip painting effects p.26
Alla Prima painting p.28
Varnishing an oil painting p.31
Archival painting p.31
Tubing oil paint p.33
Iodine number of the oil p.33
The yellow myth p.36

Sealing the support p.36
Spotty drying p.40
Heat lamps to thicken the oil p.41
Processing the oil p.42
Milk Oil Paint Milk Oil Paint- questions p.42 - 44
Jane Morris Pack- Ancient Greek Art material p.47
Chris Aerfeldt – Poetic painting p.48
Hand grinding oil paint p.49
Emulsions – a letter from Australia p.50
Safe oil painting – a letter of gratitude p.52
Testament on CSO p.52
Questions and kindness from England p.53
Hedda's Box The easy way to thicken the oil P.57 Mike's Air Stone p.60

CHAPTER TWO: Essays on Old and Modern Masters p.63
David Hockney p.63
Projection tools of the Old Masters p.65
Lenses and mirrors for tracing images p.67
Vermeer's crude optic tools p.71
Vermeer's methods p.72
Hals and Velazquez- Portrait painters p.73
Hals' face tracing method p.75
Velazquez- Las Meninas p.76
Velazquez- Portrait of the King p.76
Vermeer and the color Blue [2 parts] p.80-81
The Old Masters' Brown color p.83
Color of shadows p.84
The French Impressionists and Blue p.85
Low cost modern synthetic Blue p.85
Paul Cezanne p.86
John Singer Sargent p.86
Titian- Living glazes p.87
Rubens- Thixotropy p.87
Rubens- Varnish and Medium p.89
Modern Artists – Jean Michel Basquiat and Mark Rothko p.89
Clause Monet's cataracts p.95

CHAPTER THREE: New CSO updates, Developments and Discoveries p.97
Three CSO mucilage removal methods p.97
Thickening the oil p.107
The Thickened Emulsion Oil Paint p.109
Blue colored CSO p.112
Comparing CSO Espeso and CSO paint p.115
The math behind Pacheco's oil cleansing p.116
Cas Van Der Sluijs – New experiments in oil p.117
   extended experiment on the oil
Do not refrigerate Emulsions p.125
Cracking of CSO Egg Tempera p.125
Correction- Error in book p.126   - CSO Egg Gesso p.126

CHAPTER FOUR: Essays on various topics p.128
The movie, Tim's Vermeer p.128
False Vermeer methods p.131
Mona Lisa's hands p.134
The scientific experiment of Tim's Vermeer p.135
Anthony Van Lowenhoeck and the Microscope p.136
False Rembrandt theory p.136
How Rembrandt painted his self-portraits p.137
Poetic lighting p.138
Poetry and Painting p.139
A letter Van Gogh wrote p.139
Peter Brueghel and Design p.140
Creative Imagination p.141
A Book review on The Old Masters p.142
History of the Air Pump p.146
Polymer Sodium Polyacrylate powder p.147
Flow chart on oil pressing p.148   Vermeer's Mirror Reflection Paintings p.149

CHAPTER FIVE: Review of frequent procedures p.153
Basic CSO procedures p.153
CSO Emulsions p.154
CSO Oil out procedure p.155
Hide glue p.155
Making oil paintings dry faster p.156
Importance of Egg Glair p.157

CHAPTER SIX: Website data for future artists p.158
Benefits of CSO/Emulsions p.158
Superior oil of the Old Masters p.158
Labeling Flax – Linseed oil p.159
David Hockney's book- Secret Knowledge p.160
Paint studies of Rembrandt and Velazquez p.160
Emulsions- The Wonder medium p.161
The three objectives of CSO p.161
A history of CSO p.162
Academic Terminology p.164
French chalk p.165
The term- Oil Out p.166
Archival oil painting p.166
Emulsions p.167
A warning on the oil p.167
Frank Covino- a modern teacher and Realist artist p.168
CSO Egg Tempera p.168
Milk Oil Paint p.170

CSO Egg Tempera p.170
CSO Egg Gesso p.171
Cave paintings p.173
The Van Eyck Secret medium p.174
Vasari on Van Eyck p.174
Thin oil vs Thick oil p.178
The Magic of Psyllium Husk p.178
The traditional Old Masters' method to sun thicken the oil p.178

SPECIAL ADDITION:
THE CSO WORKSHOP GUIDEBOOK p.182
This book has its own Table of Contents

CHAPTER ONE

LETTERS FROM ARTISTS

I am grateful for the many letters I have received over the years from extraordinary artists around the world. Their letters have stimulated my thinking, resulting many times, in new directions I investigated. After creating the CSO Oil Painting method, and publishing CSO books and DVD'S, many of the letters asked for a clarification of certain topics.

In this Chapter, I include some of the most frequent inquiries. I have removed their names and edited their exact words [with exceptions]. You will note that sometimes I write in uppercase letters, and other times in lower case letters. Use of the uppercase letters is for practical reasons, and does not mean I am shouting. The artist's original questions were written in lowercase letters, and sometimes I would respond with the uppercase letters so we could both determine who was commenting. I always respond to every letter with personal comments via Email.

LETTER #1: THE CSO METHODS TO REMOVE THE MUCILAGE
The question: Which of the CSO methods is best to cleanse the oil of mucilage?

MY RESPONSE; I BELIEVE THE "CSO PSYLLIUM HUSK- ALCOHOL METHOD", THAT I CREATED BASED ON FRANCISCO PACHECO'S OLD MASTERS METHOD MUST BE CONSIDERED TO BE THE VERY BEST.

REASON NUMBER ONE:
FRANCISCO PACHECO'S METHOD FROM 1649 USED THE HOT DRY SUMMER SUN --- TO CLEANSE—AND TO THICKEN HIS OIL. -HIS OIL WAS VISCOUS AND BLEACHED. WE KNOW THAT OIL PAINT MADE WITH THICK VISCOUS POLYMERIZED OIL DRIES HARDER THAN OIL PAINT MADE WITH THIN NON-POLYMERIZED OIL.

REASON NUMBER TWO:
PACHECOS OIL STOOD OUT IN EXTREMELY HOT DRY SUMMER SUN OF SEVILLE, SPAIN. THE UV RAYS AND THE HIGH HEAT IMPACTED THE POLYMERIZATION AND BLEACHING OF THE OIL, EVAPORATING ANY MOISTURE IN THE OIL.

REASON NUMBER THREE:
PACHECO'S HOT SUMMER ENVIRONMENT ALLOWED THE OIL TO BE EXPOSED FOR AS MANY DAYS AS HE WISHED TO HOT DRY DIRECT SUN RAYS.

REASON NUMBER FOUR:
VELAZQUEZ 350 YEAR OLD OIL PAINTINGS ARE PROOF OF THE LASTING QUALITY OF PACHECO'S OIL

COMMENT:
THE ADVANTAGE OF USING THE MODERN AIR PUMP IS FOR CONVENIENCE.
--PACHECO SAID IN HIS BOOK, THAT HE LEFT HIS OIL IN THE SUN FOR 15 DAYS .
WE KNOW HOW HOT HIS AREA IN SOUTHERN SPAIN WAS.

TODAY, MANY ARTISTS LIVE IN COLD REGIONS WITH SHORT SUMMERS AND COOL SUMMERS—LACKING THE HIGH HEAT PACHECO HAD.
FOR THESE ARTISTS, THE AIR PUMP [WITH HEAT LAMPS] CAN BE USED THE YEAR AROUND. THE AIR PUMP OIL DOES NOT GET AS VISCOUS AS DOES PACHECO'S OIL, BUT IT CERTAINLY WILL DRY JUST AS FAST. - BLEACHING OF THE OIL CAN BE ADEQUATELY ACHIEVED EVEN IN NORTHERN COLD AREAS BY PLACING THE OIL IN THIN TALL JARS AND STORED IN WINDOWS THAT HAVE SUNLIGHT.- EVEN INDIRECT SUN RAYS WILL BLEACH THE OIL, THO LONGER PERIODS OF TIME ARE REQUIRED.

LETTER # 2: PSYLLIUM HUSK
A writer asked how I discovered the use of Psyllium husk for the removal of the mucilage from the unrefined flax seed oil.
(NOTE: *linseed oil is pressed from flax seeds*, **there are NO ' Lin' seeds in nature.**

MY RESPONSE
Prior to my discovery of using Psyllium husk, there was no mention in any ancient treatise, nor in any modern book, text or public source of information of psyllium husk as an ingredient to remove the mucilage from the unrefined flaxseed-linseed oil.
Psyllium husk for this purpose was completely unknown to all the Old Masters and to all subsequent historical theorists, artists, conservators and writers, including those of today.

My CSO mucilage removal recipe is based on the 17th century recipe of Francisco Pacheco who was Velazquez' teacher for six years. Pacheco did not know anything about psyllium husk.
His recipe used dried lavender flower buds combined with a powerful alcoholic liquor of 87 % ethanol and 13 % water. This strong liquor extracted the spike solvent from the lavender flower buds. After Pacheco strained the mixture to remove the flower buds, the "spike solvent" remained in the oil. Please note that "Spike oil' is not an "oil" ... it is an evaporative solvent.

In my search for "non solvent oil painting" I needed to eliminate the lavender flower buds, but I had no answer at that time.

THEN THE UNPREDICTABLE HAPPENED
At my age, I was having digestion irregularity issues. My doctor recommended I drink a high fiber 'Brand Name' laxative for this irregularity. The contents label identified it is pure Psyllium Husk with some sugar and flavoring added.

I saw that one teaspoon in an 8 ounce glass of water quickly expands to four times its size because it absorbs water. This gave me the idea to test it as a "mucilage remover" because mucilage, although a complex ingredient of oleaginous and aqueous ingredients, is basically comprised of water! To our benefit, my tests proved to be effective!

The CSO METHOD of combining liquor with psyllium husk is superior to Pacheco's method because his method leaves a small amount of water in the oil as well as a solvent.
The CSO METHOD using psyllium husk removes ALL the water and adds no solvent.

LETTER #3: MODERN BOILED 'STAND" LINSEED OIL vs THE SUPERIOR OIL OF THE OLD MASTERS –
and SEVERAL RELATED QUESTIONS
The artist's words are in lower case. My responses are in upper case letters.

QUESTION: Some of my friends prime their canvases with chalk ground mixed with boiled linseed oil.

RESPONSE: BOILED LINSEED OIL IS DECOMPOSED LINSEED OIL BECAUSE.
TO BOIL THE OIL IT NEEDS TO GET HEATED TO 343 CELSIUS.
SCIENCE SAYS THE OIL BEGINS DECOMPOSITION AT 230 CELSIUS.
ALSO....'INDUSTRIAL' BOILED LINSEED OIL AT TIMES CONTAINS METALLIC DRIERS AND THIS OIL CAUSES THE OIL PAINTS TO BECOME BRITTLE, YELLOW AND DARKER OVER TIME ...BUT NOT IN YOUR LIFETIME.

ALSO, NO MATTER WHAT YOU MIX WITH CHALK....THE CHALK REMAINS ABSORBENT.- THE OLD MASTERS TAUGHT US THEIR KNOWLEDGE ...GAINED FROM CENTURIES OF PRACTICE AND STUDIO KNOWLEDGE...THE ENTIRE REASON FOR FIRST...SEALING THE WOOD OR THE CANVAS WITH SEVERAL COATS OF HIDE GLUE ...WAS SO THE OIL...WOULD NOT GET ABSORBED BY THE WOOD OR CANVAS..BECAUSE AS THE OIL AGES, IT BECOMES ACIDIC....THIS ACIDITY WOULD ADVERSELY IMPACT [rot] THE RAW WOOD AND/ OR RAW CANVAS.

Their canvas surface is a beautiful semitransparent warm beige color similar to the sandstone buildings in Paris.
IF THE CANVAS IS OF LINEN THEN BEIGE IS THE BASE COLOR...THE CHALK MIXED WITH OIL IS 98% TRANSPARENT. SO YES, THEIR CANVAS IS A BEAUTIFUL COLOR. BUT THAT BOILED OIL WILL SEEP INTO IT AND THAT UNPROTECTED CANVAS WILL DARKEN IN TIME BY THE ACID OF THE OIL...IF THE CANVAS IS NOT FIRST 100% SEALED WITH THE HIDE GLUE.

Could I make the same kind of priming just substituting the boiled linseed oil with cold pressed and cleansed, but not sun bleached oil (maybe air pump blown)?
FOR PROPER ARCHIVAL TECHNICAL PROCEDURE, YOU MUST FIRST SEAL THE RAW WOOD OR RAW CANVAS. -APPLY 2 LIBERAL WELL SOAKED COATS OF HIDE GLUE MADE WITH THIS RATIO: The ratio is 1 vol. Ounce of dry glue granules and 10 fluid ounces of water. [Disregard those manufacturers who give a recipe of 1 vol. ounce of glue granules with 23 fluid ounces of water- I have tested that recipe and it fails to seal the raw wood or canvas] HEAT THE DRY GLUE AND WATER IN IN A DOUBLE BOILER [or one heat resistant glass jar in a second pot of water] UNTIL THE GLUE DISSOLVES, STIRRING ALL THE WHILE. - THE WATER IN THE SECOND POT WILL BOIL BUT TAKE CAUTION NOT TO BOIL THE GLUE.
[OR , ONE CAN DO THIS: APPLY ONE LIBERAL COAT OF ACRYLIC VARNISH, EITHER MATTE OR GLOSS.]
THE FINAL HIDE GLUE COAT MUST BE A THIN LAYER.- REMOVE ALL EXCESS AS SOON AS THE SUPPORT ABSORBS THE LIQUID. - THIN LAYERS OF GLUE REMAIN FLEXIBLE. AND THICK LAYERS DO NOT.

YOU CAN DUPLICATE YOUR FRIENDS METHOD, BUT USE A SUPERIOR OIL. FIRST SEAL THE CANVAS WITH TWO COATS OF HIDE GLUE AND DO NOT ADD CHALK.- ONCE THAT DRIES, THEN MIX CHALK WITH THE FASTER DRYING THICKENED POLYMERIZED FLAX OIL...DO NOT USE THE THIN UNTHICKENED OIL (it dries too slow) . ALSO, ADD A TINY AMOUNT OF DRY UMBER PIGMENT TO ACCELERATE THE DRYING, AND TO COLOR THE OIL. THIS MIXTURE WILL BE TRANSLUCENT AND THE BEIGE COLOR OF THE CANVASCAN BE STILL SEEN. THERE IS NO REQUIREMENT TO APPLY GESSO. ... IF YOU DO WISH TO APPLY A COAT OF WHITE GESSO , USE A SPATULA TO APPLY A THIN COAT OF GESSO, SCRAPING IT WELL INTO THE WEAVE OF THE CANVAS. – (on wood panel, you can apply a continuous film or several films of gesso. use a wide flat brush to apply a thin layer) ..BECAUSE THIS FILM CONTAINS CHALK IT WILL STILL BE ABSORBENT.
NOW, YOU CAN DO ONE OF TWO THINGS. [1] APPLY A COAT OF SUN THICK OIL AND LET IT DRY BEFORE OIL PAINTING, OR, [2] YOU CAN APPLY AN " OIL OUT" WITH ONE OF THE GLAIR-OIL EMULSIONS. LET IT SOAK INTO THE ABSORBENT GESSO. YOU DO NOT HAVE TO LET THE FRESH 'OIL OUT' DRY. YOU CAN NOW PAINT WITH OIL PAINTS.

BEFORE PAINTING ADDITIONAL LAYERS OF OIL PAINTS, APPLY AN 'OIL OUT' BEFORE EACH NEW PAINT LAYER [touch dry].. AND WHEN THE FINISHED PAINTING DRIES, YOU CAN APPLY A FINAL "OIL OUT" , AS THE FINISHED FINAL COAT.

YOU CAN "OIL OUT" WITH EITHER OF THE EMULSIONS OR THE AGUADO. FOLLOW THE INSTRUCTIONS IN THE BOOK OR THE DVD. IF YOU APPLY A FINISH COAT ON YOUR FINISHED PAINTING LIKE THIS, THERE IS NO NEED TO APPLY A RESIN VARNISH ON THE COMPLETED PAINTING. IF SUBSEQUENTLY, DRY SPOTS APPEAR, YOU CAN APPLY ANOTHER 'OIL OUT'. RUB IT IN SO IT IS AN ULTRA THIN FILM.WIPE IT WITH A CLEAN CLOTH TO REMOVE ALL EXCESS EMULSION.

My friends priming method seems to be a faster priming compared with hide glue gesso that has to be sealed in addition.
THE METHOD YOUR FRIENDS USE IS NOT FASTER. THE REASON A HIDE GLUE GESSO WAS APPLIED -BY MANY MASTERS - ON THE HIDE GLUE SEALED CANVAS OR WOOD...WAS BECAUSE THE ENTIRE PREPARATION CAN BE DONE IN A MATTER OF HOURS. RAPID DRYING IS DEPENDENT ON A FEW FACTORS SUCH AS MOVING AIR VENTILATION AND HOT DRY AIR.

HERE IS A ONE DAY GESSO PRIMING EXAMPLE:
FIRST STEP: 2 coats hide glue- GLUE ONLY. This dries in two hours.
SECOND STEP: 1 coat of Gesso made of chalk and hide glue. This dries in one hour.
THIRD STEP: 1 coat of hide glue to seal the gesso. This dries in one hour
FOURTH STEP: Apply an 'oil out' [oil paint on it immediately- or- wait one day for it to dry].
NOW YOU ARE READY TO PAINT YOUR PICTURE WITH OIL PAINT.
THE GETTY MUSEUM IN LOS ANGELES TECHNICAL STUDY...SHOWS TITIAN USED THIS METHOD THE LARGE CANVAS FROM THE MID 1500'S IS IN PERFECT CONDITION. (Google: THE GETTY PAINTING BY TITIAN: -VENUS AND ADONIS.).

CONTRARY TO THIS...AN OIL PRIMER GROUND...WOULD TAKE SEVERAL DAYS TO SOLIDIFY IF SLOW DRYING NON THICKENED OR INDUSTRIAL THICKENED LINSEED BOILED OIL IS USED ...A DAY OR TWO IS NEEDED DEPENDING ON THE DRYING FACTORS. = MOVING AIR VENTILATION AND HOT DRY AIR.

BY THE WAY : DONT BE FOOLED BY THE MYTH THAT AN OIL PRIMED/ GROUND MUST BE AGED FOR MONTHS BEFORE PAINTING ON IT. IT IS READY TO PAINT ON AS SOON AS IT HAS SOLIDIFIED SUFFICIENTLY SO THAT THE RUBBING OF THE "OIL OUT" DOES NOT LIFT OR SMUDGE THE LAYER. THINK OF THE PRIMER/GROUND LAYER AS JUST ANOTHER LAYER OF PAINT.

The beautiful color of my friends´ priming of course comes from the amber hue of the boiled linseed oil.
THE CHALK-OIL MIXTURE.CAN BE TONED TO ANY DESIRED COLOR.BY ADDING ANY DRY COLORED PIGMENT. IF YOU ADD SOME UMBER THIS ACCELERATES THE DRYING TOO. ALL YOU NEED IS A TINY AMOUNT SO THE MIXTURE REMAINS TRANSLUCENT, THUS, ALLOWING THE COLOR OF THE CANVAS TO BE SEEN..

THE GETTY MUSEUM: TITIAN'S METHODS AND MATERIALS
This book is free to read online.
It tells you how Titian primed / ground his canvas titled: VENUS AND ADONIS, with HIDE GLUE GESSO. I personally examined the original painting visually with a magnifying glass. It is in an excellent state of preservation. Only some glaze colors have faded, and some micro fine cracks are seen in the thick white oil paint impasto areas. This is normal.
This technical study was published by the GETTY Museum in Los Angeles, Ca.
See page 117 in their publication.

http://www.getty.edu/conservation/publications_resources/pdf_publications/pdf/historical_paintings.pdf

LETTER # 4 : THIXOTROPY
The artist asked for a clarification on Thixotropy, which is how wet paint can be painted ON TOP OF WET PAINT, without smearing the lower layer.

RESPONSE: Hello Friend, your letter is very interesting.
In the book by Ernst Van de Wetering , " Rembrandt, the painter at work", the subject of THIXOTROPY is well covered. It's a "must read" because it is explained in detail.
I will briefly discuss the basics of Thixotropic paint here.

THIXOTROPY is the overlaying of wet paint ...on top of... wet paint
without smearing the lower wet layer. It is easy to do, but you must understand how this works.

VELAZQUEZ was able to get two very different visual effects by simply waiting about 6 hours between the first layer and the subsequent layer.
If he wanted blending, smooth and soft.....He did not wait. He just immediately applied more wet paint 'alla prima', on top of the first layer of wet paint.
If he wanted a "soft" dry brush effect...he applied the first layer...waited about six hours...this allowed the first layer to get "tacky"...then...he applied the next layer.

RUBENS had a unique method of achieving MAXIMUM THIXOTROPY.
Rubens mixed a very small amount of VENICE BALSAM with his oil. In RUBENS day...they did not have or know of the word "balsam". In Rubens' day, they called a BALSAM...by the name of TURPENTINE. The ancient name is still with us. Therefore "VENICE TURPENTINE" (still sold today) IS IN FACT "VENICE BALSAM".

Our liquid turpentine of today, in Rubens' day, was called OIL OF TURPENTINE.
We know it is not an oil. It is in fact a solvent that evaporates and has no binding power. To understand Rubens' method of Thixotropic paint, it's important to know that Solvents will easily and quickly evaporate and has absolutely NO binding power. Today, it is believed Rubens' Turpentine was poorly distilled and still contained some balsam, giving it some binding power.

Rubens mixed "solvent turpentine " with balsam...to create a fluid liquid.
Then he mixed a small portion of that with the sun oil...and then mixed that with his oil paint.
Then he painted. But within minutes, the "solvent turpentine" evaporated...
leaving a very sticky tacky oil paint...made of viscous sun oil and sticky balsam.

Within minutes....this layer became almost immovable to brushing, and it was very sticky and tacky. Rubens then immediately painted a new layer on top of it.
Because of the rapid evaporation of the solvent turpentine.... he could overlay many wet paint layers one on top of the other within a couple hours....carefully, without smearing the lower wet layers. By use of this method, Rubens was able to complete a multi layered oil painting within a few hours. Calcium carbonate chalk mixed with oil has been found in Rubens' oil paint.

"CSO" CAN ACHIEVE THIXOTROPY.
BUT YOU MUST WAIT A FEW HOURS IN BETWEEN LAYERS.
IT IS NOT AS QUICK OR EFFECTIVE AS RUBENS USE OF BALSAM MIXTURES,
BUT IT IS GOOD ENOUGH , AND SAFER.
**Remember Rubens' use of "turpentine solvent" is hazardous to your lungs,
and because CSO uses no solvents, it is a fully safe method to use.**

LETTER # 5 : CANADIAN BALSAM

The artist said this: Last year I got a small bottle with a very thick, very clear resin-like solvent called Canada Balsam.

YES. ITS FROM THE AMERICAN CONTINENT. IT NEVER WAS AVAILABLE TO THE EUROPEAN OLD MASTERS.

I have had it for a little while in my studio now, but have never used it. Since I am quite sure this substance somehow is familiar to you, I wanted to ask if you have any practical experience with it, is it a safe, durable material, or does it present the same problems as the other resins do?

WELL, WE DO KNOW THAT RUBENS HAD TWO BALSAMS AVAILABLE TO HIM. ONE WAS VENICE TURPENTINE (yellowish color BALSAM) AND STRASBOURG TURPENTINE (pale clear color BALSAM) - THEY BOTH ARE PURE EXUDATES FROM TWO DIFFERENT PINE TREES...FROM DIFFERENT GEOGRAPHIC AREAS OF WEST EUROPE. -RUBENS ADDED THEM TO HIS OIL PAINT TO CREATE A VERY FAST SETTING PAINT LAYER. THIS ALLOWED HIS THIXOTROPIC PAINT. -IT ALLOWED HIM TO PAINT LAYERS OF WET PAINT ON TOP OF LAYERS OF WET PAINT - WITHOUT SMEARING THE LOWER LAYER.

THE WORD " balsam" IS A MODERN TERM, AND WAS UNKNOWN TO THE OLD MASTERS. THEY CALLED OUR BALSAM ...BY THE NAME " turpentine".

AND WHAT WE CALL TODAY AS " turpentine".... THEY CALLED " oil of turpentine". APPARENTLY THEY DID NOT HAVE THE WORD " BALSAM" IN THEIR VOCABULARY

YEARS AGO I DID TEST CANADIAN BALSAM. IT DRIES EXTRAORDINARILY FAST!!!! AND HAS A BEAUTIFUL CLEAR COLOR.

IS IT SAFE AND DURABLE? YES, IF IT IS MIXED IN A VERY SMALL RATIO WITH OUR SUPERIOR LINSEED FLAX OIL....THATS WHAT RUBENS DID - HE MIXED A BALSAM WITH HIS OIL TO GET THAT THIXOTROPIC EFFECT OF PAINTING WET PAINT OVER WET PAINT, WITHOUT SMEARING THE LOWER WET PAINT LAYER.

I have recently been reading about it, and what makes me very curious is that it is described as having excellent optical qualities - making it almost identical to glass, therefore it has for a long time been used by industry for gluing lenses and producing high quality optical devices.

YES, IVE READ SOMETHING SIMILAR

The Canada balsam has the inconvenience of being a hazardous solvent. ITS EXACTLY LIKE VENICE TURPENTINE AND STRASBOURG TURPENTINE. -BASICALLY IT IS A CRUDE EXUDATE VISCOUS PINE RESIN ....IF THEY DISTILL IT...THEY GET OUR LIQUID MODERN TURPENTINE.

It would be interesting to try a bit of it, especially when <u>"finishing areas with thin, very translucent glazes"</u> ...

CAUTION: DO NOT USE IT FOR THIN FINAL GLAZES AT ALL!!

THE CSO EMULSIONS ...NONE OF THEM...ARE INCORPORATED WITH ANY BALSAM AND NOT ANY SOLVENTS, LIKE TURPENTINE, ETC. THE WHOLE PREMISE OF CSO IS...IT USES NO SOLVENTS.

YOU CAN USE A BALSAM MIXED WITH OIL.....BY HEATNG IT GENTLY... IN A WATER BATH, OR BY PLACING IT OUTSIDE TOGETHER, IN A CLEAR GLASS JAR, IN THE HOT SUN. IT WILL INTEGRATE EITHER WAY BY SHAKING IT.

TRY THIS RATIO: ABOUT 10% BALSAM TO 100 % OIL

IF YOU DO ADD A BALSAM TO YOUR OIL, AND OIL PAINT, USE IT ONLY IN LOWER LAYERS--- THEN WHEN THE PAINTING IS DRY—APPLY A FINAL COAT OF THICKENED FLAX-LINSEED OIL AS THE FINAL COAT - AS RUBENS DID.

IF YOU MIX ANY RESIN BALSAM WITH THE OIL PAINT, AND IF IT IS USED IN THE TOP LAYERS—IT IS EASILY LIFTED BY A TURPENTINE OR ANY SOLVENT CLEANSING AT A LATER DATE.

do you consider it yourself as an unnecessary and unstable ingredient to incorporate it the emulsions?
THERE IS NO NEED TO EVER ADD ANY RESIN TO AN EMULSION. AN EMULSION IS A MIXTURE OF AN AQUEOUS [watery] INGREDIENT MIXED WITH AN OLEAGINOUS [oily] INGREDIENT. ONE INGREDIENT ENTERS THE OTHER DEPENDING ON THE RATIO, ON A MOLECULAR LEVEL. A RESIN NEVER MIXES INTO AN OIL—THEY JUST COMINGLE...LIKE A COLLOID –EVENTUALLY SEPARATING.

LETTER # 6: DID RUBENS USE MASTIC?

QUESTION: Did Rubens use 'Mastic"?
SCIENTIFICALLY MASTIC IS A GUM...NOT A RESIN....AND THOUGH SOME THINK RUBENS MADE A VARNISH FROM MASTIC....I MYSELF DO NOT THINK SO BECAUSE HE HAD NO USE FOR IT, also, GUMS ARE SOLUBLE IN WATER.

MASTIC IS FROM A TREE IN CHIOS, GREECE. I BOUGHT SOME MASTIC FROM A GREEK GROCERY STORE. - THEY TOLD ME IT IS USED IN COOKING AND THAT IT ADDS FLAVORING. THEY ALSO TOLD ME IT CAN BE CHEWED LIKE CHEWING GUM.- I TRIED IT AND IT TASTES GREAT..

IN SPANISH ...THE WORD ..." Masticar" MEANS, TO CHEW.

YET..IN OTHER ANCIENT NORTH EUROPEAN LANGUAGES,
THE WORD " mastic" IS A WORD THAT MEANS " glue".
THIS ARE THE REASONS WHY I DO NOT THINK RUBENS USED " MASTIC" GUM.

RUBENS DID USE PINE RESIN. -PINE RESIN [balsam] OOZES OUT RIGHT FROM THE KNOTS OF THE TREE...- WHEN I WAS A KID I'D CLIMB A PINE TREE AND I'D GET MY HANDS ALL STICKY. -BEING A KID, I HAD NO IDEA WHAT IT WAS,
OTHER THAN "STICKY STUFF" AND IT WAS DIFFICULT TO WASH OFF..

BUT WE KNOW RUBENS DID USE THE SAME CRUDE "STICKY" PINE RESIN a Balsam - he called "Turpentine") AND IT WAS DISTILLED TO CREATE OUR MODERN DAY WATERY THIN TURPENTINE (he called "oil of turpentine") ITS NOT AN OIL –IT'S A SOLVENT THAT EVAPORATES COMPLETELY.
WHEN RUBENS MIXED THOSE TWO WITH HIS OIL...HE CREATED A VERY FAST SETTING MEDIUM. TO CREATE A THIXOTROPIC PAINTING TECHNIQUE.

RUBENS DID NOT USE DAMMAR BECAUSE DAMMAR WAS NOT AVAILABLE TO THE OLD MASTERS. - DAMMAR IS A NEW MODERN INVENTION.

QUESTION: I use only linseed oil, either the Kremmer's one or Old Holland with a layer of oil and glair as a final coat, when finished.
I DO TOO. AND THEN WHEN IT SETS...I APPLY A FINAL COAT OF PURE GLAIR WITHOUT THE OIL ADMIXTURE..
THIS IS NOT RUBBED IN LIKE THE 'OIL/ GLAIR' EMULSION MIXTURE.
I USE A WIDE FLAT BRUSH TO APPLY IT. -IT BECOMES DRY AND HARD WITHIN SECONDS. IT IS WATER SOLUBLE....SO YOU CANNOT APPLY WATER TO IT. TIME , OXYGEN AND HEAT WILL CURE IT . -EVENTUALLY IT WILL BECOME A WATERPROOF COAT.

AS YOU KNOW...FRESHLY HARDENED OIL PAINTINGS REMAIN STICKY FOR A TIME. THE PROBLEM WITH THIS STICKINESS IS THAT FINE DUST CAN STICK TO IT IF NO CARE IS TAKEN. - THE GLAIR COAT PREVENTS DUST FROM ATTACHING TO THE SURFACE.

IVE READ THAT IN 19 th CENTURY FRANCE, (during the realist academic period) IT WAS COMMON TO APPLY A COAT OF GLAIR TO THE PAINTINGS ...IMMEDIATELY BEFORE, BEING EXHIBITED AT THE SALON....TO GIVE THE FINISHED PAINTINGS AN OVERALL SHEEN (versus 'resin varnish' which causes a strong glare shine and paintings not to be seen well).

QUESTION: What I find is the layers are fairly fragile, especially if the gallery is not careful, and they sometimes get scratched.
THAT CONCERNS ME. - WE CAN'T CONTROL THE GALLERIES. MAYBE IN YOUR CASE THE FINAL COAT CAN BE SIMPLY AN ULTRA THIN FILM OF SUN OIL WELL RUBBED IN. ---ONCE HARD… IT CAN BE DELIVERED TO THE GALLERY.-- EVEN THEN, IVE HAD MY VERY DRY OIL PAINTINGS SCRATCHED BY GALLERY ATTENDANTS.

LETTER # 7: DIFFICULTY IN RUBBING THE EMULSION.
The artist wrote to say his Tendinitis made it difficult to 'rub in' the Emulsion. He also said he preferred to paint with the non-viscous thin oil and does not care about slow drying oil paint. He uses sable brushes and other natural hairs that are softer than hog´s bristles. The long drying time is not a problem for him because he likes to paint wet in wet over several days.

He asked these specific questions:
Can I safely use the 'non viscous emulsion' as an 'oil out' on my paintings since it dries much slower? I remember you said in your book that lower layers should dry faster than top layers of paint.

MY RESPONSE:
THANK YOU. I UNDERSTAND. WE ARTISTS ALL HAVE REASONS FOR OUR PERSONAL CHOICES. YES OF COURSE. ONE CAN OIL OUT WITH EITHER THE "VE" or the " NVE"....IN FACT, IN MY BOOK I MAKE THE STATEMENT THAT ARGUABLY, ONE CAN ACHIEVE EVEN FINER MICRO FINE LINES AND DETAILS BY USE OF THE NON VISCOUS OIL EMULSION ...THAN WITH THE VISCOUS EMULSION. -THE DRAWBACK IS THAT THE ..NVE.....DRIES SLOWER...BUT AS YOU SAID...FAST DRYING IS NOT A CONCERN FOR YOU. – THE USE OF SLOW DRYING OIL PAINT IN LOWER LAYERS IS SAFE, IF YOU ALLOW IT TO DRY WELL BEFORE APPLYING NEW LAYERS ON TOP. THE KEY IS TO PAINT SLOWER DRYING COLORS ON TOP - AND PAINT FASTER DRYING COLORS ON BOTTOM LAYERS.

UMBER IS A VERY FAST DRYING COLOR. STUDY YOUR COLORS AND DETERMINE WHICH ARE THE FAST AND THE SLOW DRYING COLORS.

I get tendinitis so is there another way to the hand rubbing in the oil out? Can I use a soft leather dab (like the ones used in intaglio printing) on to an electric polisher/grinder.

TENDINITIS IS PAINFUL. -ONE ARTIST TOLD ME SHE USES A MEDICAL RUBBER GLOVE FOR SAFETY REASONS. IVE NOT TRIED THAT. SHE SAYS IT WORKS. PLEASE LET ME KNOW IF IT DOES. MAKE SURE IT HAS NO TEXTURE OR RIBBING.....IT MUST BE SMOOTH. ..WE CANNOT USE ANYTHING SUCH AS LEATHER, OR RAGS OR OTHER SUBSTANCES, BECAUSE IT WILL ABRAID AND LIFT THE UNDER-LAYERS. THE SOFT SKIN OF THE BARE HUMAN HAND,.IS ABSOLUTELY THE FINEST.

I can't buy 100% non-fat milk here [for MILK OIL PAINT].
SEVERAL ARTISTS IN OTHER COUNTRIES HAVE THAT SAME PROBLEM. OUR USA NON FAT MILK IS 100% FAT FREE. HERE IS WHAT THEY TOLD ME THEY DO. THEY BUY THE DRY POWDERED NON FAT MILK. THEN THEY ADD WATER TO THE DRY NON FAT MILK.....THEN...FOLLOWING MY INSTRUCTIONS ...THEY ADD IT TO THE DRY POWDER ...SLOWLY, TO CREATE THE ...MILK GEL......ONCE THIS IS MADE..IT MIXES VERY EASILY WITH THE TUBE OIL PAINT. ...

JUST DO NOT FORGET...YOU CANNOT APPLY ...MILK OIL PAINT (it is emulsified oil paint) ON TOP OF AN OIL PRIMED SURFACE OR OTHER OIL PAINT LAYERS. IT WILL NOT ADHERE TO OIL. BUT, IT ADHERES TO ALL GESSO PRIMED SURFACES...TRADITIONAL AND OLD MASTER.

ONCE YOU BEGIN TO PAINT WITH TRADITIONAL OIL PAINTS ON TOP OF THE MILK OIL PAINT.......YOU CANNOT PAINT ADDITIONAL LAYERS WITH MILK OIL PAINT ON TOP OF TRADITIONAL OIL PAINTS.

ITS EASY...JUST THINK OF MILK OIL PAINT AS SIMILAR TO ACRYLIC PAINTS. ACRYLIC PANTS CANNOT BE PAINTED ON TOP OF OIL PAINTS...BUT OIL PAINTS CAN BE PAINTED ON TOP OF ACRYLIC PAINTS.

I´m currently painting a portrait and the paint is drying mat on some areas. This portrait is painted only with oil and no solvents. What do you think could be a possible reason?

AS YOU ALREADY KNOW...OIL PAINT IS MADE OF PIGMENTS AND OIL. EACH DRY PIGMENT REQUIRES A CERTAIN AMOUNT OF OIL.SOME MORE THAN OTHERS.

YOU ALSO KNOW THAT WITH OIL PAINTING -USING RESINS, VARNISHES, DRIERS, ETC...ALSO CREATE ...DRY MATTE... AREAS. -THOSE WHO DO USE SOLVETS ENCOUNTER THIS SUNKEN IN EFFECT MORE OFTEN. -THEY USE A.RETOUCH VARNISH....(a simple mix of solvent and dammar resin) TO BRNG OUT THE COLOR DEPTH..

WITH CSO...WE DO NOT USE RETOUCH RESIN VARNISHES. WE APPLY A THIN COAT OF ONE OF THE CSO 'OIL OUT' MEDIUMS TO BRING OUT THE COLOR DEPTH. -ALSO, WE MUST ALWAYS APPLY AN 'OIL OUT' TO A DRY SURFACE BEFORE APPLYING A NEW LAYER. -THE REASONS ARE TO....BRING OUT THE TRUE COLOR AND TO IMPROVE THE ADHESION OF THE NEXT LAYER. -TO INCREASE BLENDING, AND FACILITATE SPREADING OF THE PAINT.
AN 'OIL OUT'...IS A LUBRICANT, AMONGST OTHER THINGS.

TO HELP AVOID THAT SUNKEN IN EFFECT, THERE IS ONE VERY IMPORTANT THING YOU MUST ATTEND TO BEFORE YOU EVER BEGIN TO APPLY OIL PAINT THAT IS THIS: THE SUPPORT SURFACE MUST FIRST BE COMPLETELY 100% SEALED WITH THE HIDE GLUE [or acrylic varnish which is a glue]..

REGARDLESS, WHETHER YOU USE CANVAS OR WOOD PANEL,. THE RAW SURFACE MUST BE FULLY SEALED WITH GLUE. IF YOU DO NOT DO THAT...IT WILL CONTINUE TO SUCK OIL FROM TOP LAYERS OF OIL PAINT, CAUSING THOSE DRY MATTE AREAS.

SADLY...ALL ACRYLIC STORE BOUGHT CANVAS AND PANELS THAT ARE PRIMED WITH MODERN ACRYLIC GESSO, ARE VERY ABSORBENT. SO.THE FIRST STEP IS TO APPLY A LAYER OF ACRYLIC " VARNISH" EITHER MATTE OR GLOSSY AND LET IT DRY.- MILK OIL PAINT WILL ADHERE TO ACRYLIC VARNISH (but not to oil varnish, oil paint, or oil primers) .

I RECOMMEND AN ULTRA-THIN, 'WELL RUBBED IN' COAT OF THE VISCOUS EMULSION AS ...THE FINAL "COATING" FOR A COMPLETED CSO OIL PAINTING.

LETTER # 8 : EMULSIONS
The writer wrote to ask about Emulsions.

MY RESPONSE:
Emulsions vary because they are made of differences of ratios...of chalk and glair.
In my book [Vol.1] I described how changing the ratios, a bit more or a bit less of either one, will change the consistency and the handling of the paint.

If painting with thick impasto oil paint, we must also add a few drops of an Emulsion to the oil paint to avoid wrinkling.

The two original CSO EMULSIONS are:
the VE [viscous emulsion]
and the NVE [non viscous emulsion]
Later I created the ESPESO emulsion which is made by adding some chalk to either of the two emulsions.

A recent Emulsion I developed is called, the THICKENED EMULSION.
The GLAIR is thickened by letting it stand exposed to air for a couple of days.
Then, by combining thickened oil and thickened glair, a 'thickened emulsion' is created.

By adding dry chalk to the thickened emulsion, a **THICK EMULSION PASTE** is created.

The **THICK EMULSION PASTE** is then mixed with tube oil paints- or with dry pigments. This new oil paint is called **THICKENED EMULSION OIL PAINT**

Each color of tube oil paint reacts differently.
Each tube color requires a different amount to be mixed with it. When it is mixed with Titanium white, the paint becomes very fluid. If it is too fluid, I mix some additional dry chalk to make it thicker. It can be mixed with the tube oil paint right on the palette…as you paint.

THE DIFFERENCES AS COMPARED WITH ESPESO.
This THICKENED EMULSION OIL PAINT remains wet on the palette for two days.
This is much longer than the drying rate of the original CSO PAINT, which becomes dry or tacky dry by the next day. Also, the Thickened Emulsion Oil Paint is more fluid as you paint.

Before beginning to paint on a dry surface, it is important to apply an **ultra thin film** 'oil out' of the VISCOUS EMULSION. The "oil out" is a lubricant and it insures adhesion of the new paint layer. CHAPTER THREE has more information on this new paint.

LETTER # 9 : ESPESO
The writer asked: What are the benefits of using ESPESO?

MY RESPONSE: As you know, ESPESO is simply the Viscous Emulsion that is mixed with additional amounts of dry chalk. There is no general ratio. You simply mix chalk into the Emulsion. If it is too liquid, you thicken it by adding and grinding more dry chalk. My book has the general ratio mixtures. You can adjust the ratio if you wish. ESPESO offers painters a bit of magic. I created it after I completed my research study of RUBENS' methods and materials.
A REMINDER::
CSO OIL PAINT (CSO mixed with tube paint) If mixed with one drop of the emulsion...the CSO oil paint stiffens. If you add several more drops....the oil paint thins and becomes more fluid ALSO, BY ADDING MORE DRY CHALK...the consistency of the paint thickens.

LETTER # 10 : THE IMPORTANCE OF GLAIR AND EMULSIONS

This letter was from an artist who complained his Emulsions dried weak and easily lifted with a fingernail. In my 15 years of CSO/EMULSIONS work, and hundreds of letters from artists, **I've never had this complaint before**. Even though my original book gives complete instructions, I thought to repeat the information on making the emulsions because the CSO EMULSIONS are fully archival and – I believe- one half of the Van Eyck Secret Medium.

MY RESPONSE
The correct use of EMULSIONS is of paramount importance.

1. Do not use packaged, powdered dried egg whites. Do not use egg whites that are sold in ready to use liquid form and refrigerated. These have been STERILIZED in conformity with health laws.

2. You must use a fresh chicken egg. The fresher, the better. Some sellers sell very old eggs.

3. You must make sure ... that none of the yolk...enters the clear of the egg. We do not use any of the yolk. DO NOT USE YOLK. Yolk is very slow and soft on drying, and easily lifted and scratched ... with a fingernail.

4. The clear of the egg as two components. A very thick mass, and lots of thin liquid. Both are important. Do not separate the two. The clear is made of 85% water which does evaporate eventually if left alone. The remaining 15% is albumen, which if left alone will become brittle crystals....and useless.

5. Do not froth the egg white with an electrical beater. It will...evaporate the water. We need the entire egg white with its components.

6. Beat and froth the white with a metal spoon and a bowl. As it froths, remove the froth, and place it in a jar. Repeat this until all the egg white is frothed. Discard any ligaments that remain.

7. Let the froth slowly stand so it will drip and distill...you must move the froth to the side, or it will seal the jar and stop the distillation..... Finally, after 20 or 40 minutes, the distillation will cease and the remaining froth will dry hard and can be discarded...or left there, but pushed aside.

8. Make sure the emulsion has the correct ratio. The oil is 3 parts oil and the glair is 2 parts. If the oil sticks to the spoon, add a bit more oil to compensate. The ideal ratio is 3 parts oil & 2 parts of glair...but you can use 4 oil & 2 glair if needed. Under all circumstances, do not use more glair than oil. You must always have more oil than glair.

9. Mix the oil and glair well by stirring it briskly or capping the jar and shaking it vigorously. It will turn white opaque as you see it in the jar in concentration...But, when it is spread out and rubbed in on anything, it becomes fully transparent like clear glass.

This, I believe, is indeed ONE HALF of the Van Eyck Secret WONDER MEDIUM.
The second half is the correct application of the RUBBING TO AN ULTRA-THIN FILM.

I continuously receive letters from all parts of the world, testifying and telling me that this emulsion is amazing. When used together with CSO OIL PAINT, it indeed gives you full mastery of the oil paint medium

----

LETTER 11 : LIQUIDITY OF OIL PAINT

This letter asked how much thinned and liquid the CSO oil paint can be made.
The writer asked if large amounts of the VE can be used with a blob of paint and still have good bonding and drying properties.

MY RESPONSE
YOU DO NOT NEED TO WORRY ABOUT BONDING/ADHESION - THAT IS NOT AN ISSUE FOR 'CSO OIL PAINT'. BECAUSE OIL PAINT MIXED WITH CHALK CREATES A MIXTURE SIMILAR TO CEMENT OR PLASTER.

YOU **DO** - NEED TO BE CONCERNED ABOUT ...DRIPPING.
THAT IS THE REAL PROBLEM. THE PAINT DRIPPING DOWN...- AND THE OTHER PROBLEM IS EXCESS FLOW BLEEDING, WHICH RESULTS IN LOSS OF YOUR DEFINITION BRUSH MARKS.
TO STOP THIS, CSO USES ONE OR BOTH OF THE TWO STABILIZERS, WHICH ARE : CHALK AND GLAIR.

IN MY BOOK [Vol. 1] YOU CAN READ ABOUT THE PROS AND CONS OF THE THICK VISCOUS OIL......ONE PRO IS IT DRIES FAST......BUT ONE CON, IS IT FLOWS TOO MUCH AND LOSES DEFINITION OF BRUSH MARKS OR PALETTE KNIFE MARKS IF YOU DONT ADD A STABILIZER (CHALK OR GLAIR EMULSION , OR BOTH).

IN MY BOOK [Vol.1]- IF YOU ARE GOING ...TO LIQUIFY ...THE CSO OIL PAINT....DO NOT USE THE THICKENED OIL...
ITS BEST TO USE THE THIN OIL....BECAUSE THIN OIL DOES NOT DRIP, FLOW OR SPREAD -AS MUCH AS THE THICK VISCOUS OIL.
YOU CAN ALSO MAKE THE AGUADO AND THE EMULSION WITH THE THIN OIL, FOR OUTDOORS ' PLEIN AIRE' PAINTING ...AND USE THE AGUADO MADE WITH THIN OIL AS THE ' OIL OUT'.

Sometimes when I'm painting large canvases outdoors, I need thin flowing paint.
YOU MUST JUST ACCEPT THAT THE THIN PAINT WILL DRY SLOWER.....
BUT YOU CAN DO A COUPLE OF THINGS TO ACCELERATE THE DRYING.
1. Add a slight amount of dry umber pigment to the tube oil paints
2 . Add a small amount of dry umber pigment to the thin oil that is used in making the Emulsion and the Aguado.
3 . Add some dry umber pigment to the emulsion used in the oil out.
4. Place the finished painting outdoors exposed to the wind even if it's cold outside.
If the painting is indoors, place a fan on it. The moving air helps drying greatly.

LETTER # 12: MODERN PAINTING WITH DRIP EFFECTS
The artist said he enjoys the CSO oil painting, but asked about how it could be used for modern styles that use drips and splashes in their creative goals.

MY RESPONSE
Thank you for the letter. I recommend you do not use solvents to create drips and splashes. Here are some recommendations. You must experiment to find answers.

To achieve a safe, non-solvent, archival painting, I suggest you begin the painting with Tempera paints. Since ALL Temperas are water based you can effortlessly achieve those drips without any hazards. By adding more liquid to your tempera paint , you could get all the drips you desire. Once done with all your tempera underwork, you can seal it with a coat of oil and paint on it with oils

SINCE CSO WAS DESIGNED ... NOT TO DRIP......ARTISTS MUST EXPERIMENT...AND KEEP AN OPEN MIND. -THE ANSWERS WILL BE FOUND THROUGH EXPLORATION.
I RECOMMEND EXPLORING THIS PROCEDURE:

HERE IS ONE METHOD TO EXPLORE:
START WITH " MILK OIL PAINT" [see my DVD that is free on YouTube – also see the letter from an artist below] THIS MULTI MEDIA METHOD IS USED IN LOWER LAYERS...NOT ON TOP LAYERS UNLESS YOU WANT TO GET A " RESIST" EFFECT (not archival) OF CRAWL, AND BEADING (an indication of poor adhesion).

USE FRESH REFRIGERATED NON FAT MILK ONLY... (DO NOT USE CANNED MILK ... NOR MILK REQUIRING NO REFRIGERATION. THEY ADD NON DRYING PALM OIL. TO INCREASE BODY - ADD SOME CHALK - TO LOOSEN FOR MORE FLUIDITY, ADD MORE MILK. -EXPERIMENTATION IS THE KEY.

PLEASE NOTE THIS.....ONCE FINISHED WITH THE "MILK OIL PAINT, PAINTING, AND IT IS DRY, IT MUST BE SEALED WITH FAST DRYING THICKENED OIL.
I RECOMMEND THAT WHEN YOU ARE FINISHED PAINTING YOU THEN APPLY A COAT OF THICKENED OIL OVER THE ENTIRE SURFACE. RUB IT IN WELL. THEN REMOVE ALL EXCESS WITH A CLEAN TOWEL. LET THAT OIL COAT, DRY WELL.
NOW...APPLY AN "OIL OUT", AND FINISH THE PAINTING WITH OIL PAINTS

ONCE FINISHED WITH THE ' MILK OIL PAINT' - EXPERIMENT WITH THESE OIL PAINT METHODS

APPLY AN "OIL OUT", OF THIN OIL OR OF THICKENED OIL LIBERALLY – IF YOU STILL WANT DRIPS AND SPLATTERS. -BRUSH IT ALL OVER THE CANVAS WITH A WIDE FLAT BRUSH. KEEP THE CANVAS VERTICAL TO INCREASE THE DRIPS AND RUNS.

DO NOT USE AN EMULSION, DO NOT USE CHALK, AS THESE ARE STABILIZERS.

PUT YOUR TUBE PAINT IN A SMALL JAR. ADD MORE OIL. AND STIR IT WELL WITH ALL OF THE ABOVE....USED TOGETHER..YOU WILL GET THE DRIPS

CSO HAS TWO STABILIZERS THAT STOP DRIP.
ONE IS EGG GLAIR MIXED WITH OIL IN A MIXTURE OF THREE PARTS OIL AND TWO PARTS GLAIR. -IT IS AN EMULSION.
THE SECOND IS ADDING CHALK, CALCIUM CARBONATE POWDER, TO THE OIL - WHEN MADE FLUID, THIS IS CALLED AGUADO.

WHEN YOU DO NOT WANT DRIPS ... SWITCH BACK TO THE ORIGINAL CSO MIXTURES TO CONTINUE TO PAINT WITHOUT DRIPS.

YOU CAN ALWAYS ALTERNATE BETWEEN CSO. AND THIN OILS
BUT, ONCE YOU APPLY OIL PAINTS ON TOP OF THE MILK PAINT.
REMEMBER, DO NOT APPLY MILK PAINT ON TOP OF OIL PAINT. IT WILL PEEL OFF.
I DO NOT LIKE TELLING CREATIVE ARTISTS WHAT TO DO—PERHAPS YOU WANT THE PAINT TO PEEL OFF?- TO GET A USED WORN EFFECT?

HERE IS AN ALTERNATE METHOD BEGINNING WITH A TEMPERA:
Begin your painting with simple mixtures of non-fat milk, mixed with dry pigments to the desired consistency. Once finished, let the paint dry completely.
[NOTE: this is milk mixed with dry pigments- this is NOT "MILK OIL PAINT"].

Next... continue with a second type of TEMPERA .What you do here is make the second tempera out of eggs because EGGS will not lift MILK, but, MILK WILL LIFT EGGS.
The egg tempera can be painted on top of A WELL DRIED LAYER OF non-fat milk tempera without lifting or blurring the milk tempera.

Next, scramble some eggs. Do not separate the yolk from the white...use the entire egg.
ADD a bit of water. You must experiment how little or how much water to add.
Beat it with a spoon or mix it briefly in a blender. Filter it through cheese cloth to remove any ligaments from the yolk sack. Then mix it with dry pigments just as you did with the non-fat milk. Experiment as to consistency.

REMINDER AND CONCLUSION
Experiment with the amounts of water to add to the egg tempera.
EGG TEMPERA WILL NOT LIFT NOR BLUR A WELL DRIED LAYER OF MILK TEMPERA, BUT MILK TEMPERA WILL LIFT OR BLUR EGG TEMPERA.
SO MAKE SURE THE FIRST LAYER IS MILK TEMPERA -AND WELL DRIED.
THE SECOND LAYER IS EGG TEMPERA
THEN AFTER THE FINISHED EGG TEMPERA PAINTING HAS DRIED HARD, **SEAL IT** WITH THE FAST DRYING THICKENED SUPERIOR FLAX-LINSEED OIL. -WIPE OFF ALL EXCESS OIL WITH A TOWEL.
DO NOT SEAL WITH VARNISH - NOR OTHER SEALANTS BECAUSE THEY STOP THE ENTRY OF OXYGEN.
USE LINSEED OIL ONLY BECAUSE OILS BREATHE, AND RESIN VARNISHES DO NOT BREATHE
AND THE TEMPERAS DO NEED AIR TO CURE
ONCE THE **OIL SEALANT** IS TOUCH DRY, YOU CAN APPLY AN " OIL OUT", AND PAINT WITH OILS ON TOP [OF THE TEMPERA UNDER WORK].

LETTER #13 : ALLA PRIMA PAINTING
This letter asked about Alla Prima painting.

MY RESPONSE
Simply defined, **Alla Prima painting**, is painting " wet-in-wet" to achieve the final effect. However there are two types. The first is the **Traditional Alla Prima** which uses a monotone under painting as a guide for the beautiful colors to be painted on top of it , and the other is the French Impressionist 19th Century **Modern Alla Prima** method which has NO under painting. This modern Alla Prima painting method on the white canvas is also called DIRECT painting.

THE TRADITIONAL ALLA PRIMA METHOD

Oil paint was known for centuries before the Van Eycks used oil paints in the 1300-1400's. As Theophilus wrote in the 1100's, oil paints were not used in commerce because they dried too slow. For centuries before the Renaissance, Tempera paints (egg, casein, or glue binders) were in wide use because Tempera paint dries almost instantly. In the generations between the exclusive use of Tempera paints ....and later use of oil paints [the 1300's], some Old Master painters would sometimes apply slower drying oil paint on top of fast drying Tempera paints. The oil paint on top allowed easier blending of colors.

Once oil paints were in common use (late 1300's and onwards) , due to making oil paints dry faster, artists also made mixtures of oil paint and Tempera paints to create **Tempera Grassa,** which is an **aqueous-oleaginous Emulsion paint**. Tempera Grassa paint dried slower than a Tempera paint, but faster than an oil paint.

The TRADITIONAL ALLA PRIMA oil painting method

was used since the beginning. Many Old Masters like the Van Eycks painted ALLA PRIMA on white surfaces, but they first drew an intricate drawing in pencil, ink or Tempera.
In effect, they " colored in" the shapes within the outlines with thin veils of oil paint colors.

Many other Old Masters, like Rembrandt, did not paint on white surfaces (there are exceptions as most painters, sometimes did paint on white surfaces). Most chose to paint on " colored" surfaces and they did not always make intricate drawings to begin a painting .

Some, to include Vermeer, Rembrandt, Velazquez, Hals and many others, chose to begin a painting by painting a flat brownish or greenish colored image, called the **monotone**. Another term for the monotone was, "the DEAD COLOR". On this monotone they sometimes painted a "GRISAILLE", meaning a three dimensional image in black, white and grays.

This traditional GRISAILLE was painted ALLA PRIMA, and this method allowed artists to create a three dimensional image with only three values of one color or various values of just black and white paint [monotone means ' one color'] Once dry, the artists would apply thin veils of color glazes on the white areas of the grisaille, that would be as effective as the Van Eyck pure method of painting on white surfaces. Titian in the 1500's was a master of this grisaille method. This method can also ignore the grisaille, and immediately paint ALLA PRIMA in full colors on top of the monotone.

REMBRANDT SOMETHIMES USED THE ALLA PRIMA METHOD

Rembrandt experimented with many paint application methods. The greatest example of the Traditional Alla Prima method is his portrait of Jan Six, which appears to be a simple two step painting: A brownish monotone was painted on an ocher colored ground first, followed by full colors ALLA PRIMA. Rembrandt's thick viscous oil paint shows an extraordinary bravura and virtuosity of brush strokes which is vastly different from the Van Eyck's thin paint, alla prima method.

THE OLD MASTER ALLA PRIMA METHOD, IN SUMMARY:
The Old Master ALLA PRIMA METHOD had a pre-planned design. It was either an intricate outline drawing [like Van Eyck] ... or just a flat brownish (or greenish colored) monotone [like Rembrandt]. For artists using either of these, they served as a "guide" for the coloring and/or subsequent exploration of paint textures. This method was known as "a division of labor" between DISEGNO and COLORE" (design and color).

THE MODERN ALLA PRIMA METHOD
As stated, Alla Prima painting is basically direct painting "wet-in-wet" to achieve the final effect at once. The first modern era major exploration of ALLA PRIMA oil painting as used today was by the French Impressionists of the 1870's.

Van Gogh learned from the Impressionists, and he is called a "Post-Impressionist". All his later paintings were painted ALLA PRIMA but he would first sketch in the scene with bright blue paint. It looked like a 'paint-by-numbers' canvas. He then painted with thick oil paint colors into this wet bright blue oil paint outline.

Generally in the modern Impressionist ALLA PRIMA method, the color of the canvas was white. Many times the white surface was left exposed and served as white areas in the final painting. Velazquez in the 17th century, sometimes in his last years, painted ALLA PRIMA with a combination of very thin oil paint colors and thicker oil paint brush strokes on an off-white surface . Because of this, he is called the first Impressionist painter in history. The French Impressionists of the 1870's recognized and followed Velazquez' paint application method.

Many modern artists today paint ALLA PRIMA on a white surface, like the Van Eycks did 700 years before, but without an outline. The other major difference is that most modern artists today do not use thin glazes, preferring to use thick impasto oil paint.

LETTER # 14: MUST WE VARNISH AN OIL PAINTING?
The writer asked: "Must we varnish an oil painting?"

RESPONSE:
There are several reasons why or why not to varnish an oil painting.
REASONS FOR VARNISHING: A final coat gives an equal shine to the finished oil painting. As the painting is in progress, some portions dry matte. Matte spots are caused by many reasons. The final varnish coat should be a **removable** varnish, like Dammar, because natural resin varnishes will yellow over time. Synthetic varnishes become gray in time. Another reason for varnishing is to protect the oil paint itself, from damage, moisture, and especially dirt and grime accumulation.

REASONS FOR NOT VARNISHING: Throughout art history, all oil paintings were varnished after completion, and they have lasted over 600 years. In today's world, many do not want the oil painting varnished because the glossy reflective glare makes the paintings hard to see in a home. Therefore, many use techniques so the final oil painting dries matte. This is unfortunate because matte oil paint is not archival. Matte dried oil paint lacks sufficient oil binder which is important to hold the pigment particles together.

ALTERNATIVE MIXTURES FOR 'VARNISHING".
My recommendation for giving the finished painting a PROTECTIVE FILM is based on the practice of Rubens [died 1640], as published by the London National Gallery. Their 1983 report can be found online.
The conclusion is that Rubens painted with a thickened viscous oil that dried lustrous and shiny, and that **Rubens DID NOT varnish his completed paintings with a resin varnish.**
Rubens' oil paintings are some of the very best preserved in all of Art history. My recommendation is in line with Rubens. I believe the completed oil painting should be given a final ultra-thin layer of either an emulsion, like the CSO VISCOUS EMULSION or a film of the AGUADO, or a film of pure thickened oil.. These must be ULTR-THIN applications. All excess must be wiped off. This is applied NOT WITH A BRUSH [brushes leave a thick coat]. They should be well rubbed in by the bare hand.
I repeat again, all excess oil must be wiped off with a towel and removed.

LETTER # 15: HOW TO PAINT AN ARCHIVAL PAINTING

RESPONSE:
The MOST IMPORTANT FIRST STEP ....in oil painting.....is to 100% fully seal... the wood or canvas...before ever applying oil paint. Oil paintings on metal, like copper, need not to be sealed. Even after hundreds of years, oil paintings on copper develop no cracks at all.

ALL GESSOS...old master chalk and glue...or...modern acrylic gesso ...ARE ABSORBENT.
Do not apply oil paint until the gesso has been 100% fully sealed.

Since we have no idea if art store GESSOED canvas were first sealed with glue, we then must SEAL THE GESSO.

To seal acrylic gesso...we can do a couple things.
One method is to apply two liberal coats of non-fat milk. Let the first coat dry before the other milk coat is applied. This takes a few hours to complete both coats.
The second method....is to apply one coat of acrylic varnish, either matte or gloss.
It dries quickly (1 hour or less) and oil paints can then be applied.

To seal traditional Old Master gesso we can do this:
If we use Old Master hide glue and chalk gesso, we can apply two coats of warm hide glue to the canvas first before applying the gesso. Let the first glue coat dry hard, before applying the second glue coat. Touch the first coat with your finger. If it feels cold or damp, it's not yet dry.

Do not use solvents with oil painting.
Solvents are one cause for matte oil paint drying. The CSO method uses no solvents.

As we paint with CSO... we will notice some layers drying matte between layers.
This is because each pigment is of a different chemical and each requires a different amount of oil. When a CSO layer dries matte, all we need do is to OIL OUT the dry matte area with the emulsion before applying a new layer of oil paint.

When the painting is finished, wait three days...and apply a final coat of the emulsion (VE) as your final 'coating'. Or, you can choose a different CSO mixture to use as the final coat.
The VE results in a silky shiny final coat
The NVE results in a silky less shiny coat
The AGUADO. Results in an even lesser shiny coat

If you varnish with any resin varnish, like dammar, the resin will yellow over time.
Resin varnishes have a high gloss that is disturbing to the eyes as we look at the painting.

LETTER # 16 : TUBING CSO MIXED WITH LEAD OIL PAINT

The artist asked if he could premix his lead white oil paint with CSO and the Viscous Emulsion and then place it in tubes for instant use.

PLEASE NOTE: CSO does not recommend using any LEAD PIGMENTS.
This artists has made a personal choice to use them.

RESPONSE:

AS YOU KNOW, CSO DOES NOT RECOMMEND USE OF ANY LEAD OR DANGEROUS OIL PAINTS. HOWEVER, IN YOUR PAST LETTER, YOU SAID THAT YOU HAND GRIND FLAKE LEAD WHITE DRY PIGMENT AND THAT YOU ADD THE 'VE' VISCOUS EMULSION.

I INITIALLY SAID THAT SINCE THE EGG WILL DECOMPOSE AND HAVE A BAD ODOR, YOU CAN ADD VINEGAR AS A PRESERVATIVE.
I MUST CHANGE THAT- PLEASE DO NOT USE THE VINEGAR DROPS TO LEAD WHITE PAINT, AND INSTEAD ADD A COUPLE DROPS OF ANY CLEAR NON COLOR LIQUOR..LIKE VODKA, GIN, WHISKEY..ETC.

HERE IS THE REASON.

SINCE YOU ARE USING A METALLIC..LEAD WHITE POWDER, THE VINEGAR (used to stopping putrefaction of the egg) JUST MIGHT REACT AND DARKEN THE METALLIC WHITE LEAD PIGMENT.- IT WOULD BE SAFER TO USE THE ALCOHOL LIQUOR....IT WILL NOT CAUSE ANY CORROSIVE REACTION.

LETTER # 17 : IODINE NUMBER OF FLAX LINSEED OIL

The artists asked how some oils are classified as ' drying oils' and others are not.
Also a question on the removal of the mucilage.

RESPONSE:

AFTER MANY YEARS OF OBSERVATIONAL LOGICAL TESTING..I'VE ALWAYS KNOWN THAT *THE ONLY TRUE ANSWERS* AS TO THE EFFECTIVENESS OF THE REMOVAL OF MUCILAGE CAN ONLY BE RESOLVED BY A MODERN SCIENTIFIC LABORATORY.

LIKE MYSELF, NONE OF THE OLD MASTERS HAD OUR MODERN LABORATORIES YET THEIR PAINTINGS ARE ARCHIVAL. -THE COLORS ARE BRIGHT AND CLEAR

TO MY KNOWLEDGE, NO ONE TODAY..HAS YET HAS DONE THE LABORATORY TESTING, OF THE ART STORE LINSEED OIL...-MEANING: ALKALI REFINED OIL . HOWEVER, YEARS AGO I MADE A TEST OF A BRAND NAME ALKALI REFINED LINSEED OIL, AND FOUND THAT MUCILAGE WAS IN THE OIL. THE TEST I USED IT IS CALLED "THE WATER SEDIMENT TEST". ALL ONE DOES IS PLACE ABOUT 2 FLUID OUNCES OF THE OIL ON ABOUT 4 FLUID OUNCES OF WATER. **DO NOT** SHAKE THE TWO. -SHAKING CREATES A COLLOID OF OIL, WATER AND AIR. - TO DO THE TEST, JUST GENTLY ADD THE WATER TO THE OIL AND ALLOW IT TO STAND STILL. -IT TAKES TIME, UP TO 45 DAYS.

ALSO, TO MY KNOWLEDGE, NO ONE HAS USED A LABORATORY TO EVALUATE THE HAND PROCESSED OIL USED BY THE OLD MASTER METHODS.
MY EMPIRICAL TESTS SHOW THAT I CAN REMOVE 99% OF THE MUCILAGE-

I TEST THIS BY USE OF THE "WATER SEDIMENT" TEST- THE WEAKNESS IN OUR HAND CLEANSED OIL IS THE FILTER WE USE.- IT IS NOT PERFECT- I ALWAYS RECOMMEND THAT ARTISTS DO A SECOND FILTERING OF THE OIL.

EVEN HIGH TECH DUST VACUUM CLEANERS NEVER SAY THEY CAN REMOVE 100% OF THE DUST FROM A RUG. THEY ALWAYS SAY THEY CAN REMOVE 99%.

AS TO THE DRYING OF THE OIL, PREVIOUS SCIENTISTS LIKE ARTHUR CHURCH **(**1909), PROVED AND KNEW THAT OIL, ONCE PRESSED, GOES THROUGH THREE STAGES OF DRYING.-(I use the word "drying".to mean how the oil hardens. It cures over time by contact with oxygen) THE OIL POLYMERIZES AS THE MOLEQULES CROSS-LINK TO FORM A HARDENED SURFACE.

IN THE FIRST STAGE...THE OIL IS VERY SLOW TO DRY. AS THE POLYMERIZATION (thickening) CROSS LINKING OF THE MOLECULES, BEGINS..SLOWLY ... TAKING SEVERAL DAYS.

THE NEXT STAGE IS RAPID HARDENING.....THE OIL QUICKLY BECOMES HARD TO THE TOUCH.... THIS HAPPENS VERY FAST AFTER THE LONG WET DAYS OF THE FIRST STAGE HAVE PASSED..

THE THIRD STAGE TAKES HUNDREDS OF YEARS TO FINALLY END. AND EVEN THEN..- MR. CHURCH CORRECTLY IDENTIFIED ALL OF THE MANY FATTY ACIDS IN THE OIL…HE ALSO IDENTIFIED OLEIC FATTY ACID ..AS ONE FATTY ACID THAT NEVER FULLY DRIES (cures).THIS ADDS A DEGREE OF PLIABILITY TO THE FULLY DRIED PAINT FILM.

VEGETABLE OILS AND THEIR IODINE NUMBER
Artists, since time immemorial have made paint with various vegetable oils that harden over time. Today's science tells why some oils will harden while others will not:

The various oils are categorized as being, "Drying", "Semi-drying" and " Non-drying".
Vegetable oils such as Flax-Linseed oil, are made of glycerol tri-esters of fatty acids.
The oils have many fatty acids. The important one for drying, is the alpha-linolenic acid.
Vegetable oils are measured by their "iodine number".
Drying oils have an iodine number greater than 130.
Semi-drying oils have an iodine number between 115 to130.
Non-drying oils have an iodine number measuring less than 115.
Olive oil is an example of a non-drying oil.

THIS KNOWLEDGE ABOUT THE " IODINE NUMBER "IS LEADING TO NEW TESTS.
IT HAS BEEN MENTIONED THAT MODERN INDUSTRIAL ALKALI REFINEMENT PROCESS REMOVES QUANTITIES OF THE " IODINE" FROM THE OIL,
THIS ALTERING OF THE IODINE NUMBER CREATES A SLOW DRYING OIL.

ONE DEFECT OF MODERN ALKALI REFINED LINSEED "STAND LINSEED OIL" IS THAT IT IS HEATED FAR ABOVE THE SAFETY TEMPERATURE OF 230 CELSIUS.
ANOTHER DEFECT OF THIS MODERN OIL, IS THAT IT IS HEATED WITHOUT EXPOSURE TO OXYGEN. IT IS OXYGEN THAT PROMOTES DRYING (curing, hardening).
IN PLAIN ENGLSH..THEIR MODERN ALKALI REFINED " STAND" OIL HAS NEVER BEEN ALLOWED TO "STAND STILL". IT SHOULD BE CALLED **" BOILED OIL".**

MODERN STAND LINSEED OIL IS NOT LIKE THE OLD MASTERS " STAND" OIL THE OIL OF THE OLD MASTERS DID INDEED STAND OUT IN THE SUN FOR SEVERAL WEEEKS.
THE MODERN ARTISTS STAND LINSEED OIL IS SIMPLY...**BOILED OIL** (oil boils at 340 Celsius).
THE OLD MASTERS KNEW BETTER THAN TO BOIL THE OIL BECAUSE IT BECOMES BROWN! - ONE EXAMPLE IS BURNT PLATE OIL.

LETTER # 18 : THE YELLOWING 'MYTH" OF LINSEED OIL
This writer asked about the 'yellowing' of the linseed oil.

MY RESPONSE:
Linseed –Flax oil IF CORRECTLY CLEANSED of its natural mucilage will appear to be yellowish in the jar. The reason is, because it is being seen in thick concentration. A simple test will prove that the SUPERIOR OIL is completely transparent without any yellow color.
TEST: Place one drop on a pure white glazed ceramic plate and rub it in. IF the thin rubbed in oil film is yellow, then it has not either been cleansed correctly nor bleached.
Henry Levison, a chemist made an in depth test in the 1970's of the yellowing of the oil. Please read the two sources for in depth information.

HENRY W. LEVISON
An internet article : http://cool.conservation-us.org/jaic/articles/jaic24-02-002.html
Mr. Levison published a rare pamphlet that can be found on Amazon
"Artists' pigments: Lightfastness tests and ratings : the permanency of artists' colors and an evaluation of modern pigments" Paperback – 1976 -by Henry W Levison (Author)

The real problem with LINSEED-FLAX oil is this:
If the raw unrefined oil is not correctly cleansed of its mucilage, the mucilage will ferment, decompose and turn a dark brown umber color over the years. This dirty oil will cause all the beautiful colors to become brownish. This condition is IRREVERSIBLE and PERMANENT. Photos of this 'browning', are on my website.

LETTER # 19: SEALING THE CANVAS OR WOOD
The question was asked about sealing the canvas or wood support we artists paint on.

MY RESPONSE:
Hello Friend
THANK YOU FOR YOUR LETTER...AND FOR ASKING MY VIEWS ON SEALING THE SUPPORT.
ILL RESPOND WITH WHAT I KNOW FROM MY RESEARCH AND EXPERIENCE AND LOGIC AND HISTORICAL FACT .- EVEN IF CONTRADICTORY TO SOME CONSERVATORS.

THE FINEST BEST PRESERVED OIL PAINTINGS IN ALL OF HISTORY....ARE THOSE PAINTED ON COPPER.
THE PROOF IS THERE TO BE SEEN.. IN MUSEUMS AND DATE BACK TO PRE RENAISSANCE.
THEY APPEAR TO HAVE BEEN PAINTED YESTERDAY..THE PAINT HAS ABSOLUTELY NO CRACKS, AND THE COLORS ARE PURE. THERE IS NO PAINT LOSS

COPPER WAS USED BY MANY ARTISTS - IN HIS YOUTH, REMBRANDT PAINTED THREE VERY SMALL PAINTINGS ON COPPER. THIS APPEARS TO HAVE BEEN AN EXPERIMENT. WE KNOW HIS MAIN USE FOR COPPER WAS FOR ETCHNG PLATES. THE MAIN OBJECTION FOR COPPER AS A SUPPORT, WAS THE COST (as compared to low cost wood and lower cost canvas) AND THE WEIGHT BECAME HEAVIER AS THE SIZE INCREASED. ALSO COPPER CAN BE BENT EASILY IF TOO THIN.

WHY ARE THESE PAINTINGS ON COPPER SO WELL PRESERVED?
THERE IS ABSOLUTELY NO ABSORPTION OF THE OIL FROM THE OIL PAINT BY METAL. THERE IS NO GLUE APPLIED AS A SEALANT. THERE IS NO GESSO. THE PREPARATION IS SIMPLE. - THE COPPER IS CLEANSED OF HUMAN OILS AND ANY DIRT WITH ALCOHOL. THE SURFACE IS ABRADED SLIGHTLY JUST ENOUGH TO CREATE A MECHANICAL TOOTH THAT WILL HOLD THE PRIMER/GROUND..THIS WAS LEAD WHITE OIL PAINT.
THIS LEAD WHITE WAS POUNCED ON, INTO THE TOOTH....AND ALLOWED TO DRY WELL (it's a myth that it had to dry for months) ALL IT NEEDS IS TO SET AND BECOME HARD TO THE TOUCH, MEANING IT DRIED THROUGHOUT ITS THICKNESS. THE LEAD WHITE POWDER WAS GROUND IN A FAST DRYING THICKENED POLYMERIZED FLAX LINSEED OIL. TWO THIN COATS WERE FASTER DRYING THAN ONE THICKER COAT. A SMALL AMOUNT OF UMBER (manganese) WAS ADDED TO ACCELERATE THE INTERNAL DRYING. THIS THEN WAS A SUPPORT WITH ABSOLUTELY NO OIL IN ITS CONTENT. THE OIL PAINT HAD NO ADVERSE EFFECT ON THE METAL.
WE MIGHT ASK A CHEMIST WHY COPPER IS NOT AFFECTED BY THE ACIDIC OIL, AND IF IRON MIGHT BE? THE CHEMISTRY OF THE TWO METALS IS DIFFERENT.
THE PROOF OF ARCHIVAL ENDURANCE IS PROVEN BY THE EXISTANT PAINTINGS.

MY RESEARCH IS THAT OLD MASTER PAINTINGS WERE SEALED FROM ABSORBING OIL.
THOSE THAT WERE PAINTED ON WOOD, ALWAYS RECEIVED A FEW COATS OF HIDE GLUE.
IN EXPERIENCE WE SEE THAT RAW UNTREATED WOOD IS HIGHLY ABSORBENT.
IN PRACTICE, ...GLUE BEING A MIXTURE OF WATER AND ANIMAL HIDE THAT IS BOILED INTO A GELATINOUS SUBSTANCE, ...ONE SEES THE RAW WOOD ABSORB IT READILY, JUST AS RAW WOOD WILL ABSORB PURE WATER. BUT, THE EVAPORATION OF THE WATER CONTENT LEAVES THE GLUE IN THE WOOD CELLS. A SECOND AND EVEN A THIRD COAT..(depending if a hard wood or a softer wood is used) ARE NEEDED UNTIL ONE SEES ....NO MORE ABSORPTION, AND ONE SEES A GLAZE LIKE SHINY APPEARANCE TO THE DRY GLUE APPLICATION.....TESTING TO SEE IF THE SEALANT IS COMPLETE IS EASY...PLACE THE WOOD BOARD HORIZONTALLY AND PLACE SOME OIL DROPS ON TOP. -ALLOW THIS TO STAND. IF THE SEALANT IS COMPLETE, THE OIL DROPS WILL NOT SEEP INTO THE WOOD. IF NOT COMPLETE, THE OIL GETS ABSORBED, AND SPREADS OUT.

BY READING CONSERVATION BOOKS, ONE LEARNS THAT WHEN OLD MASTER PAINTINGS ON WOOD ARE EXAMINED, THE VARIOUS LAYERS CAN BE SEEN. CONSERVATIONISTS HAVE WRITTEN THAT THE GESSO......WHICH WAS APPLIED ON TOP OF THE GLUE COATS, WAS ALSO SEALED WITH MORE COATS OF HIDE GLUE, AND THAT THESE LAYERS OF THE GESSO
...(glue mixed with either calcium carbonate or calcium sulphate) ARE COMPLETELY WHITE AND NOT YELLOWED NOR COLORED BY OIL OR OIL PAINT COLOR ABSORPTION.- CONFIRMING THE GESSO WAS SEALED BEFORE ANY OIL PAINT WAS APPLIED ON THE GESSO PRIMER/GROUND LAYERS.
BESIDES PROTECTION FROM ACIDIC OIL, THE EARLY FLEMISH PAINTERS PRESERVED THE PURITY OF THE BRILLIANT WHITE COLOR OF THE GESSO AS IMPORTANT FOR THE " inner light" IT GAVE THE THIN COLOR GLAZES ....CREATING THAT " jewel-like" BEAUTY WE STILL ADMIRE TODAY, 700 YEARS LATER.

SO MANY CANVAS PAINTINGS BY THE OLD MASTERS HAVE SUFFERED DAMAGE.
THIS IS BECAUSE OF THE HYGROSCOPIC NATURE OF FLAX OR FIBER CANVASES. MOST HAVE BEEN RELINED BECAUSE OF THE ROTTED CANVAS. WOOD TOO IS HYGROSCOPIC AND SUBJECT TO WOOD WORMS. CANVAS IS SUBJECT TO TEARING. THE EXPANSION AND CONTRACTION OF THESE ...WOOD AND CANVAS....ARE THE CAUSE OF MOST OF THE CRACKING.
THERE HAS ALWAYS BEEN THE DEBATE...SHOULD OR SHOULD NOT THE WOOD AND THE CANVAS BE SEALED ON ALL SIDES? I BELIEVE THE ANSWER IS.." Yes" .
THOSE WHO ARGUE THAT THE SUPPORT MUST " breathe" ARE EXPECTING THE SUPPORT TO BE KEPT IN A MODERN BUILDING WHERE THERE IS NO EXPANSION OR CONTRACTION.
THEY FORGET MOST PAINTINGS OVER THE. CENTURIES WERE EXPOSED TO TERRIBLE ENVIRONMENTAL CONDITIONS OF DAMP WALLS, EXCESSIVE HEAT , ETC.
REMBRANDT'S ANATOMY LESSON OF DR TULP IS AN EXCELLENT EXAMPLE OF EXTENSIVE CONSERVATION REPAIR EFFORTS.

LINSEED FLAX OIL...AND THE PAINT MADE WITH IT....BECOMES INCREASINGLY ACIDIC.
THIS IS NORMAL, AS THE MOLECULES CROSS LINK. THIS POLYMERIZATION IS HOW THE OIL HARDENS AS IT CURES. NEITHER WOOD NOR CANVAS IS BENEFITED IF THIS ACIDIC ELEMENT IS ALLOWED INTO ITS CONTENT. -OF THE TWO, THE CANVAS IS THE ONE THAT IS MOST DAMAGED BY THE ACID...OVER MUCH TIME (centuries) .

A GREAT AMERICAN ARTIST OF THE 1900'S WAS JAMES MCNEIL WHISTLER ...
FAMOUS FOR HIS PAINTING " Whistlers mother"-. A COMPOSITION, IN BLACK WHITE AND GRAYS. - THERE IS A CONSERVATION REPORT ON HOW MUCH CONSERVATION EFFORT WAS NEEDED TO KEEP THIS FRAGILE 100 YEAR OLD PAINTING INTACT AND CLOSE TO WHAT IT LOOKED LIKE WHEN HE PAINTED IT.
REMEMBER THAT THE EARLY FLEMISH PAINTINGS ARE IN EXCELLENT CONDITION AND THEY ARE 700 YEARS OLD.
WHISTLER WAS A GREAT ARTIST YES...BUT HE WAS A TERRIBLE TECHNICAL PAINTER. HIS MAIN " paint liquid medium " WAS TURPENTINE. -WE KNOW THS IS THE WORST OF ALL LIQUIDS TO MIX WITH OIL PAINT. I COULD EXPAND ON THIS WITH MUCH DETAIL...BUT I WOULD BE REPEATING WHAT MY BOOK CONTAINS.

QUESTION: I called a conservator at the national gallery about that because I have had problems with oil being visible on the back side of the canvas. He said I wasn't supposed to seal the back. I think I have asked 3 or 4 conservators about those oil stains on the back of my canvases. They all said it doesn't matter because I have glued the canvas very well (with rabbit skin glue) so the canvas will not rot.

I BELIEVE THE INFORMATION IS FALSE.. THE REMBRANDT I WROTE ABOUT ABOVE, HUNG IN A DAMP ROOM, THE CANVAS ROTTED FROM THE BACK. HAD IT BEEN SEALED FROM THE BACK, THIS WOULD NOT HAVE HAPPENED TO SUCH A DEGREE. A COAT OF GLUE TO THE BACK WOULD HAVE MINIMIZED THE HYGROSCOPIC CONTRACTIONS ALSO.
NOT YO MENTION THE ROTTING OF THE FIBERS...OVER LONG PERIODS OF TIME.

QUESTION: I doubt their judgement. I think it is wrong that the oil sucks through and is visible on the backside.

YOUR INTUITION AND EXPERIENCE ARE ACCURATE. MY LIBRARY HAS A RATHER RECENT PUBLICATION BOOK...ON THE POOR JUDGEMENTS BY PAINTING CONSERVATIONISTS.OVER THE YEARS. EVEN THEY ADMIT THAT THEY ARE NOT ALWAYS MAKING THE BEST DECISIONS.
I TRUST THE OLD MASTER KNOWLEDGE...MORE THAN THESE PERSONS.

QUESTION: What do you think is the best way?

MY COMMENTS ABOVE ANSWER THAT QUESTION.
THE BEST METHOD IS WHAT THE OLD MASTERS USED... BEGIN WITH SEVERAL VERY LIBERAL GLUE LAYERS ON BOTH SIDES OF THE RAW WOOD OR CANVAS. THIS IS WELL RUBBED INTO THE SUPPORT, SO IT SUCKS UP THE GLUE. - THEN APPLY SEVERAL THIN LAYERS OF THEIR HIDE GLUE ON THE DRY GESSO...THE SAME GLUE THEY MADE THE GESSO WITH.

QUESTION: I work on CANVAS. I need some oil in it. The fat free milk is not an option, what about glair?.

DO NOT USE GLAIR, AND NOT PAINT WITH MILK ON AN OIL GROUND. THEY WILL NOT ADHERE. THIS GOES BACK TO THE BEGINNING.
STEP ONE: FIRST, ON RAW CANVAS. APPLY THE GLUE ON FRONT AND ON THE BACK. APPLY TO BOTH FRONT AND BACK AT THE SAME TIME TO COUNTER ANY WARP. - SEVERAL COATS, WITH DRYING IN BETWEEN LAYERS, LIBERALLY APPLIED. KEEP THE CANVAS VERTICAL TO AVOID PUDDLES. APPLY THE GLUE IN HORIZONTAL STROKES BEGINNING AT THE TOP. -YOU NEED AT LEAST TWO GOOD LIBERAL COATS.
ON THIS DRY GLUE SEALED SUPPORT ...YOU CAN APPLY OIL PAINT DIRECTLY AND PAINT YOUR PICTURE.....THERE IS NO REQUIREMENT TO APPLY AN OIL OR GESSO PRIMER OR A GROUND AT ALL.- -PRIMERS AND GROUNDS WERE APPLIED TO FILL IN AN EXCESSIVE WEAVE,..OR TO CREATE A PURE WHITE SURFACE, OR A COLORED SURFACES.
SINGLE OR DOUBLE COLORED GROUNDS ON CANVAS WERE APPLIED FOR COLORISTIC REASONS EXAMPLES ...COLORED GROUNDS ON CANVAS...ARE MANY:
EL GRECO'S COLORED GROUND WAS A BRICK RED.- GOYAS SOMETIMES USED A BRIGHT ORANGE. – VELAZQUEZ' LATER WORK WAS A PASTEL PINK OR GRAY OR OFF WHITE. - REMBRANDT SOMETIMES USED A DOUBLE GROUND OF A FAWN COLOR ON TOP OF A DARKER REDDISH BROWN. THE GROUND COLOR CHOICES ARE ENDLESS.

PART TWO:

ON CANVAS SUPPORTS.... THE GESSO LAYES ARE APPLIED THINLY
AND ARE NOT APPLIED WITH A BRUSH... THEY ARE SCRAPED ON WITH A PALETTE KNIFE ..TO SOMEWHAT FILL THE WEAVE IF DESIRED...TO CREATE THE LIGHT OR TONED COLOR IF DESIRED ...AND MOST IMPORTANT...TO AVOID.A CONTINUOUS FILM OF GESSO...WHICH WILL...CRACK OVER TIME.
SOME OLD MASTERS ADDED HONEY OR FIG BRANCH JUICE AS A METHOD OF ADDING AN ELASTIC INGREDIENT THAT GIVES THE DRY GESSO SOME PLIABILITY TO AVOID FUTURE CRACKING ...CAUSED BY HYGROSCOPIC CONTRACTIONS OF WOOD OR CANVAS SUPPORTS, CAUSED BY HUMIDITY OR DRY AIR .

LETTER # 20: SPOTTY DRYING

An artist wrote to say his CSO painting dries " SPOTTY", some areas are shiny, others are matte.

MY RESPONSE
THE FIRST REQUIREMENT is that the support, whether it is raw wood or raw canvas, MUST FIRST BE SEALED 100% and made.to be made isolated and non-absorbent.

There are two ways.
One, is two liberal coats of old master hide glue/ or/ rabbit skin glue allowing each application to soak in. Let the first coat dry before applying the second coat.
The other way...one liberal coat of acrylic varnish (It is called a varnish, but it is also a glue - use either gloss or matte)

Both will seal the raw support, 100% .
Unfortunately, ready-made art supply canvases are NOT SEALED before they coat it with acrylic gesso.
ALL GESSOS.....either old master or modern acrylic are VERY ABSORBENT.
Thus....if you do not seal that gesso first, it will absorb...oil out of the oil paint. It then dries spotty or matte.

IF YOU BEGAN WITH A RAW SUPPORT , BUT YOU DID NOT SEAL IT.
THEN you must seal the gesso...use the acrylic varnish for acrylic gesso.
And use the hide glue for old master hide glue gesso.

NEXT REQUIREMENT
As you paint. Layers may dry spotty. This is normal because different colors require more oil. To solve this, you need to apply any one of the CSO "Oil Out" mediums to the dry spots. Rub them in well. Wipe off any excess. Use either the VE...the NVE ... or the AGUADO.
You can let this dry or you can paint on it while it is damp.

THE FINAL REQUIREMENT.
When the painting is finished......
Let it dry three days...(in normal weather) ..so it is not in danger of paint being smeared.
Then rub in by hand [only by hand] AN ULTRA THIN FILM ...ALL OVER....
Using either of the same three 'oil out' mediums.
THE VE : This gives a silky shine
THE NVE : This gives a less silky shine
THE AGUADO: It gives a lesser shine, almost matte, but not matte.

LETTER # 21: HEAT LAMP BOX TO THICKEN THE OIL IN COLD WEATHER CLIMATES

The artist Matthew J. Campbell, wrote to tell me how he made an INDOOR HEAT LAMP BOX, made wood and the types of heat bulbs he used . - I myself have no experience with use of heat lamps because I live in sunny California. For those who live in northern colder climates his ideas might be very helpful to thicken the oil in winter. I cannot vouch for the effectiveness of the content of this letter. I do know other artists are experimenting with heat lamps to thicken their oil.

WARNING: Artists must be careful not to burn themselves, endanger family and pets and to be sure there are no hazardous fire conditions, nor hazardous air fumes. Do this at your own risk.

THIS IS WHAT Mr. CAMPBELL WROTE:
Lizard lamps are used with an aluminum type reflector that the UV bulb sits in , this helps reflect the UV light to the reptile ....in this case it is the flax/Linseed oil.
The optimum for infrared light is white type & the optimum for UV is an aluminum
Infrared light bulb with white reflector, but this can easily overheat oil in confined spaces.

I built a box from plywood to thicken my oil. I measured the hole in the plywood from both sides.The hole outside of the box is made smaller than the hole on the Inside of the box , which faces the Oil, which is larger.
I cut the hole for the reflector and pushed the reflector in the box from the inside, that will make sure the reflector sits in place , as the outside hole is smaller.
The inside of the box is lined with aluminum foil to maximize the light.

The first light box I made was with 2 UV lights & One Infrared light. I made the original light box completely light tight as a bit of safety overkill.
WARNING: It is not safe to stare at UV lights.
Now I just drape plenty of aluminum foil over the top of the box
At first I tried using an infrared light. The Oil got particularly thick.
After 5 Days the oil got so thick it could be called a solid. It was a firm blob of Linseed oil which I was barely able to pull out of the neck of the bottle.
I got rid of the Infrared light as I think it cooked the oil ... it's too hot.

Since then I have used two low wattage UVB lamps for lizards.
These have a large % of UV perhaps 10% or 12%.
This is better than the Infrared heat lamp I first tried out.
The oil is kept in transparent fused quartz containers as fused quartz doesn't block UV light .
The last several batches of flax/Linseed with the 2 UV lights without the Infrared have worked well, and there has been no excessive heat . The oil appears pale straw in color and the heat is similar to a comfortable room temperature

All the best,
Matthew J. Campbell

LETTER 22# THE PROCESSING OF FLAX LINSEED OIL

My good friend Leandro Cassiano from Norway , sent me this EXCELLENT
Article on FLAX SEED- LINSEED OIL. The entire article is excellent, but for us artists, Section 2 is of great interest. It is brief but full of details.

http://flaxcouncil.ca/wp-content/uploads/2015/02/Flax-Feed-Industry-Guide-Final.pdf

PLEASE SEE SECTION 2: PROCESSING

The first part is: SOLVENT EXTRACTION
This discusses non-edible oil for modern industry.

The second part is: MECHANICAL EXTRACTION
This discusses: Human edible grade-cold pressed flax oil..
Because of the manner of extraction, this is the same oil the Old Masters used.

LETTER # 23 : MILK OIL PAINT
An artist asked about the new ' Milk Oil Paint'.

I created 'Milk oil paint' to be used as a fast drying archival paint for use in underpainting. Milk Oil Paint is an EMULSION OIL PAINT, meaning, part oil and part water based paint. Please see my YOUTUBE VIDEO on this paint. It is full length and FREE. To locate it, type in the words: CSO VELASQUEZ in the search box. The YOUTUBE version is the beginners version. A Professional level DVD, is available on Amazon.

HERE ARE THE REQUIREMENTS

1. Make the MILK GEL. A simple mixture of LIQUID non-fat milk and DRY POWDERED non fat milk....Do not use canned milk. It has non-drying Palm oil and sugar added for preservation. There is no accurate mixture ratio. Mix it so it gets a "stand up" appearance, ..much like the tube oil paint.

2. Mix an equal amount of tube oil paint with the MILK GEL. It mixes easy and quick.

ONCE YOU MIX THE TWO TOGETHER....YOU NOW HAVE
'MILK OIL PAINT'. IT IS A TRUE EMULSION PAINT MADE OF AQUEOUS CASEIN PAINT AND OLEAGINOUS OIL PAINT.
ONCE IT IS MIXED.....YOU CAN DO ANYTHING YOU WANT, WITHIN REASON.

You can add more liquid milk to paint with washes that dry in five minutes.
Or, you can add more dry milk powder ... to add body to make the paint thicker.
BE CAREFUL NOT TO MAKE IT TOO DRY.

DO NOT WORRY ABOUT ... "FAT ON LEAN" ... IT DOES NOT APPLY BECAUSE......
MILK OIL PAINT IS LEANER THAN THE ....PURE OIL PAINT YOU WILL BE APPLYING ON THE ...'OVER PAINT' STAGE

ONCE YOU BEGIN TO USE ...PURE OIL PAINT ON TOP OF THE MILK OIL PAINT YOU CANNOT RETURN TO PAINT WITH MILK OIL PAINT ON TOP OF THE OIL PAINT.

SIMILARLY
YOU CANNOT PAINT WITH MILK OIL PAINT ON TOP OF AN OIL PRIMERED CANVAS OR PANEL SURFACE. IT MUST BE A GESSO SURFACE FOR IT TO ADHERE.

ALSO
TO PROTECT THE FINISHED MILK OIL PAINTING, YOU MUST...SEAL THE ENTIRE SURFACE WITH A LIBERAL APPLICATION OF SUN OIL.....RUB IT IN........THEN WIPE OFF ALL THE EXCESS. LET THIS OIL LAYER DRY.

DO NOT APPLY ANY SEALER CONTAINING A SOLVENT TO THE MILK OIL PAINT LAYER.

ON FLEXIBLE CANVAS,USE 'MILK OIL PAINT' THINLY.
ON RIGID BOARD..USE IT AS THICK AS YOU WANT.

WHEN PAINTING WITH MILK OIL PAINT....YOU CAN STOP ....AND RESTART..OVER AND OVER AGAIN.......UNTIL YOU GET IT THE WAY YOU WANT IT.
YOU CAN ALSO DRAW ON IT WITH INKS, THEN SEAL IT WITH THE SUN OIL

THIS IS THE BASIC INFORMATION.
I RECOMMEND YOU WATCH THE FREE DVD ON YOUTUBE

LETTER # 24: MORE ON MILK OIL PAINT

I recently bought your dvd, "The New Milk Oil Paint and the Van Eyck Secret Medium", as well as your book, "Oil Painting Lessons with Rembrandt".
THANK YOU.

I have found both to be full of many different kinds of very helpful information.
IT IS A LOT TO DIGEST. TAKE YOUR TIME ...READ IT CAREFULLY… DONT SPEED READ.
You point out, in the DVD, that one can paint simply with skim milk mixed with dry pigment.
ITS TRUE ...BUT THE GROUND MUST BE ABSORBENT ....USE A REGULAR GESSO, EITHER TRADITIONAL OLD MASTER OF CHALK AND GLUE..OR ACRYLIC GESSO..

NOW… THIS IS VERY IMPORTANT. IF YOU WILL BE PAINTING A FINAL LAYER OF OIL PAINTS ON TOP… YOU MUST FIRST BEGIN WITH TWO COATS OF HIDE GLUE ON THE BARE WOOD OR BARE CANVAS OR BARE PAPER. IF YOU WANT YOU CAN APPLY ONLY ONE COAT OF ACRYLIC VARNISH, GLOSS OR MATTE.

THEN, APPLY THE GESSO. -THEN USE THE MILK MIXED WITH DRY PIGMENT ....OR TRY THE NEW 'MILK OIL PAINT'.

I love the gentle, yet rich look it has when dry. I prefer it's beauty to any other form of casein.

YES. PART OF CREATIVE ARTWORK IS GETTING VERY FAMILIAR WITH THE VARIOUS MEDIA...MANY OLD MASTERS UNDER PAINTED IN TEMPERA (either glue, or egg, or milk) OR AS IN A RECENT YALE UNIVERSITY SCIENTIFIC STUDY SHOWED ..USE OF TEMPERA GRASSA...WHICH IS A TEMPERA MIXED WITH OIL...AS IN MY MILK OIL PAINT.

YOU BOUGHT THE DVD, "THE VAN EYCK SECRET" ... AND IF YOU GO ON YOUTUBE ...SEARCH....**CSO VELASQUEZ**. THERE FIND THE BEGINNERS VERSION OF 'MILK OIL PAINT' AND THE STUDY OF RUBENS. ..BOTH ARE FREE. THEN GO TO MY WEBSITE... www.calcitesunoil.com

AND READ ABOUT OTHER TOPICS ...WRITE ME WITH QUESTIONS. I RESPOND TO ALL EMAIL INQUIRES.

But one thing worries me: While I can find plenty of evidence on the internet that casein extracted from skim milk is archival, I have never found anything about skim milk itself.

SKIM MILK IS ALSO CALLED ... FAT FREE MILK ..OR ... NON FAT MILK. ITS WHOLE MILK WITH ALL THE FATTY BUTTER REMOVED. -WHATS LEFT IS CASEIN . -MILK FAT [AKA BUTTER], NEVER DRIES. BUT ONCE REMOVED, THE CASEIN DRIES DURABLE AND ARCHIVAL ...BUT AS I WROTE ABOVE..IT WILL NOT ADHERE TO AN OILY SURFACE. -ALSO, ALL GESSOS ARE ABSORBENT AND ALL THE TEMPERAS ALL STICK WELL TO IT.

I have read that skim milk contains more than just casein - it also contains significant amounts of whey and lactose sugar. Are they archival? Could they yellow/crack/peel off or some other kind of problem?

WHEY IS THE WATERY PORTION OF THE NON FAT MILK. THE QUARK IS THE SOLID PORTION. YOU NEED BOTH. SUGAR, IS A PRESERVATIVE......AS IS SALT.

BEFORE REFRIGERATION WAS INVENTED, MILK WAS KEPT FROM DECOMPOSING AND REMAINED EDIBLE BY ADDING LOTS OF SUGAR.- IT IS CANNED MILK.

THE GROUND SUPPORT (gesso) MUST BE ABSORBENT. IT NEED NOT HAVE ANY TEXTURE. -NO MECHANICAL LOCK IS NEEDED.

Since I hope to sell my paintings, I feel a responsibility to ensure they will last.

OF COURSE - THEN..DO NOT USE ZINC WHITE. IT BECOMES BRITTLE WITH AGE ...AND DON'T USE ANY OILS EXCEPT FOR WALNUT AND FLAX-LINSEED...-AVOID OIL PAINTS GROUND WITH SAFFLOWER OR OTHER OILS. -RECENT STUDIES SHOW DRIPPING OF DRIED PAINT LAYERS , YEARS LATER ..ILL TRY TO LCCATE THAT STUDY FOR YOU. ITS BURIED...IN MY EMAILS.

I want to be able to provide credible evidence that skim milk is just as archival as pure casein, to satisfy any skepticism or criticism.

WHEN YOU STUDY MY DVD ON EGG TEMPERA......STUDY HOW THE DEVELOPMENT CAME ABOUT. ..THEN ASK ME SOME SPECIFIC QUESTIONS.. I'M HAPPY TO GO OVER ALL YOUR QUESTIONS. FOR INSTANCE, THE ANCIENT EGG TEMPERA METHOD OF THE RENAISSANCE AND PRE RENAISSANCE ...CANNOT USE ANY IMPASTO...IT WILL CRACK AND PEEL........THE NEW CSO EGG TEMPERA CAN . THE DVD EXPLAINS WHY... AS DOES MY BOOK.

Do you have historical evidence that would reassure buyers/conservators/other painters that skim milk, even with its whey and lactose sugar, is just as archival as pure casein?

I HAVE NO HISTORICAL CITATIONS FOR YOU. -I KNOW THEY WOULD BE IMPORTANT TO YOU. ...IN LINE WITH THAT… -ERNST VAN DE WETERING'S BOOK..."REMBRANDT: THE PAINTER AT WORK" ...PUBLISHED A TRUE STUDIO SECRET - DISCOVERED BY MODERN SCIENTIFIC TESTS - THAT HAS NO HISTORICAL WRITTEN RECORD. –IT IS THE USE BY MANY OLD MASTERS , OF EMULSIONS. MY BOOK COVERS THE TOPIC COMPLETELY.

Even if you don't have anything to offer, please know that I am enormously delighted and grateful to you for your idea of using skim milk. If nothing else, it will make a terrific medium for practicing in.

I THINK YOU WILL ENJOY THE NEW...'MILK OIL PAINT'...THAT I DEVELOPED. HERE IS THE LINK ON YOUTUBE, TO THE BEGINNER'S VERSION:

Here : https://m.youtube.com/watch?v=MpvGnfEUZ0Q

AND THE RUBENS DVD IS HERE: : https://m.youtube.com/watch?v=Ktwca5ov7D0

THANK YOU FOR YOUR LETTER

LETTER # 25: JANE MORRIS PACK on ANCIENT GREEK ART MATERIAL

Jane Morris Pack has lived in Greece for over 20 years. She is a Teacher and Fine Artist herself. She runs an Art school along with her husband there in Greece.
[Google: The Aegean Center, on the island of Paros, Greece].
Part of the year, her school moves to Pistoia, Italy, in Tuscany.
She teaches CSO to her students that attend her school from many different countries.
She once told me **her students refer to CSO in Greek, as 'LAKI'.**

Jane sent me this letter with interesting information of a mixture that closely resembles my own CSO EGG GESSO mixture.

SEPT. 4, 2016, From Jane Morris Pack
Hi Louis,
I stumbled on two things recently that might interest you. One is a quote from a webpage about Greek temples. In it they mention the use of marble dust and egg white for a painting base. The second is a photo from the museum in Crete of ancient palettes from 2000 BC for painting and grinding pigments. All of this relates back to your work and discoveries.

Με χαρά
With joy,
Jane

JANE'S LETTER CONTAINS COPYRIGHT PROTECTED INFORMATION, SO I CANNOT QUOTE IT EXACTLY. YOU CAN READ THE ARTICLE AT THE LINK BELOW. HOWEVER, I WILL SUMMARIZE IMPORTANT POINTS FROM THAT RESEARCH.

Ancient Grecian Materials and Construction:
1. The earlier temples were chiefly built of stone
2. Coarse local stones were frequently used.
3. The stone was coated with a thin skin of very fine hard cement, usually made of lime and powdered marble or white stone, mixed with white of egg, milk, or some natural size, such as the sap of trees.
3. This cement-like mixture was almost as hard, and white, and durable as marble itself.
4. This marble cement, protected soft stone from the weather and made it look as if it had been built of real marble
5. It also formed a slightly absorbent surface for later added painted decorations.
6. Even when the temple was built of solid marble, it was not uncommon to coat it with a thin skin or priming of 'marble dust cement' for later paint decoration.
From the following website.....
http://www.hellenicaworld.com/Greece/WS/en/Temenos.html

Hello Louis,
Thank you for your letter and of course I am happy for you to include both my letter and the link to the information I sent to you earlier on Greek temples. It's so interesting how many threads lead back to your work. I am once again teaching the CSO method to students and once again grateful for your research. I always direct them to your website for more information.

You might mention in your book that LAKI is an acronym for the Greek word for oil (ladi) and chalk (kimolia). Also, Murphy Soap was introduced to me by a student and it cleans brushes, floors and jars up beautifully from even hardened, dried oil.

Με χαρά,
Jane

LETTER # 26: CHRIS AERFELDT and POETIC PAINTING

Chris and I have exchanged many letters over recent years. Chris is one of the most creative artists I have met through my CSO website. Please view her website to learn the steps she takes in creating a fine painting. You will learn many tips and will be as inspired by her work as I am.
This is from her website: RE: Old master methods and materials.
Her words echo what I continuously say to artists who are new to CSO.

"Over the past few years I have been researching old master methods and materials, not because I want to paint old fashioned pictures but because learning new skills and techniques expands my painting vocabulary. As a result I now refine my own linseed oil (the raw cold ground version) using gin or vodka and a kind of bran [psyllium husk], and then thicken it in the summer sun just like Rembrandt and Velasquez. This makes for a much nicer painting medium which makes the paint dry faster and blend better. I have also totally eliminated solvents from my oil painting practice. I now mix my tube paints with the special refined and thickened oil, beaten egg white, and chalk from the Champagne region. All of this information can be found in a book by Louis Velasquez (no relation) or on YouTube. He has called this old master 'medium' Calcite Sun Oil. It takes a while to get your head around the new way of working but it's actually very simple.

SEE HER very engaging paintings at :
http://www.chrisaerfeldt.com/blog/2016/10/14/blood-sweat-and-tears-part-2

LETTER # 27: HAND GRINDING OIL PAINT AND ISSUES OF WALNUT OIL.

I have had several questions about hand grinding oil paint, and questions about oil paint made with walnut oil. Here are some responses I've sent to artists.

HAND GRINDING OIL PAINTS.
1. Generally the dry pigment is ground in THIN OIL...not thickened oil.
This will slow down the drying., as thin oils (non thickened) dry much slower than the sun thickened oils.

2. Adding 50/50 mixture of CSO...to that grind of pigments ground in thin oil...will increase the drying... Because CSO is a mixture of SUN THICK OIL AND CHALK...

3. Grinding dry pigment with THICKENED. FASTER DRYING OIL ...creates a excessively flowing oil paint that spreads and drips....hence, the grinding with thin oil.
If you do hand grind with sun thickened oil, add just a small amount of the CSO and then add a few drops of the NVE.....grind this well together. This non viscous emulsion will stop the drip and the excessive flow and will prevent wrinkling.

4. ALSO, for normal daily use of oil painting, you do not need a muller to grind the paint.
A flexible partially stiff palette knife is adequate. It should have a STRAIGHT blade about 5 or 6 inches long, 1/2 inch wide, and a round tip. DO NOT use a palette knife with a crooked neck.

5. The first step is to gently MIX the oil and the dry pigment powder. Then, once it is wetted, you must GRIND with pressure for a couple of minutes. Some dry pigments RESIST being wetted. If so, you can first add a few drops of liquor (white wine or whiskey, vodka etc) to wet the dry pigment, then add the oil.

WALNUT OIL
This beautiful oil dries so slow as to be useless. A friend of mine in Australia ...knows the manufacturer of walnut oil paint He said the owner told him privately: WE MUST ADD DRIERS TO THE PAINT OR THE ARTISTS WILL HANG US....it takes so long to dry.

MY TEST OF WALNUT OIL PAINT
I did a concurrent dry test of several brand name tube oil paints.
That included a tube of a famous walnut oil paint brand.....
This tube of walnut oil paint died just as fast as the other oil paints made with linseed oil.
Then I did a separate comparison test of this tube oil paint.

This test made conducted concurrent with a self-ground dry pigment of the same color with RAW CLEANSED WALNUT OIL ... that I made into paint.
The famous walnut oil paint brand dried normally in a couple days.
My pure walnut oil ....with no driers added ...was not dry 5 days later ...it was still wet as the day I made it. The test indicates that the brand name walnut oil paint has driers added to it.

ALSO: Do not believe those who say walnut oil paint will not wrinkle. Any impasto oil paint mixed with excessive fast drying oil, will wrinkle.

LETTER # 28 : EMULSIONS FROM AUSTRALIA
Mr. John W. is from Australia. This kind letter specifically discusses the merits of CSO and the Emulsions. John writes in lower case—I WRITE IN UPPER CASE.

DEAR JOHN, YOU WROTE THIS:
   Although your CSO mix does make the paint quite workable, I wanted to thin it a little more, so I made some glair too. Too lazy to beat the whites by hand, I put them through my blender instead!
   I was amazed. I confess that I had reservations about your system of glair for thinning and oiling out, since it seemed to me that the watery egg yolk would never properly mix with the oil; Oil and water??!!! But to my surprise it blended in perfectly with the paint/CSO mixture. I added more; still no problem; nice smooth even paint that went on beautifully and held its shape. What was going on here?
   I did some research on-line, learning that egg white is more than 90% water!!! But the list of proteins it contains goes on and on. Then I started thinking about emulsions and what was possibly happening. I haven't had the time yet to see if your claims that thick paint won't wrinkle or skin, but I've no doubt they're true. Everything else you've asserted has been!!!
   May I respectfully add the fruits of my ponderings to your body of knowledge, if you think them worthy?

You say that the glair slows down the drying of the paint and maybe that's true, but I think that the crux of the matter is that the whole body of the paint can dry out evenly rather than just the outer layer. Thick paint wrinkles because it forms a skin, which seals and shrinks as it dries, trapping the more moist inner paint and deforming to form ripples or wrinkles. By introducing glair/water oil emulsion and all of the proteins contained in egg white, into the body of the paint, and homogeneously distributing it within, a matrix is formed composed of the paint and an almost infinite mass of microscopic pathways through which air and water can pass. These pathways extend in every direction and connect amongst themselves and the exterior like breathing passageways. Instead of only the exterior layer drying, the whole body of paint/emulsion is able to dry out evenly. Furthermore, due to the firm, but elastic nature of the egg white (meringue, blancmange etc.) there is no sagging or dripping and paint strokes remain as they were applied. I hope my little imagined expose meets with your approval.

All the best and thanks again.
John W. Australia

DEAR FRIEND JOHN,
THEY ARE MOST CERTAINLY WORTHY. WHAT YOU WROTE ..IS A CLEAR CONCISE EXPLANATION OF WHAT I CONSIDER TO BE THE ONE THING I AM MOST PROUD OF HAVING DISCOVERED. -- WHICH IS: THAT THE GREAT REMBRANDT...WHO SCIENTIFIC EXAMS OF HIS PAINTINGS PROVE...DID NOT USE ANY RESINS (outside of experiments). CONTROLLED HIS THICK VISCOUS LEAD WHIRE PAINT AND IMPASTO....FROM WRINKLING.. AND PREVENTED THE VISCOUS OIL PAINT FROM DRIPPING, SAGGING, OR SPREADING... BY ADDING ONE DROP OR TWO, OF AN OIL/ GLAIR EMULSION...TO THE PAINT.

YOU SO WELL EXPLAIN EXACTLY WHAT HAPPENS...WHEN IT IS MIXED INTO THE THICK VISCOUS OIL PAINT....AND BY THAT ACTION.....ALLOWS THE ENTIRE BODY OF THE THICK PAINT TO DRY EQUALLY THROUGHOUT...NOT JUST THE SKIN, WHICH WOULD WRINKLE.

ADDITIONALLY THIS........IF YOU ADD ONLY ONE OR TWO DROPS TO A NUT SIZED AMOUNT OF OIL PAINT...THE PAINT REMAINS FIXED SO YOU CAN PAINT IMPASTO.....IF YOU ADD MORE DROPS OF THE EMULSION..THE PAINT BECOMES FLUID, USEFUL FOR OTHER EFFECTS. IN EITHER CASE...THE GLAIR OIL EMULSION HOLDS THE STROKES , LIBES ETC..EXACTLY AS YOU PUT THEM...BUT YOU CAN EASILY BLEND..THIS IS CALLED THIXOTROPY. MOVE IT--- STOP IT....BY BRUSHING

ONE MORE THING... THE OIL PAINT MIXED WITH THE GLAIR OIL EMULSION..WILL " set up " AS QUICKLY AS THE OIL PAINT WITHOUT IT...BUT ..IN MY TESTS...IT TAKES THREE DAYS TO HARDEN..THIS IS BECAUSE AS YOU POINT OUT...THE DRYING IS FROM INSIDE EQUALLY THROUGHOYT.

THANK YOU JOHN...YOU MADE MY DAY
THANK YOU FOR YOUR ASTUTE OBSERVATIONS
BEST LOUIS

LETTER # 29: A LETTER FOR SAFE OIL PAINTING

Louis,
Thank you for your great book, "Solvent Free Oil Painting" and videos that I bought in late September 2012. I am so grateful to you. You have given me a future as an oil painter. I have a home studio and the fumes were killing me. I knew I had to quit. I was devastated, then I found you. I am painting better, much better, and the paints dry so fast I am able to complete a painting while I still have the inspiration! My new paintings have a rich glow never before seen in my work. Thank you, thank you!!! I am having trouble cleaning the oil and sun thickening it. I am a vegetable gardener and have a JUMP START windowsill heat mat, 7.3 watts 120 volts, information at www.hydrofarm.com. It is to start seeds at a very low heat. I think that the heat mat and the air pump should do the trick in cold winters. I do organic gardening and your methods are exactly the way that I want to live and paint.

-MJB, California USA

LETTER# 30: TESTAMENT TO CSO

I receive many letters from artists from all parts of the world. This one is especially poetic and touching. These letters really lift my spirits and cause me to continue my work in helping others.

Louis,
I am finally reaching a level of finish, and that is because of your wonderful and continual work. I hope to have enough pieces by the end of the year to approach a gallery and see where it takes me. I hope to keep in contact more. I will take some photos soon to show you some of my progress, which would have been impossible without your brilliant book.

I suppose the best way I can describe what you have done for me is to say that, prior to finding your book it was as though I was in a dark room crawling around, searching for that elusive something I knew was out there but couldn't see. You saw me searching in the shadows, smiled and turned on the light. For that I will be forever grateful. :)

With the warmest wishes and unwavering gratitude,
Michael M.
Melbourne , Australia

LETTER # 31: A KIND LETTER and questions from England

Sometimes a letter expresses gratitude for the CSO knowledge, and within the letter, the writer tells why. This letter includes several good questions at the end.

Hello Louis
HELLO, I READ YOUR LETTER...IM HUMBLED BY THE KINDNESS...
THANK YOU VERY MUCH.

I have just bought your book and have been deeply immersed in it. It is probably the best £15 I have ever spent! WOW is all I can say!
I HOPE THE BOOK...THE DVDS AND MY WEBSITE WILL CONTINUE TO BE OF GOOD HELP FOR YOU OVER THE YEARS. PLEASE KNOW, I CONTINUE MY RESEARCH DAILY, AND I DO NOT KNOW EVERYTHING...NO ONE DOES..BUT YES....THE BOOK DOES CONTAIN MUCH USEFUL INFORMATION FOR THOSE WHO WISH TO LEARN THE CRAFT OF THE OLD MASTERS.

ALSO KNOW THIS. - ONCE YOU MASTER THE SIMPLE CSO KNOWLEDGE...YOU CAN THEN..DO YOUR OWN EXPERIMENTS...AND LEARN MORE BY YOURSELF..
IT IS WHAT I CALL...***"INTIMATE KNOWLEDGE."***...BY USING THE MATERIALS.
THERE IS A GREAT DEAL OF KNOWLEDGE IN THE BOOK...THIS WILL TAKE TIME.
THEN ONE DAY...YOU WILL LAUGH AT HOW UTTERLY SIMPLE IT ALL IS.
YOU CAN WRITE TO ME WITH AS MANY LETTERS AND QUESTIONS AS YOU WISH FOR AS LONG AS I BREATHE ...ILL RESPOND ...ILL BE AGE 73 THIS YEAR.

I'm 20 years old, and live in the United Kingdom.
NICE TO MEET YOU...I AM AMAZED AT YOUR YOUTHFUL AGE… YOUR FINE PAINTINGS YOU SHARED WITH ME, AND OF BEING SO WELL EXPRESSED...AND THE GOALS AND DETERMINATION YOU HAVE.

I am a self taught painter, specializing in oil painting. Like most painters, I've learnt how to paint mostly by looking at the work of others. This also involves making copies of their work to find out exactly how they were made- I have always had a deep fascination with the materials they used. I am interested in artists from the 15th century right up to the modern day. I have a particular love for Rembrandt, Rubens, Anthony Van Dyck, Constable, Turner, Jean Baptiste Camille Corot, Degas, Monet, Bonnard, Vuillard.....and the list goes on.

YOUR PARAGRAPH DESCRIBES EXACTLY HOW I LEARNED TO PAINT.
I WAS TEN YEARS OLD... MY MOM BOUGHT US A CHILDRENS VERSION ..18 VOLUMES OF THE WORLD BOOK ENCYCLOPEDIA..ONE DAY..IN THE "P" VOLUME.. UBDER " PAINTINGS" , I FOUND FULL COLOR REPROS OF ALL THE GREAT OLD AND MODERN MASTERS . BY AGE 13, I WAS SPENDING ALL MY TIME IN THE PUBLIC LIBRARY AFTER SCHOOL, READING AND POURING OVER THE ILLUSTRATIONS IN THE ART BOOKS.

I am currently still developing my own style and way of perceiving the world in which we live. Yet I continue to make copies of older paintings (or my own in their style). This gives me much more intimate knowledge of how they thought and painted. It is a vital part of my education!

THERE IS THAT WORD *"INTIMATE KNOWLEDGE"* THAT YOU USED THAT TELLS ME YOU ARE A BRILLIANT YOUNG MAN! THAT MAGIC WORD YOU USED COMES FROM CONTINUED EFFORT TO LEARN AND ..TO UNDERSTAND.- BRAVO!

I have been experimenting with materials for years, with a particular interest in achieving similar paint characteristics to the old masters. Like many oil painters, I have looked at old masters, and have wondered how they could possibly achieve such effects. The paints, canvas and mediums bought at the art store simply can't produce something so superior and beautiful, no matter how hard you try.

YOU ARE CORRECT.- A MAN FROM AUSTRALIA CAME TO VISIT ME SOME YEARS AGO. HE SAID THE SAME THING YOU SAID. HE SAID THAT WHEN HE READ MY WEBSITE---HE DID NOT BELIEVE A WORD I WROTE BECAUSE HE THOUGHT IT WAS ALL ADVERTISING-—UNTIL THE BOOK ARRIVED.
HE TOO WAS SELF TAUGHT AND TRIED EVERYTHING. HE ALMOST GAVE UP OIL PAINTING. HE BECAME A GOOD FRIEND AFTER ALL THESE YEARS.

I read Ralph Mayer's Artists Handbook back to front many times, trying out different mixtures of oils (which I now know were alkali refined), resins, driers, solvents etc. Of course, none of them seemed to achieve what I wanted. Then one day I discovered sun thickened oil by mistake when a little oil had thickened on my palette. I loved its viscosity, stickiness and fast drying time.

I TOO HAVE DONE WHAT YOUVE DONE....AS I GREW FROM TEENAGER TO ADULT. SELF LEARNING..INTIMATE KNOWLEDGE.

IN SALVADOR DALI'S BOOK.....
http://www.amazon.com/Secrets-Magic-Craftsmanship-Dover-History/dp/0486271323/ref=sr_1_9?s=books&ie=UTF8&qid=1430014545&sr=1-9&keywords=salvador+dali

DALI SAYS SOMETHING SIMILAR TO YOUR PERSONAL EXPERIENCE..HIS OIL JAR HAD REMAINED IN THE WINDOW SILL.....A WASP HAD FALLEN IN....HE SAW THE **BRILLIANCY** OF THE COLORS YELLOW AND BLACK - IT WAS THE VISCOUS OIL'S APPEARANCE AND THE COLOR DEPTH AND UNBELIEVABLE OPTICAL CLARITY.....OF THE SUN THICKENED OIL!!! THAT GAVE IT THAT BEAUTY. DALI LATER SAID: *"Today in 1948, we can build a H-Bomb…but no one knows what Vermeer's painting medium was".* WELL, DALI DID NOT KNOW, BUT TODAY WE DO KNOW. IT IS SOMETHING LIKE 'CSO'. DALI DID FIND A SUBSTITUTE ... IT WAS FREDERIC TAUBES "COPAL PAINTING MEDIUMS" DALI LOVED USING THEM..
FREDERIC TAUBES' BOOKS WERE MY TEACHER TOO.

I then researched it and decided to make a large quantity of it (still using the alkali refined oil). It took 5 months or so to thicken but it sure was worth it. I could never go back to using anything else- I was hooked!
YES.....NOW WITH THE CSO METHODS..IT WILL BE EASIER.
THE AIR PUMP WAS A PROBLEM AS IVE TRIED TO POINT OUT...
THE AIR MUST BE DRY......ANY HUMIDITY IN THE AIR ....WILL CAUSE THE AIR PUMP TO BLOW MOISTURE INTO THE OIL..CAUSING SLOW DRYING OIL

NOW, WITH THE HELP OF A DUTCH ARTIST WE FOUND A WAY TO PREVENT THE MOIST HUMID AIR FROM GETTING INTO THE OIL. The METHOD IS CALLED
" The CSO Psyllium Husk [Velasquez-Travenier] Method. IT USES NO ALCOHOL, AND YOU CAN READ ABOUT IT ON MY WEBSITE AND IN THIS BOOK.

I then came across your website and was amazed at the wealth of information on there. You're a true pioneer in this field of research. I have already tried combining the sun thickened alkali refined oil with chalk, marble dust etc. and have seen how incredible the paint handling and effects are.
THANKS TO SCIENCE OF 1988.. PUBLISHED BY THE LONDON. NATIONAL GALLERY..IN THE BOOK. "REMBRANDT: ART IN THE MAKING" YOUR BRITISH SCIENTISTS FOUND THAT REMBRANDT USED THE CHALK...THEN IN 1990...THE PRADO IN SPAIN... FOUND THAT VELASQUEZ USED CHALK AND CALCITE..ALONE OR TOGETHER..AS THEY ANALYZED OVER 50 OF VELAZQUEZ' PAINTINGS...THEN IN LATER SCIENCE STUDIES....RUBENS WAS FOUND TO HAVE USED CHALK TOO

I have just read most your book and can't wait to make and use the superior sun thickened flax oil, with the added knowledge of CSO, emulsions, oil outs etc. as you have described. I have a few questions:

THE EMULSIONS ARE ONE VERY IMPORTANT KEY.
PLEASE PLAY AROUND WITH THEM. -.PLEASE FIRST..USE THEM AS I INSTRUCT, THEN… EXPERIMENT AND BRANCH OUT.
THEY ARE TRUELY A MAGICAL INGREDIENT.- IN MY EXPERIENCE AND OPINION, IT IS 1/2 OF THE VAN EYCK SECRET MEDIUM…..THE OTHER HALF IS KNOWING HOW TO RUB IT IN….INTO AN ULTRA THIN FILM…THEN APPLY THE CSO OIL PAINT WHILE THE 'OIL OUT' FILM IS DAMP.

1. Regarding the air pump oil: will the plastic tubing react chemically with the oil after being submerged in it for long periods of time?
2. NOT AT ALL FOR THE 10 to 15 DAYS… BUT DO NOT STORE YOUR OIL IN PLASTIC BOTTLES. USE GLASS.
3. Do I need to sterilize the glass jars containing the flax oil and emulsions, or can i simply wash them with soap and water?
4. ONCE YOU USE EGG IN A JAR..THROW IT AWAY. DONT REUSE IT.
5. Can I safely use tap water to cleanse my oil using the psyllium husk-water method?
6. YES, BUT I RECOMMEND THE CSO PSYLLIUM HUSK-ALCOHOL METHOD or the VELAZQUEZ-TRANENIER [non- alcohol] AIR PUMP METHOD AS BEING MORE EFFECTIVE
7. Would I be able to use the 10 day air pump oil for the Aguado oil out, CSO mix, and the Viscious Emulsion?
8. YES. 10 DAYS IS ALL YOU NEED—BUT YOU CAN USE THE AIR PUMP FOR UP TO 18 DAYS, NOT MORE.
9. Would it be wise to add a drop of VE to my 50% CSO / 50% Tube oil paint mix?
10. ONLY IF YOU WILL BE USING IMPASTO……..THIN OIL PAINT, DOES NOT NEED IT BECAUSE THIN PAINT DOES NOT WRINKLE…..ONLY IMPASTO WILL WRINKLE. THE 1 or 2 DROPS OF THE EMULSION WILL PREVENT ANY WRINKLING OF THE IMPASTO THICK PAINT

With this new knowledge of the old masters' materials and methods of application, which you have provided me, I aim to produce some accurate copies of old master paintings- with their underpaintings, layers, textures, glazes and scumbles. I think Ii will try a Rembrandt self-portrait first! I will email you an image of it when it is completed- give me a few months though!

DEAR FRIEND
I AM EXCITED IN SEEING YOUR PAINTINGS.
YES..WRITE WITH ALL THE QUESTIONS THAT COME UP
CORDIALLY AND BEST WISHES, LOUIS VELASQUEZ

LETTER # 32: THE EASY WAY TO THICKEN THE CLEANSED OIL – HEDDA'S BOX

HEDDA GJERPEN is a gifted fine artist from Norway. She is fortunate to also live in Rome, Italy part of the year. She knows firsthand the two distinct geographical areas that vary greatly in temperature , sunlight and humidity.
Over the years, by meeting artists from around the world, it became clear that the CSO procedures on processing the raw oil, must be slightly altered according to ones geographic area.

HEDDA wrote me a letter [2015] with photos (see them on my website) of the oil sitting inside a large clear plastic file/ storage box with a lid. This introduces a simple low cost method to thicken the cleansed oil, without the worry or concern that dust, bugs, rain or other forms of moisture getting into the oil as it thickens.

HEDDAS LETTER is included here for us all to learn. Her words confirm important observation I too have noted about the thickening and the bleaching of the oil once cleansed of the mucilage. My only suggestion to her idea, was to drill several 1/2 inch wide holes 2 inches from the bottom, to allow more air circulation and to prevent moisture condensation.

HEDDAS WORDS ARE IN LOWER CASE. MINE ARE IN CAPS.
I'm happy more people are using the box… there is absolutely zero work with it.
IT IS A BRILLIANT IDEA FOR THE MANY REASONS YOU MENTION. I TOO HAVE HAD SPILLS, MESSES, GRIME, DIRT IN THE OIL, LEAVES AND BUGS ..ETC ETC. THE BOX SOLVES ALL THAT .

But I absolutely do NOT recommend making any holes in it… in that case they must be very tiny.

I READ YOUR REASONS BELOW.....YOU MAKE A GREAT POINT. IT ALL DEPENDS ON YOUR GEOGRAPHIC/ CLIMATE AREA..WHEN I FIRST BEGAN THE CSO RESEARCH......ITS THE ONE THING THAT BECAME CLEAR.....
WE ALL LIVE IN DIFFERENT TEMPERATURE ZONES...HUMIDITY...SUNLIGHT....
AND THESE ARE IMPORTANT ENVIRONMENTAL FACTORS AND VARIABLES THAT DIRECTLY IMPACT THE RESULTS OF OUR OIL

Here in Italy the rain is crazy sometimes.. like a tropical storm or something..
it's raining in all directions including upwards when the drops hit the floor.
WHEN I WAS AGE 20 I WENT TO THE STATE OF GEORGA.....THAT REGION IS CALLED...THE SOUTH. IT WOULD RAIN SO HARD..IT WOULD KICK MUD UP AT THE WALLS!!!!! SO I CAN FULLY UNDERSTAND YOUR ITALIAN RAIN!!!
THANK YOU
Probably people must test this a little bit in their own area.. I have no holes
Actually the lid isn't 100% tight so some air will always enter anyway
GOOD POINT. YES. EACH IN THEIR OWN AREA

If the box is big enough.. there will be space around the containers inside the box and that is an extra protection against infiltration of water on the sides
YES. GOOD POINT
I have never seen any condensation at all… but that could be different with another type of box or in another climate.in this case maybe my very cheap boxes are good because the lid isn't super tight
YES...ANOTHER GOOD POINT...THE VARIABLES WE EACH MUST FIND OUT FOR OUR AREA AND BOX CONSTRUCTION

I keep the lids on more or less all the time now.. I have a plastic glove under the lid in one corner to let in some air.
YES. OXYGEN IS NECESSARY FOR THICKENING...CANNOT DO WITHOUT IT

The weather is unpredictable here too right now so if it starts to rain with no warning I still don't get an accident because the rain won't enter under the lid with glove before it rains like crazy.. maybe
THANK YOU...GOOD

another benefit is that if you have an accident while moving the boxes.. the oil spill ends up inside the box and can be saved.
THAT IS VERY IMPORTANT..ONCE I SPILLED AN ENTIRE 16 OUNCE JAR OF...FINISHED OIL!!! WHAT A MESS...AND I HAD TO SOMEHOW RECOVER IT. THE OIL WAS EVERYWHERE.

when the top of the lid is full of water I put a towel on top and let it suck up the water repeatedly till its dry… do not open the lid when there is water left on it.
CREATIVE SOLUTIONS...GREAT.
OTHERS WILL FIND USE OF THE BOX, TO BE VERY IMPORTANT

I did a drying test with the oil made in the boxes and the one that was completely free without lid last year and they dry identically fast.
EXCELLENT TEST...THIS IS GOOD EVIDENCE FOR USING THE BOX

I think the air and heat is more important than the sunrays actually.. air for the bleaching and heat/air for the drying.
YOUR OBSERVATION IS VERY IMPORTANT. THE AIR PUMP METHOD PROVED WHAT YOU JUST SAID ABOUT HOW THE AIR...CONTINUOUS MOVING AIR..WILL HELP TO RAPIDLY BLEACH THE OIL...THE OXYGEN IS ALSO IMPORTANT FOR THE THICKENING..THE SUN UV RAYS ALSO PLAY AN IMPORTANT PART..THE HEAT TOO....MOTHER NATURE IS VERY PROFOUND.

I have bottles with oil from before xmas that is only cleaned and has not been in the sun.. . only in the room in bottles and the more air there is in the bottle the more the oil looses it's color.
GREAT OBSERVATION...WE KNOW THAT SUNS RAYS BOUNCE ALL OVER THE WORLD..EVEN INTO SHADOWS. BUT THEY CANT ENTER INTO DARK ROOMS. HOWEVER.....I HAVE NOTED THAT CLOSED BOTTLES HALF FULL WITH OIL AND LOTS OF AIR....KEPT IN THE DARK ROOM...WILL NOT BLEACH...THEY REMAIN YELLOW OIL

It's this oil I use for making paints.. so there will be more and more air in the bottles as I use the oil .
I UNDERSTAND...I RECOMMEND PUTTING THE GLASS JARS OF OIL IN A WELL LIGHTED WINDOW. ...OVER TIME THE OIL BLEACHES.

the same goes for uncleaned oil… with mucilage… lots of air.. leads to less color (but this oil doesn't dry as we know)
YES TRUE..OIL WITH MUCILAGE WILL NOT DRY WELL...IT DRIES VERY SLOWLY BECAUSE MUCILAGE HAS A LOT OF MOISTURE.

If some drops of water should enter the oil I can't see the big problem with it… the sun will dry that water up in no time!
A FEW DROPS OF MOISTURE IS NOT A PROBLEM. SOME OLD MASTERS WOULD " temporarily" PLACE THEIR FRESH OIL PAINT UNDER WATER..SO IT WOULD NOT DRY OUT……BUT I FOUND OUT THAT IF CSO…IS ADDED TO THE OIL PAINT….AND KEPT UNDER WATER..THE CHALK BECOMES OPAQUE BY ABSORBING THE WATER, AND THE PAINT COLOR BECOMES A PASTEL COLOR. THOSE EXPERMENTS ARE IN MY BOOK.

- Hedda
THANK YOU AGAIN, LOUIS

LETTER # 33: WHAT IS AN AIR STONE?

An Air Stone is a simple small object sold at pet stores for aquariums. It can be easily attached to the Air Pump. It is like a shower head that sprays the water through numerous tiny air jets. It is valuable for the AIR pump we use , but necessary. You will read how it is effective to stopping the oil from splashing. This letter includes other aspects of the Air pump's effectiveness.

Louis,
Your book and methods are just fantastic! My first batch of air pump sun oil was a success.

DEAR FRIEND..I CANT TAKE ALL THE CREDIT…….IT'S AN EVOLVING METHOD THAT I'VE BEEN WORKING ON FOR 15 + YEARS ON MY PART.

I FIRST READ ABOUT CALCIUM CARBONATE CHALK IN 1988 … IN THE LONDON NATL GALLERY BOOK OF REMBRANDT'S PAINT BINDER AND PIGMENTS.

YES ... I HAVE DONE LOTS OF TESTING AND THEY ARE IN MY BOOK…BUT EVEN THEN … NEW INFO HAS COME IN …VERY SLOWLY…OVER THE YEARS ... AND I THANK ALL MY ART FIRNDS ACROSS THE GLOBE WHO HAVE INSPIRED ME.

I'M ALMOST FNISHED WITH VOLUME TWO OF MY BOOK. IT HAS LOTS OF NEW INFORMATION …TO GUIDE AND INSPIRE ARTISTS TODAY AND FUTURE.

It's still warm here in Salinas, California, and when I started the 14-15 day pump stretch the humidity shot up to 85-90%. Very rare, for around here. A second fast wash removed the hazy moisture easily and the oil came out clear again. The pump ran for 10 days when the humidity shot up.

YES. THAT BECAME THE BIG CRITICAL ISSUE WITH THE AIR PUMP. AN ARTIST IN HOT SUMMER VERY MUGGY WEATHER IN FLORIDA WAS THE FIRST TO TELL ME THAT HIS OIL WAS FILLED WITH MOISTURE BY THE AIR PUMP PUMPING WET AIR. SO, THAT'S WHY WE NOW ADD SOME DRY PSYLLUUM HUSK AS THE PUMP IS PUMPING AIR. IT ABSORBS THE MOISTURE FROM THE HUMIDITY.

I used a double air pump from Walmart, and air stones on my tubing lines into the jar, and it greatly reduced the splashing of oil up through the vent hole. I tried with and without air stones in a 16oz batch in a 32oz jar. Just the tubing created splash through and oil was mysteriously migrating through the vent. The air stones eliminated this minor detail.

YES. THAT DOES WORK. I'M SURE OTHER ARTISTS WILL BENEFIT FROM READING YOUR LETTER AND YOUR CREATIVE SOLUTIONS, TO THE TECHNICAL NEEDS.

I'm very happy with the results. The oil is not water clear but I am letting it sit jarred, in the sun. I guess I will find out how long it will take with the shorter days of winter although it's still warm.

I did rid the oil of the humidity with a second washing for sure using the second cleansing method with. It is no longer slightly hazy but "light straw yellow clear". I'll let the sun bleach it longer.

ALSO TRY THIS METHOD- BECAUSE OF THAT HIGH HUMIDITY YOU HAD

PUT 1/2 VOLUME OUNCE PSYLLIUM HUSK IN THE OIL JAR ... CAP AND SHAKE VIGOROUSLY FOR A FEW MINUTES, SO ALL IS WELL MXED. WAIT TEN MINUTES THEN REPEAT ANOTHER VIGOROUS SHAKE. LET STAND SEVERAL MINUTES. THEN USE A COLANDER TO SEPARATE THE OIL AND THE HUSK

THEN FILTER IT THROUGH THE FUNNEL WITH THE COTTON BALL. ONCE FILTERED, CAP THE JAR AND PLACE IN THE REFRIGERATOR. DO NOT PLACE IN THE FREEZER. -LEAVE IT IN THE REFRIGERATOR FOR A FEW HOURS ONLY. THIS OIL SHOULD NOW BE MOISTURE FREE...AND FULLY TRANSPARENT WITHOUT ANY CLOUDINESS...NO MATTER HOW LONG IT'S LEFT THERE.

I did a test with some Winton oil colors. The CSO/Titanium white mix dried overnight. Amazing. The burnt umber, burnt sienna, yellow ocher, ultramarine blue all dried very quick.

EXCELLENT, IF YOU MIX THE OIL WITH DRY PIGMENTS, SOME COLORS WILL DRY WITHIN 6 HOURS.

The calcium carbonate I used was the champagne chalk from Kremer as you advised.

YES, IT'S THE HIGHEST QUALITY AND NOT EXPENSIVE

I watched for wrinkling and have not seen any.

IF YOU DO SEE WRINKLING THE SOLUTION IS SIMPLE. MAKE THE EMULSION FROM GLAIR AND OIL. THEN, ADD A FEW DROPS ...GRIND IT IN WELL. THE WRINKLING HAPPENS ON VERY FAST DRYING PAINT, IF...THE PAINT IS THICKLY APPLIED.

The nonfat powdered milk under painting was successful too. I still need to get used to the fast dry time of this. It kind of reminds me of acrylics.

IT WAS DESIGNED FOR FAST DRYNG OF UNDER PAINTING ... IT DRIES FASTER THAN ACRYLICS

I read a testimonial on your web page about how the cso/paint mixture, "was like liquid glass". It is true!

YES. IT IS REALLY AMAZING - AND SO COUNTER INTUITIVE- WHEN THE EMULSION IS MADE OF MIXING OIL AND EGG GLAIR IT IS PURE WHITE AND OPAQUE. BUT THEN, WHEN RUBBED INTO THE SURFACE – IT BECOMES AS FULLY TRANSPARENT AS GLASS!

Thank you very much,
Mike Wilson
Salinas, California

CHAPTER TWO:

ESSAYS ON OLD and MODERN MASTERS
CREATIVE ARTISTS PAINT "IDEAS".

Our paintings are a record of our lives.
"ART IS A WINDOW AND ART IS A MIRROR"-
PAINTINGS ARE A WINDOW TO OUR PAST,
AND A MIRROR OF OUR PRESNT.

The purpose of this chapter is to stimulate creative artists to think "outside of their normal sphere". My books have focused on the technical aspects of the art materials.
However, I realized long ago that <u>Aesthetics and Technical issues</u> are related.

Even the greatest masters like Velazquez and Vermeer, who focused on painting extraordinary realism, DID NOT simply copy EXACTLY what they saw, even when they traced the projected images by concave mirrors or lenses , with or without the 'camara obscura'.
They did what all creative artists do, THEY EDITED the visual reality they saw and CONSTRUCTED meaningful expressions of their aesthetic ideas.

I believe the working methods of some Old Masters are an inspiration for contemporary artists.
My hope is the reader will be inspired to <u>think and imagine</u>… before they paint.
We all have personal ideas and as creative artists, we can share our personal ideas in paintings, as they define who we are as individuals.

ESSAY #1: DAVID HOCKNEY
THE USE OF MIRRORS AND LENSES TO TRACE IMAGES

DAVID HOCKNEY: THE SECRET KNOWLEDGE OF THE OLD MASTERS
To begin this chapter, I begin with the research by David Hockney, who published in about 2001, on the "Secrets of the Old Masters". His landmark work has exposed the hidden tracing/projection/collage methods used by SOME— [BUT NOT ALL] —Old Masters.

In the year 2001, David Hockney's book, 'Secret Knowledge', and Philip Steadman's book, "Vermeer's Camera", were published. The "hidden secret" was that many Old Masters traced projected images and these two men exposed those methods. These books changed my thoughts and beliefs about the masterpieces. AT FIRST, I felt the magic of the paintings was gone. It was a let-down that took me years to understand. Today, Years later I am comfortable with the truth exposed by Hockney and Steadman.

TRACING IS NOT CHEATING
I never felt the artists "cheated" by using optics and projections to trace the images. Had their tracing methods not been kept a secret and known to all, I would not have cared and I might have used projections too. However I felt cheated.
I felt cheated because they purposely hid their methods. Initially, I saw my heroes as LIARS.
I felt tricked into believing the highly accurate details had been drawn freehand.

VERMEER traced as did VELAZQUEZ and HALS.
REMBRANDT sometimes did it, as did many others. By tracing projected images, these great artists created some of the most moving masterpieces.

MANY OF THE GREATEST MASTERS DID NOT TRACE.
El Greco didn't, neither did Bosch, nor Michelangelo, nor Botticelli and many others.
Their artistic visions had no need for tracing. Their images came from their heart and soul.

THE REASONS FOR TRACING
In time, I better understood the reasons the Old Masters had for hiding the "secret methods" from others. It was simple commerce and elimination of competition. Even today, Trade secrets, in many aspects of commercial enterprises are guarded to protect their product from cheap duplication and to insure steady profits.

One other reason for tracing is that it saved a lot of time.
Tracings are quickly made, while freehand drawings take a lot of time.
In addition, the degree of accuracy and details is made easier.

KNOWLEDGE AND FREEDOM
With the "secret methods" publicly exposed and understood, artists can better appreciate the masterpieces as being commercial products. Much of the "magic" is gone forever.
However, the paintings can now be more accurately evaluated.

Another aspect of the Old Masters business of making and selling paintings involves the " workshop". The painting of hand painted pictures was a full blown industry, with the goal being, to sell and make a profit. A workshop solves the simple economic principle of Supply and Demand. Most of the great Masters had many talented assistants to help them paint the commissioned paintings.

This fact that "paid employees" helped in painting the pictures, was never hidden. It was openly discussed in letters of the times. Knowing this today allows us to better appreciate the huge number of paintings that some artists, like Peter Paul Rubens, were able to deliver to their patrons. Once paintings by Rubens became highly sought after, he painted few pictures entirely by himself. He mostly added the final touches on the many "Rubens paintings".

OPTICS, MIRRORS, PROJECTIONS AND TRACINGS
Today, hyper-realist style artists use modern cameras and projectors. Their paintings look EXACTLY like photographs. The crude optical lenses and mirrors used by the Old Masters are no longer sought after for projecting images and for tracing.

PROJECTED IMAGES WILL NOT MAKE MASTERPIECES BY THEMSELVES
When one looks at the great modern paintings of Van Gogh, Dali, Picasso ...OR, the great Old Master paintings of Botticelli, Bosch, and others, one understands that use of projection tools are simply TOOLS. They are not needed for creating great masterpieces. Rembrandt knew of projections used by his contemporaries. He may have experimented with them also. There is a statement attributed to him in which he says, "I am not a dyer". This means he did not project, to trace, and then "color in" the outlines like a child's paint by number set, or coloring book..

ESSAY # 2 : THE OLD MASTERS' TWO PROJECTION TOOLS

DAVID HOCKNEY conclusively proved that two projection tools were used in European painting by the Old Masters. Yes, I know there are those that do not accept his findings. I am a painter and my experience for over 50 years, tells me Mr. Hockney's theory is correct.

The first projection tool to be used was a **concave mirror** and this occurred in about 1420. The second one was **optical lenses** as used in eye glass spectacles. These lenses became common in the late 1500's when microscopes and telescopes were created using high quality magnification glass lenses.

1420: The concave mirror will project an image that can be traced under specific conditions in daylight. The required daylight conditions are that the projection surface [the paper] must be in shade or shadow, and the subject [the person being drawn] must be in very bright sun light. The one problem was that these images were projected upside down, but it is important that they were not mirror reversed. The projected image was not perfect. The circular shaped projected image became blurry as the image receded from the central axis. Distortions were common.

1500's: The use of lenses for artistic projections required the use of a dark room, or a shaded box. The lens was placed stationary in one wall, and the images of the subjects illuminated by the sun, were projected through the glass lens and onto the wall inside the dark room (the word Camara Obscura means Dark Room).

The Camara Obscura, with its dark room projection had two problems . The projected image on the far vertical wall was upside down and mirror reversed.

If the artist traced this image, any images and words were backwards. Artists could deal with upside down images but needed to try different things to correct the mirror reversal so the tracing would accurately represent the subject.

SOLVING THE CAMARA OBSCURA MIRROR REVERSED IMAGE:
Creative artists tried many arrangements and combinations of lenses and mirrors to correct the mirror reversed image. Sometimes they used several one or more flat mirrors to correct a mirror reversed image.

One solution to the upside down, mirror reversed projected image , was to simply place a flat mirror at a 45 degree angle to a 'stationary' lens that projected the image into the dark room. This offered three benefits. [1] The first was to correct the mirror reversal and [2] the image was projected downwards and flat onto a horizontal table. [3] This downward horizontal projection allowed the artist to sit in a chair at the table and to carefully trace the image while in a comfortable position.

THE IMPORTANCE OF THE TRACING
Artists create images in their mind by use of their gift of imagination, originality, and personal atheistic sensibilities. Once this is done the next step is to further develop the idea in a tangible form that can be seen by others. Many great masters would make numerous compositional sketches and drawings. Michelangelo, Rembrandt and others left us proof of this creative method by their surviving drawings. These show us how the finished painting was first begun as an idea.

Vermeer left no drawings and Velazquez left only a few. Other masters who used projection devices, like Hals and Caravaggio, also left no drawings. The reason they left few or no drawings was because they composed the paintings in front of the CAMARA OBSCURA by moving the objects around. There was no need to draw.

The use of projection devices such as mirrors and lenses allowed creative artists to circumvent the making of drawings and sketches as the main method to compose the idea of the planned painting. Once the tracing was finished, the artist still had to paint the picture..

LIMITATIONS AND REQUIREMENTS OF THE CAMARA OBSCURA
1. The Camara Obscura requires the subject to be in bright light. The brighter...the better.
2. The inside of the Camara Obscura can function, in low light or even studio light [I call this the Daylight Camera]. They serve the important purpose of establishing the composition, and for painting a brown monotone, or for drawing the composition, as many artists did under-draw with pencils and charcoal and ink.
3. The Camara Obscura does not allow an artist to paint bright colors...in the dark
4. The Camara Obscura needs THREE implements to serve the artist better.
The first is a flat mirror inside the dark room, placed at a 45 degree angle to the lens, to project a corrected mirror-reversed image downwards and onto a horizontal table. This set-up removes the obstruction to the projection, caused by the artists body, and allows artists who does detailed tracing to sit down.
The second is a " focus lens" , that allows the projected image to be focused into high resolution. This is the same principal used in telescopes and microscopes.
The third is the placement of mirrors INSIDE THE STUDIO, appropriately arranged, for directing sunlight (spotlighting) onto specific areas of the model, for illuminating details.

ESSAY #3; THE USE OF LENS AND MIRRORS FOR PAINTING

This essay presents my study of the paintings of Velazquez and Vermeer.
The paintings of Velazquez and Vermeer are easily recognized because they are so different.
The unique quality – they share in common- is how they both painted light and shade.
I conclude that both achieved this uniqueness of light and shade, by painting a reflected image they saw in in a flat mirror – OR– by use of a glass lens to project the image – OR- both..

LEONARDO DA VINCI'S USE OF MIRRORS
The image we can see in a mirror has been written about by several artists in history. The most meaningful observation, for artists, were written by Leonardo Da Vinci in the 1500's. In brief, he recommended artists should place their painting- alongside and next to - a flat mirror that was reflecting the subject being painted to compare the painting to the mirror reflection.
An example would be a portrait of a woman. By seeing her image in the mirror and her image in the painting, at the same time - the differences in coloring, light and shade are instantly seen.

Da Vinci's writings were known by many artists who followed him.
Even today, we can use Da Vinci's instructions to our own benefit - IF we wish to paint in a style that is " photo realism". Once the differences are seen through comparison in the mirror, the artist can make the needed corrections to lighting, shading and coloring in the painting.

Having said that, I note that the MONA LISA, is not a "photo realist" painting. Her hands are like sculpted marble and her face is not "photographic" and neither are other components of the painting. She does not look like a reflection in a mirror.

DaVinci's comments about comparing a painting with a mirror reflection are meant to instruct artists on how exact a mirror reflection can be to reality.

VELAZQUEZ' AND VERMEER'S AESTHETICS
VERMEER: With Vermeer's extraordinary realism, we recognize a sense of peace and serenity **as if the persons are frozen in time**. We note Vermeer's masterful paint application which is seen to be <u>meticulous, careful and controlled</u>. It is similar to that of many other 17th century Dutch Masters who also painted "photographic-like realism" of flowers and still lifes.

VELAZQUEZ: Unlike Vermeer's frozen stillness, Velazquez' "photographic-like realism" has a sense of motion **as if the persons were alive and breathing**. We sense the wind blowing in their hair. Velazquez' masterful paint application is <u>loose, free, sketchy, spontaneous, and alive</u>. His virtuoso paint application is also highly controlled, and has only been equaled by Rubens and Hals in the history of oil painting.

VELAZQUEZ' AND VERMEER'S REALISM
Through study, one can reasonably conclude there is no question but that both masters used optical lenses and mirrors - as legitimate tools (it is not cheating)- to help them achieve their photographic-like realism.
These tools allowed them to TRACE a projected image.
This insured that the SPATIAL positions of figures and other items were accurately represented, and followed linear perspective exactly as seen in nature.[Note; lenses did distort perspective lines- but the artists did correct these geometrically with straight edges].

HOW DID THEY ACHIEVE THEIR HIGH DEGREE OF REALISM?

A. I believe it was because they consciously tried to COPY the color values of the images they saw reflected in a mirror. Their effort to "accurately" COPY the values and colors they saw as REFLECTED in a mirror is different from what an artist 'knows' of reality when not looking at images reflected in a mirror.

B. It is important to know they could NOT COPY THE EXACT values they saw reflected in a mirror BECAUSE natures lights and shades are in constant change. However they had intellectual means and tools - memory and "value scales" (wet and dry), to assist them in approximating the values and colors.

C. Vermeer and Velazquez also differed in the way they applied the oil paint. Vermeer applied his paint carefully and meticulously like a miniaturist painter. In dramatic contrast, Velazquez used broad vigorous sketchy applications of the paint. Yet, both achieved a high degree of realism... approaching photo-realist effects.

HOW DID THE TWO MASTERS COMPOSE THEIR PAINTINGS?

Most Master painters made "composition" drawings as they determined the composition/ design of their paintings. These drawings survive and are valued works of art in themselves. Only a few portrait drawings by Velazquez exist, and no drawings by Vermeer exist. This suggests these two masters composed their paintings as they looked at the reflections in the mirrors.

A mirror has a frame and this frame allows us to see a tiny slice of life. Mirrors come in all shapes but for this essay, we are using a rectangular shaped mirror. This "rectangle" shape of a flat mirror functions like viewfinders used by modern photographers.

A mirror, or a photographer's viewfinder, blocks out everything else outside the frame/ viewfinder. Modern photographers do not make drawings in order to design and comprise their photos. They use a viewfinder and move themselves around or they move the subjects around, until they get the desired composition. Vermeer and Velazquez did the same as they moved things around, in the reflected surface of the mirror.

HOW DID VERMEER AND VELAZQUEZ DIFFER IN THEIR USE OF A MIRROR?

A flat mirror reflects a "mirror reversed" image of reality. Van Gogh cut off his left ear, and then painted a self- portrait of the injury. Since he copied what he saw in a mirror, it appears to us that his right ear was the one he cut off (due to the mirror reversed image).

Velazquez' painting of "Las Meninas" is a painting of what Velazquez saw reflected in a huge flat mirror. It is a reverse image of reality.
Vermeer's paintings are NOT mirror reversed images. He did this by combining a flat mirror placed at a 45 degree angle to an optical stationary lens, to create a "corrected" projected image. This combination of lens and mirror corrects the mirror reversed image.

Velazquez, at times, also used combinations of mirrors and optical lenses. However, he did something unique when he painted "Las Meninas". Here he painted a "reverse image" on purpose because it is such a huge painting (ten feet tall). It would be impossible to compose or paint such a huge painting in a Camara Obscura.

I believe he poised the figures in front of the large flat mirror with their backs to him. He then positioned himself and his portable "box camera" at the [viewers] far left and behind the figures. He placed the huge canvas we see reflected in the painting, in front of his camera to hide it, so the camera would not be reflected in the huge mirror. In simple terms, the huge canvas hides the camera.

The exact position of Velazquez' camera is further proven by the fact that the Princess' eyes are looking to her right and <u>straight at Velazquez and his camera</u>. Photographers often tell their subjects, "look at me, look at the camera", right before they snap the shutter.
Velazquez did the same, but he had no shutter, and had to trace.

Velazquez' own self-portrait figure in the painting shows him leaning over to his left side, so he is visible to the artist (himself) making the tracing of the scene in the mirror's reflection. It appears to me that he later painted his two arms from memory as to how they would look with brushes and palette in hand , or used a model.

IN WHAT OTHER WAY DID VERMEER AND VELAZQUEZ USE A MIRROR?
Velazquez and Vermeer, saw the same reality of life as we can see it today. The image we see in a mirror is FLATTENED to our human eyes, because the reflected image is within a frame. All reality outside the mirror's frame is cut off and is sufficiently eliminated from our eyes. Because of this, we are able to focus completely on the image inside the frame. It is similar to looking at a painting in a frame. The frame of the painting separates its contents from the side and background objects of the world. This allows our eyes to see the contents of the painting as a world within itself.

Do this experiment to demonstrate how visual reality is flattened to our eyes and mind, when we look in a flat mirror.

First. Sit in a room with furnishings and stare straight ahead. Your vision will focus on the object directly in front of you, YET, your peripheral vision is actually observing all items in the room that are within 180 degrees from your left to your right and up and down. Only the items directly in front of your eyes are in sharp focus. Everything above or below your focus point, or to the left and right of it, are out of focus, but are still visible.

Note that YOU HAVE A HIGH DEGREE of SENSATION OF DEPTH and a very accurate sense of 'sense of depth', and clear sensation of a three dimensional roundness of objects. This includes all objects you can see within this 180 degree wide panorama of sight. Nothing in this view is flattened and all objects are experienced to exist in three dimensions of depth, height and width. Please note that for this to be, you must have two eyes with adequately accurate vision. If you close one eye - you will immediately notice that the things you see lose much of their three dimensionality, and what you see will appear to be flattened , much like what one sees reflected in a flat plane mirror.

Now. Look at a reflected image in a mirror, in the same room. Regardless of the size of the mirror, everything outside its frame is cut off and separated from the reflected mirror's image. Although the items in the mirror are still seen as being in three dimensions, there is no more peripheral vision, either up, down or sideways. The contained surface area of the mirror allows the human eyes to see all items inside the mirror together as one, ALL AT ONCE, all in a sharper focus, as when compared to the broad 180 degree reality without a mirror. This gives us the effect that all items in the mirror have been flattened out. This is how we look at and appreciate paintings that are of small or medium size. Huge paintings, those covering walls, are hard to "see" as a single unit when we are too close to it. What we do is back away so the dimension of the huge painting is reduced. This allows us to see the entire content as a single whole.

This flattening of images seen in a mirror is a great assist to the artist in composing. When items are flattened, artists see them as abstracted forms of positive and negative spaces. The artist's intuition plays an important part in arranging items within the two dimensional space of the mirror. As previously said, there was never a need for Vermeer or Velazquez to make any compositional drawings. Once things were arranged and clearly visible in the mirror, the artist traced the images by use of crude camera projections.

ESSAY # 4; VERMEER'S CRUDE OPTICS

It is certain Vermeer explored and tested various optical lenses and mirror projection arrangements ....and also experimented with various arrangements of these optical materials. Did he conceive of some arrangement similar to Tim Jenison's? No one knows.
We know these instruments were available in his era.

1. Short barreled telescopes using two lenses can focus the image to be sharper or less sharp. This telescope was invented in The Netherlands over 30 years before Vermeer was born. Documents in the archives of The Netherlands, before 1600, report a Patent infringement lawsuit over the discovery of the telescope. Please note one of the lens of the short barrel telescope -was a movable FOCUS LENS!
2. Microscopes also used various lenses in combination with mirrors as a light source, and made the image sharper or less sharp. I REPEAT: of the two glass lenses- one is used as the FOCUS LENS. Vermeer's neighbor was a maker of lenses and microscopes.
3. Optical lenses of various size, shape, thickness and focal length, that could be used alone or in combination.
4. The concave mirror was used as a projector of images for tracing. It projects inverted images, BUT, the images are accurate images (not mirror reversed). This method projects an image that becomes blurry as the image spreads away from the central axis point of the center projected area.

5. Various forms and sizes of the Camara Obscura... fixed, or portable , with various arrangements and positions of one or more lens ...and mirrors .inside, outside, top, and even both sides. Optical lenses in the Camara Obscura as a projector of mirror reversed and inverted images. The additional use of a flat mirror at a 45 degree angle to the lenses, will correct the mirror-reversals and inversions of the projected images. By use of the flat mirror, the projected image is cast downwards onto a horizontal table for easier working.

6. Flat mirrors as reflectors of images that are right side up, BUT are mirror reversed images. They were used alone to paint mirror reversed images, or in combination with other mirrors to correct the mirror reversed image.

7. Use of mirrors..(like the ancient Egyptians did)..to DIRECT bright beams of exterior sources of sunlight...into dark areas ... being a crude but effective SPOTLIGHT...for the purpose of illuminating nature's details, so as to allow tracing fine line details that are projected into the dark Camara Obscura .

9. The " daylight camera" as a projector. This tracing box is simple to make. The box is kept in shadow of a well-lighted studio. A Focus lens will make the projected image highly detailed onto a horizontal surface. See my Youtube video on the "Daylight Camera".
Search: CSO VELASQUEZ to locate it.

ESSAY # 5 : VERMEER'S METHODS
I propose Vermeer used the following technical painting methods in creating his paintings.

Scientific tests show Vermeer applied an aqueous glue chalk gesso ground on his canvas and not an oil ground. I think this argues that he began the under layer of his paintings with a tempera paint medium. I theorize this because it was normal to put an oil ground on a canvas and had Vermeer done so, he could not use a Tempera paint as it does not adhere to an oil surface. There are important technical reasons why he would have chosen to use a water based Tempera paint in the painting of the monotone, [the lowest layer of paint].

Following are my reasons in support.

Tempera paint dries almost instantly and all fine lines and details are captured as painted. There is no flow nor distortion to the paint. The fast drying Tempera paint also allows easy instant corrections. Because Tempera paint is thin as watercolor paint, there is never any objectionable paint impasto build-up. Layers are equal, and edges and contours are undetectable and seamless. The Tempera paint has no objectionable odor when working. This lack of odor is important when working in the enclosed space of a Camara Obscura.

There are three basic Tempera paints known in Vermeer's time that he could have used. Hide Glue, Egg, and Milk Casein. Whether or not sufficient laboratory examinations have been conducted on the 36 Vermeer paintings, I do not know. Whether or not current investigative equipment could or could not determine if Egg or Casein were used by Vermeer in the lower Monotone layer, I do not know.

However the Tempera of hide glue could have been used and would be virtually undetectable because it becomes a part of the hide glue gesso primer on the canvas. In the past, I eliminated Glue Tempera as a possible Tempera because Hide Glue Tempera congeals when cold, making brushing fine details difficult, if not impossible. **Recently I learned that if wine is added to Hide Glue, the hide glue will not congeal and remains as liquid as watercolor paints.** This would be my choice as to which Tempera paint he used. When applied on top of Hide Glue Gesso, the adhesion is permanent and because the Tempera paint binder is the same, it would be undetectable.

I am a professional artist painter in many paint media. This experience of over 50 years allows me to propose the following application method of the Tempera paint.
Certainly, Vermeer traced/painted the monotone with the aid of a crude camera and its projection of the subject. The application of a Tempera paint for the monotone would be a mix of broad and very fine paint applications.

Once the monotone was completed, the painting was removed from the Camera Obscura. I propose Vermeer made a calculated effort to paint in the style of what I will name as the " FLAT MIRROR REFLECTION STYLE". There are two Master painters who I identify as consciously using this style, Velazquez, and Vermeer.

The "FLAT MIRROR REFLECTION STYLE" is what gives the paintings of Velazquez and Vermeer that easily recognized photographic look, with its focus on subtle values from black to white. Even today, simply by looking in any flat mirror - we can see the very same range of abstracted values that Vermeer and Velazquez saw reflected - in their flat mirrors.

ESSAY # 6 : HALS' PROJECTION METHODS
BOTH BEGAN THEIR PAINTINGS BY TRACING WITH PAINT [THEY DID NOT USE A PENCIL] . THEY TRACED THEIR PROJECTED IMAGES WITH A BROWN MONOTONE OIL PAINT.- THEY HAD 2 PROJECTION METHODS AVAILABLE TO CHOOSE FROM.
ONE WAS A LENS..THE OTHER WAS A CONCAVE MIRROR.
THE TWO PROJECTION METHODS WERE USED SEPARATELY INDIVIDUALLY, OR TOGETHER ... AS NEEDED.

PROJECTION METHOD #1.
THIS IS MY YET UNPROVEN THEORY ON HOW FRANZ HALS PAINTED HIS PORTRAITS OF OTHERS:
I BELIEVE HALS BEGAN WITH A LARGE WALK-IN SIZED DARK ROOM WITH A STATIONARY LENS (Camara obscura) AND A FOCUS LENS.
THIS HE USED FOR PAINTING FULL BODY, LIFE SIZED PORTRAITS.
THE PROJECTED IMAGE, WAS TRACE PAINTED ONTO PAPER WITH OIL PAINT...VERTICALLY TAPED TO THE REAR WALL. IT WAS PAINTED ON PAPER BECAUSE A LENS PROJECTION IS UPSIDE DOWN AND IS A REVERSED MIRROR IMAGE. THIS PAINTED TRACING, WAS THEN SUBSEQUENTLY TRANSFERRED TO THE CANVAS BY 'PRESSING AND RUBBING' THE BACK OF THE PAPER..IN ORDER TO TRANSFER THE WET OIL PAINT IMAGE ONTO THE CANVAS.

MY ARTIST FRIEND, JANE JELLY, OF ENGLAND, INSPIRED ME IN THIS THEORY. SHE HAS PUBLISHED HER THEORY AND IT CAN BE LOCATED VIA GOOGLE.

I BELIEVE HALS TRACED- PAINTED THE IMAGE ON A PAPER ...THAT WAS TAPED TO THE DARK ROOM WALL.. - I BELIEVE HALS PAINTED/TRACED THE PROJECTED IMAGE WITH **BROWN, THICK VISCOUS OIL PAINT (thin oil paint does not transfer well, while thick oil paint does)** . IT MUST BE THICK VISCOUS OIL PAINT.
THE LENS PROJECTED IMAGE WAS UPSIDE DOWN AND MIRROR REVERSED, BUT THE TRANSFERRING CORRECTS THE MIRROR REVERSED IMAGE.

THE OIL PAINTED LINES SEEP THROUGH THE PAPER, THUS, MAKING THE DRAWING VISIBLE FROM THE BACK. THIS ALLOWS ACCURATE POSITIONING ON THE CANVAS.
THEN...WHEN HALS WAS PAINTING HIS CIVIC GUARD PORTRAITS MADE OF MANY PERSONS, HE COLLAGED THE VARIOUS WET PAINTED FACES-IMAGES...BY POSITIONING AND TAPING THE IMAGE TO THE CANVAS MUCH LIKE A COLLAGE. HE PRESSED THE BACK OF THE PAPER TO TRANSFER THE IMAGE ONTO THE CANVAS.
THIS CREATED A BROWN PAINT MONOTONE. - ONCE DRY - HE THEN PAINTED THE COLORS IN ALLA PRIMA, USING HIS SKETCHY FASHION.

PROJECTION METHOD #2.
A DARK ROOM WITH A CONCAVE MIRROR (no lens, but still a Camara obscura)
THIS METHOD WAS DEMONSTRATED BY DAVID HOCKNEY IN THE BBC DOCUMENTARY "SECRET KNOWLEDGE" AVAILABLE ON YOUTUBE.
IT WAS USED FOR SMALL SIZED PORTRAITS (single head or 3/4 head and shoulders).
HALS PAINTED WITH A BROWN OIL PAINT, A MONOTONE DIRECTLY ON THE CANVAS, NOT ONTO PAPER.

ONCE THE MONOTONE DRIED, THEN HE EITHER PAINTED AN INTERMEDIATE GRISAILLE, - FOLLOWED BY A COLOR LAYER ON TOP -
OR WHEN THE MONOTONE WAS DRY, HE DID NOT PAINT THE GRISAILLE, AND SIMPLY PAINTED THE TOP COLOR LAYER ALLA PRIMA.

ESSAY #7 : HALS' 'FACE TRACING' PORTRAIT STUDIO

HALS CERTAINLY EXPERIMENTED WITH THE MANY WAYS OF PROJECTING AND TRACING. A LENS OR A CONCAVE MIRROR WILL PROJECT IMAGES.
THIS HELPED HIM TO QUICKLY AND ACCURATELY PAINT MANY PORTRAITS..

THE PROOF THAT HALS DID PROJECT AND TRACE IMAGES, WAS DEMONSTRATED BY DAVID HOCKNEY IN THE BBC DOCUMENTARY. HE SHOWS THAT ALL THE PERSONS IN A PAINTING ARE LEFT HANDED—INCLUDING A LEFT HANDED MONKEY! THIS IS DUE TO THE PROJECTION BEING MIRROR REVERSED IMAGES.

HALS BEGAN WITH A BROWN THIN PAINT MONOTONE ON THE CANVAS, PAINTING THE 'GENERAL COMPOSITION' FREESTYLE WITHOUT A PROJECTION.
-HE LEFT A 'RESERVE SPACE' FOR EACH FACE AND HEAD.
THEN THE HEADS WERE PROJECTED ON PAPER WITH A CAMARA OBSCURA, AND TRANSFERRED, OR...DRAWN ON PAPER WITH A MIRROR GRID METHOD
THEN TRANSFERRED, OR THEY WERE PROJECTED WITH A CONCAVE MIRROR

HALS MADE SURE THE LIGHTING WAS STRONG. HE POSSIBLY HAD AN OUTDOOR SHADE TENT OR HE HAD A PHOTOGRAPHERS STUDIO, WITH SEVERAL FLAT MIRRORS ARRANGED TO BOUNCE LIGHT, INTO THE ROOM FROM OUTSIDE PROJECTING PORTRAITS REQUIRED STRONG LIGHTING

HALS PROJECTED OR TRANSFERRED THE IMAGE ONTO THE CANVAS AND PAINTED THE BROWN MONOTONE LIVE – **WITH THICK VISCOUS OIL PAINT**

AFTER THE BROWN MONOTONE DRIED, HE THEN APPLIED, AN 'OIL OUT'.
HE THEN PAINTED A GRISAILLE - FOLLOWED BY PAINTING THE COLORS

ESSAY # 8: DIEGO VELAZQUEZ [1599-1661]
HOW VELAZQUEZ MAY HAVE PAINTED LAS MENINAS
[my opinion based on my experiences]

LIKE HALS, VELAZQUEZ TOO WAS A "PHOTOGRAPHER" PORTRAIT PAINTER
HE USED A CAMARA OBSCURA TO TRACE THE ARCHITECTURE OF A ROOM INTERIOR. HE THEN USED A GRID EXPANSION METHOD TO PAINT THE ROOM...THIS ROOM WAS HIS "BACK DROP" FOR THE PORTRAIT FIGURES.

VELAZQUEZ THEN USED A LENS/CONCAVE MIRROR PROJECTOR LIKE HALS, TO PROJECT AND TRACE THE PEOPLE ONE BY ONE... THEN ON TOP OF THE DRIED BACK DROP OF THE ROOM...HE TRANSFERRED THE TRACINGS, THEN USING LIVE MODELS, HE PAINTED THE MONOTONE BROWN UNDER PAINTING, THEN WHEN THE MONOTONE WAS DRIED, AGAIN WITH THE LIVE MODELS ONE BY ONE, HE PAINTED FULL COLOR ALLA PRIMA/ OR PAINTED A GRISAILLE FOLLOWED BY COLORS

I propose that Velazquez painted Las Meninas by this procedure.

1. He did NOT use sight size methods to draw the persons and architecture on the canvas nor on paper ...with everyone posing in position.
HE USED A TRACING METHOD TO TRACE THE FACES.

2. He DID use a projection tool, to project the real image, persons and architecture,
and he DID trace it. He may have used a "daylight lens" crude camera

3. Because the painting is so large [10ft x 8 feet] he could not project the full image DIRECTLY ONTO the canvas. He did it piecemeal, like a collage. He HAD to have used a grid enlargement method.

4. A lens....can project an image of live subjects...inside a Camara Obscura
That will appear onto a vertical wall...but the image will be reversed and inverted.
And projecting a ten foot tall image directly onto a huge canvas is not feasible
His choice was to use a portable sized crude 'day light camera', to trace the image possibly onto a paper for making an accurate drawing that could be enlarged by the grid method.

5: A "mirror reversed" lens projection can be "mirror reversed corrected " by placing a flat mirror at 45 degrees to the lens. By using a "daylight camera" set up... (this can also be done in a dark room, Camara Obscura)...The flat mirror will project the image downwards horizontally onto a table ...so it is not upside down- ..and so the image will not be reversed.
But this projection cannot be projected onto a horizontal ten foot tall canvas.
Therefore, this is not a feasible set up.

6. Since the image was not projected DIRECTLY to the large ten foot tall canvas, for tracing, VELAZQUEZ must have projected it onto a smaller sized paper, and traced it. Then, this small tracing would later be transferred onto the large canvas, by use of a grid transfer method. This is the same way Michelangelo had done it for his huge Sistine Chapel ceiling. Michelangelo and all the great muralists made medium sized drawings on paper [called a Cartoon] that were later enlarged by a grid method and transferred to huge walls.

7: I propose Velazquez used a portable 3 foot wide, daylight camera...using a lens, and a flat mirror . This would let him project the image horizontally onto a paper on a table. This allowed him to trace the full image... on the paper measuring about 30 X 30 inches in size. This type of projection is easy to do and the tracing is very accurate because there is no parallax distortion.

HOW DID HE COMPOSE THE PAINTING, LAS MENINAS?
I propose he composed the painting in steps.
The first step was to use his imagination in creating and making a freehand sketch of the design. He did this from his imagination ---which was inspired by what he saw reflected in the large flat mirror. Las Meninas was painted in 1656 when Velazquez was 57 years old and very experienced in creating and painting pictures by use of optical /projection tools.

WHERE DID HE PLACE THE CAMERA?
His portable daylight camera was placed in a specific place facing the huge flat mirror. I propose it was placed **behind the canvas seen in the painting**. The large canvas hides the camera...and it is not reflected in the mirror.

The camera was placed so figures would not obstruct any drawing of the subjects who were facing the large flat mirror. It was placed at a very slight angle to the flat mirror, just enough to avoid distortion.

NOTICE THIS IMPORTANT OBSERVATION: Notice the eyes of the princess are looking at the cameras position where Velazquez is also standing , which is right behind the canvas.
The canvas covers the camera so we cannot see it reflected in the mirror. . Velazquez self portrait (body) we see in the painting is a male model, but with Velazquez' facial features later added.

HOW DID HE PLACE THE MODELS?
He used a large flat mirror that reflected the room that was BEHIND HIMSELF.
I propose he began by projecting, tracing, and outlining the architecture of the room (as the stage setting) onto the large paper having the grid.
He then positioned the models facing the large flat mirror.
He stood behind the models who are in the foreground.
Using his portable daylight camera, he copied/ traced the reflected image seen in the mirror

He collaged (moved things around) to position the different figures.
He positioned and outlined the different persons , at different times, onto their predetermined design position on the paper.
While inside the Camera Box, he was able to move the paper to the left or right, or up or down, to make adjustments of the position of the figures in the design

He first outlined the princess and the two Lady Meninas, as a single group.
Then, in their absence, he outlined the two dwarfs
First the large dwarf by herself, followed by the thin dwarf with his foot on a stool.
He then drew the dog freehand without a projection or tracing.
He then positioned and outlined the three background figures.

X-rays show there was a young woman initially at the place where he painted his own self portrait. He painted her out, and painted himself in that spot.
I have read that the young woman was the Kings grown daughter from an earlier marriage, and not appreciated by the current Queen. This offered the opportunity to paint himself in her place.

ONCE THE DRAWING WAS COMPLETE
A GRID WAS DRAWN ON THE PAPER PENCIL DRAWING
AND A GRID WAS DRAWN ON THE PROPORTIONAL LARGE TEN FOOT TALL CANVAS

He made a grid on the paper and on the canvas. He had assistants enlarge and transfer the smaller sized drawing from the paper image, onto the canvas.
They drew the outlines of the persons and details of the room, and the grid **with calcium carbonate chalk which will disappear when oil paint is applied.**
The drawing was done on a on a mid-toned ground .
He then used oil paints to paint the loose sketchy brown monotone on the dry chalk outlines
After the brown monotone dried, He then painted a gray-white grisaille underpainting
After this dried he finished the painting in full colors, by painting individual portraits from life, and the costumes were worn by models.

NOTE:
The Large version of Las Meninas in the Prado museum in Madrid, Spain measures:
318cm= 125 13/16 inches= 10 ft 4 inches by 276 CM =108 21/32inches = 9feet 3/4 inch

A smaller version of Las Meninas is in England at the Kingston Lacy collection.
It is reputed to be the first draft of the larger famous painting. Its size is 142cm = 56 inches 122cm= 48 inches. Some scholars disagree as to it being by Velazquez. Francisco Goya saw it and said it was an authentic Velazquez maquette.

ESSAY # 9: VELAZQUEZ' PAINTING KING PHILLIP 4th

I continuously receive many letters about the methods and materials of Velazquez. His paintings, like Rembrandt's, seem to touch many of us.

One of my all-time favorite paintings in history, is Velazquez' LIFE SIZED painting of his King Phillip 4th. It is in the FRICK MUSEUM in NYC .The historical report is that he painted it in 3 days...at a battlefield. Then he brought it back to his studio for a few touch ups. X-rays show it has just a couple minor alterations.

HOW DID HE DO IT?
It's like asking how did Shakesphere, Einstein, Rembrandt, Ali the boxer, Tiger Woods the golfer, and other greats in their fields ....did what they did. HOW did they do it?
Obviously....it's his intellectual genius (some call it talent). Great painters are great thinkers.

BUT he used a basically simple technical method and materials to facilitate and allow the speed and to achieve the result. Following is my thoughts on how he painted it.

DAY ONE: On a well prepared canvas ...with a well prepared pale mid tone ground primer, he painted a brownish monotone of three values .....using fast drying thickened oil....using the natural drying of manganese brown umber. .. and the lead white of his era (which I believe is not needed).. Plus an emulsion and a chalk/calcite additive to stabile the oil paint.

DAY TWO: Ideally, with low humidity weather...the brownish monotone would be sufficiently non-smearing tacky dried within 6 hours ... and ready for an "oil out". On the brown monotone ...he used oil paint to paint " Alla Prima" in full coloring....with his virtuoso, unparalleled, shorthand "impressionistic" manner.
By this method, he effectively completed the painting in the second day,

DAY THREE: Minor touch ups and corrections. Later in the studio he made minor corrections over the next several days.

RUBENS was as effectively a virtuoso as was VELAZQUEZ. ..and by a very unique and specific use of a THIXOTROPIC medium... Rubens could complete a painting of many layers...in one day. (Thixoptropy is where a wet layer can be painted on top of a wet layer without disrupting the lower wet layer)
Studies show VELAZQUEZ , REMBRANDT, and RUBENS used emulsions.
RUBENS THIXOTROPIC medium is explained in my DVD free on YouTube.

A recent academic video posted on YOUTUBE by Yale university states that science shows REMBRANDT (meaning certainly others too) used a MULTIMEDIA construction of the oil paintings, to increase drying and accelerate their completion . The science states REMBRANDTS **brownish colored under painting was an emulsion made by mixing a protein liquid and an oil.**

INTERESTING FACTS ABOUT A MIRROR REFLECTION OF YOUR FACE
Stand an arm's length in front of a large mirror. Use a marker to mark the mirror by placing a horizontal line at the top of your head, and a line at the level of the chin.

If you measure your actual head from top to chin you will see that a 9 inch high head, when seen in the mirror, is one half the size of your actual face. The mirror reflection will be 4 1/2 inches But this is an illusion. As you move back away from the mirror, your head will remain within the same markings you made on the mirror. Because you are backing away, the 4 & ½ inch head becomes smaller in line with the size of the mirror becoming also smaller in size.

ESSAY# 10 : JOHANNES VERMEER'S USE OF BLUE PART ONE

Much has been written about the photographic appearance of Vermeer's true to life accurate " light and shade values" , seen in his paintings. I will try to explain why Vermeer's use of ultramarine blue is important to understanding the unique beauty of light we see in his paintings, and how by using blue, he achieved the accurate representation of nature's colored light and bluish colored shade values.

Just yesterday, I took a walk outside under a bright blue sky, and by observing nature's brilliant light, I conformed what I will say about Vermeer's use of blue. At the conclusion of this essay you can read about my walk in my garden, and how it relates to what I have written here. I must first lay a foundation by discussing major artists, schools of painting, and the historical development of oil paints.

The walk I took outside confirmed what I had realized in theory about what Vermeer and Velazquez and the Impressionists also saw with their two good eyes.
In my garden, I saw the living light of nature in all it's true glory of colors. Trees and flowers bathed in colored lights and with bluish colored shadows. The white light came from our sun. The light was palpable and gleaming, and existed in three dimensions as I was also able to perceive its depth. Nature's light is not flat nor are its nuances hidden from, nor invisible to my retina. As I moved my focus, the colors of nature's living colored lights and bluish colored shadows were beautifully and accurately perceptible. I as an artist have always known that the sun's light beams bounce everywhere. The light livens up the deepest shadows and makes the lightest areas of things sparkle as if covered with dew.

In my garden I saw the innumerable blue hues of nature. Many more blues and far more profound than Vermeer's simple ultramarine blue hue. And, mixed within, was the warm colorful light from the sun. Such was Vermeer's , Velazquez' and the Impressionist's secret of using the color blue to accurately represent nature's living lights and shadows.
- Louis R. Velasquez November 10, 2014

JOHANNES VERMEER'S USE OF BLUE
PART TWO

INTRODUCTION
This essay is focused on how Vermeer used color ....as well as how he used light in creating his paintings. Light and color can be discussed separately by artists, but are one and the same because we cannot see colors without light.

To better express my thoughts, I wish to describe a recent visual experience I had that was related to the weather ... as well as the time of day ... and the month of the year.

In my recent studies of Vermeer's paintings, the focus by artists and historians has been on his use of LIGHT. Some refer to the "tonal" qualities in describing his paintings. The scientific studies of his pigments , by the London National Gallery Museum, shows Vermeer used blue pigment systematically, and that blue is mixed with almost all of his other colors. I have noted that the color blue is the underlying color of our natural air - and the fact that air envelops everything, the color blue is visually evident everywhere in nature as we see it.

I believe Vermeer also experienced the same visual experience I had, and on several occasions. I too have experienced it on several occasions throughout my life, but I never before related it to the light and color I see in Vermeer's paintings.
I recognize my perception of this experience as an epiphany.

A REVELATION
Yesterday I drove my car eastbound, in San Diego, California (my home). The setting sun was behind me. It was late afternoon. A slight rain had cleared the air and the air was crystal clear. Please remember those descriptive words' " crystal clear". This crystal clarity caused by the rain combined with the late hour of the afternoon was further enhanced by the brilliant rays of the setting sun. Everything, including the details on trees on distant mountains were seen in hyper sharp detail. The clouds ... in the distant brightly lit eastern sky ... were of various colors of purple and gray and salmon pink and orange. The buildings and homes on the hills were illuminated by a magical light emanating from the setting sun. Highlights on the structures glistened like diamonds, as if spot lighted . They contrasted with the muted grays of the shadows of hills, trees and other structures obstructed by the light. The total effect of multiple colors and glistening light was surreal and magical.

MAGICAL COLORS AND LIGHT
I once lived in San Francisco, California. The magical effect I saw yesterday in San Diego I had frequently seen in San Francisco. This extraordinary beauty of light and colors is commonly seen in the City of San Francisco because of its geographical location. It is 500 miles to the north of San Diego. The Pacific Ocean is at the very edge of the city of San Francisco. The air is generally moist with fog being a part of the early morning or evening air, and it is more common in certain seasons of the year. Once the morning sun burns off the marine air and fog, the extraordinary colors and lighting are EXACTLY the very same colors and lights I see in the paintings of Vermeer, and those I saw in San Diego. The Netherlands have air that is also very moist.

DELFT IN VERMEER'S TIME
Holland is a beautiful country. Like all modern cities today around the world, we accept today's smog and air contamination. Also, today, because of so many electrical lights, we can see only a fraction of the stars at night. Years ago I was in Australia's outback, 600 miles fram a city. An area that is completely isolated. One night, I saw the trillions of stars of our Milky Way galaxy like I had never seen before. They seemed so close and the rotation of the Earth was powerfully felt. The pristine air magnified the clarity of the bright stars.

The point I make is that 350 years ago, Vermeer lived in an age of pristine beauty of planet Earth. He experienced the trillions of stars each clear night of his life. He experienced the most extraordinary colors and lighting each and every day when the conditions were right.

VERMEER EMULATED NATURE'S BEAUTY
Vermeer was undoubtedly motivated in representing the pictorial TONAL effects we see in his paintings, by the beauty of light and colors he saw daily. Velazquez too, was undoubtedly motivated to capture the beauty of lights and colors he personally experienced. Many years before my interest in Vermeer's paintings, I was enthralled by the colors and lighting I saw in the 16th century Italian Venetian paintings by Titian and others of his circle. Titian too, was influenced by natures PRISTINE colors and lights that he saw daily in his home in Venice, Italy. Venice, like San Francisco , is surrounded by ocean waters that create an extraordinary and unique visual experience caused by moist air.

TODAY'S ARTISTS
Today's artists living in certain geographical or urban areas are missing the PRISTINE beauty of nature the Old Masters knew. Van Gogh, relocated from modern Holland to the LIGHT and COLORS of southern France. David Hockney is another who left his birth home in Britain, whose colors he described as being "gray", to the colorful areas of California's coastal region.
--Louis R. Velasquez December 1, 2014

ESSAY # 11: THE OLD MASTERS' BROWN

THE COLOR OF NATURES SHADOWS
The Old Masters , including early Velazquez and early Vermeer, relied on the color brown as the color of shadows . Caravaggio was the leader of the brown colored shadows. Those who followed him used his model of chiaroscuro, with high contrasts of light and shade. Caravaggio's followers included many great masters, Rubens, Rembrandt, Van Dyck, early Velazquez, early Vermeer and many others. The color brown was their choice for the color of shadows. It is important to say that brown earth colors were and still are very cheap. In contrast, mineral ultramarine blue was, and continues to be exceedingly expensive.

Every great master has a personally felt, individual " color scheme". It is not a rigid scheme, as there is creative variance within it. Vermeer's basic color scheme is yellow, blue, gray, black and white. These few colors are the color backbone of his paintings. Velazquez' basic color scheme is pink, gray, black and white. Rembrandt's is dull reds, bright reds, several browns, several yellows, grays, black and white. He never used ultramarine blue. These basic color schemes are not always rigidly applied, but they are, creatively applied. These color schemes are as unique and personal as the artist's fingerprint or voice.

REMBRANDT
I now temporarily leave Rembrandt out of the discussion, and focus on Vermeer and Velazquez, because of their highly concentrated focus on representing ...accurate colored values of light and shade, as seen in nature. They both found the secret that others missed or ignored because of other personal reasons and goals. The focus by Velazquez and Vermeer on the accurate colored values observed in natures living light, makes their paintings appear to be "real". Both achieved this by using grays and blues.

JOHN SINGER SERGEANT'S teacher told all his students to study Velazquez, because it was Velazquez' use of values that made his paintings appear so realistic. Sargent (born 1856) studied how many Old Masters painted light and shade values, and being unsatisfied, focused on Velazquez .

THE IMPRESSIONISTS
Later, Sergeant became interested in the paintings of the Impressionists because of how they painted light and shade by using color. The French Impressionists of the late 1800's excluded the color black from their palette and greatly reduced the use of browns. Note that the leading painters of the French Academy of the same era, were still using browns as the color of natures shade and shadows. Also note their paintings are dark, heavy, listless and do not reflect the accurate colors of nature's lights and shadows.

We note that both Vermeer and Velazquez throughout their lives, continued to use the color black. They used black because it is indispensable to the simulation of the extraordinary range of nature's profound light effects.

ESSAY# 12 : THE COLOR OF SHADOWS

VELAZQUEZ (1599- 1661) AND THE BLUISH COLOR OF NATURE'S SHADOWS
In 1628, Five years before Vermeer's birth, Velazquez made a major change to the ground/primer color of his canvas, thanks to Rubens' advice. In addition, Velazquez' paint became as thin as watercolors in many places. He added chalk to his dark colors to make them more translucent so as to make them more lively. Grays and blues became mixed with his browns in an attempt to create the bluish color of nature's shadows. Velazquez' use of pure black and pure white, combined with the grays and the bluish color seen in nature's values of light and shade, allowed him to create the lively realism seen in his paintings. The Light and shade in his paintings sparkle with life.

VERMEER (1632- 1675) AND THE BLUISH COLOR OF NATURE'S SHADOWS.
Like early Rubens, early Velazquez, and many great masters, early Vermeer also used brown as the color of nature's shade color. At some point, Vermeer , like Rubens and Velazquez, also realized that the color brown caused an "artificial" appearance of light and shade to his paintings. Like Velazquez, the color blue and grays became more prominent in Vermeer's paintings. The aura of blue white light seen in his paintings is not related to use of optical tools. It is his effort to create living light effects that anyone with two good eyes, can easily see in nature. Vermeer combined blue with all other colors, and used pure black and pure white as accents. This, combined with his focus on nature's values of light and shade, make his paintings sparkle. It is his use of ultramarine blue mixtures, alone and in mixtures, that creates an accurate representation of the color of nature's living light and shadows. These color mixtures are what gives his paintings their unique beauty, aside from his extraordinary design and workmanship..

THE NATIONAL GALLERY : VERMEERS USE OF ULTRAMARINE BLUE
The National Gallery's studies showed that Vermeer added ultramarine blue to most of his colors. Ultramarine means ' beyond the sea", because it was extracted from the semi-precious stone lapis lazuli imported to Europe from Afghanistan.

Ultramarine was extremely expensive. It was used sparingly but Vermeer used it liberally in his paintings by mixing it into many of his colors. This unified the overall coloristic effect and created an atmospheric sense of light and shade..

REMBRANDT [1606-1669] AND THE COLOR OF NATURE'S SHADOWS

Like many other great masters, Rembrandt used browns as the color of his shadows throughout his life. One must note that he did use many subtle grays in shadows, instead of blue. But, contrary to Vermeer and Velazquez, Rembrandt's goals were like Caravaggio's, focusing on the **high drama** created by chiaroscuro effects. Rembrandt did not use ultramarine blue but did use some azurite blue in his paintings, and when used, it was in small minor areas. **He created the illusion of blue by mixing bone black with white**. Ultramarine blue was an extremely expensive color for any of the Old Masters. Yet, Vermeer did use it, as he wished his paintings to have an "accurate" and not an "artificial appearance" of nature's lights and shades.

ESSAY# 13: THE IMPRESSIONISTS AND THE COLOR BLUE

When the Impressionist movement began in the 1870's, synthetic pigments made many colors affordable, especially the blues.
The French Impressionists got rid of the brown shadows seen in many earlier Old Master paintings. It was unknown to many of them that this golden brown coloring was nothing more than numerous layers of YELLOWED RESIN VARNISHES. Rembrandt's 'Night Watch' was so dark by the 19th century that it looked like a night scene. Once the many layers of varnish were removed, Rembrandt's beautiful color harmonies and nuances were seen again.

Still, the Impressionists explored painting without the brown and other dark colors. Their goal was use of the primary colors with pure white to create the IMPRESSION [hence their name as Impressionists] of natural light. They explored the use of blues in the shadow areas of their paintings much like Velazquez and Vermeer had done. In addition many Impressionists also used purples in their shadow areas. This was a step forward from the earlier Masters, because the newer Masters had no concern for duplicating photographic images of nature as Vermeer had.

ESSAY # 14 : LOW COST SYNTHETIC BLUE

The Impressionists did not use the color black. They mixed ultramarine blue with umber to create a dark color that substituted for black. It was a trade-off because by eliminating black, they reduced their accurate representation of nature's darks, as black is crucial to creating accurate realism. It is important to say the Impressionists were not concerned with realistic effects. Both Vermeer and Velazquez used black because both were concerned with realistic effects.

By the 1800's, chemists were producing low cost synthetic colors. Ultramarine blue became very cheap in price. For the Impressionists and for painters to follow, the new inexpensive synthetic blue color became the color of nature's shadow, and their paintings glistened and sparkled with the impressions of life itself.

The Impressionists mixed the synthetic ultramarine blue to create grays - accurate grays of nature's lights and shadows - as both Vermeer and Velazquez had also discovered.
Velazquez has been called art history's first Impressionist- 200 years before the Impressionists began their exploration of colored shadows and light.

ESSAY# 15: CEZANNE, BLUE AND THE OLD MASTERS

Cezanne is sometimes called the father of Modern Art. Cezanne adopted the color blue in shadows and in light of the Impressionists, but combined it with the compositional structure of the Old Masters. When we look at a Cezanne painting, it cannot be called photographic. He uses various perspective viewpoints that conflict with reality. He distorts contours, colors and everything else. Nothing is "real"... except for the accurate representation of nature's living colored light and living shadows, created by the use of ultramarine blue and other hues of blue in color mixtures.

Cezanne's paintings use numerous individual broken patches of separate values of light and shade, combined with touches of pure black and touches of pure white. We get the same sensation as we get from a Vermeer. Both painted accurate representation of nature's lights and shadows by the use of the color blue.
Cezanne differs only in that Vermeer painted with realism and Cezanne did not care for realism effects. The modern camera made that goal obsolete for painters.

We marvel at Vermeer's minute meticulous touches of paint of realistic representation of the numerous changing values of light we see on a white wall. Cezanne, was equally as meticulous and as accomplished as Vermeer. We marvel at the accurate and numerous changing values of light and bluish colored shade on a white table cloth, although it is represented non-realistically.

ESSAY# 16: JOHN SINGER SARGEANT : THE COLOR BLUE

John Singer Sargent's teacher...Carolus Duran kept saying to John (paraphrased) VELASQUEZ, VELASQUEZ...VALUES, VALUES ... no one does them better!!

John took his advice and studied Velazquez at the Prado in Madrid. He used the lessons of VALUES all his life. True. No one does them better than Velazquez...and he just used his TWO GOOD EYES and no doubt the VALUE SCALE taught to him by his teacher Francisco Pacheco....as he looked at reflections in a flat mirror ... just like Pacheco wrote about Da Vinci's instruction ...also found in Pacheco's book.

In John Singer Sargent's letters is one where he says he went to meet Monet in France The color blue plays an important part of Monets' color studies of nature.. He painted Monet's portrait....and in the studio he saw over 50 canvases of Monet's experiments of how light and color changes with the minutes and hours of the day and its weather.....these are MONET'S famous haystack series.

ESSAY # 17: TITIAN: THE LIVING COLOR OF GLAZES

The Italian masters were influenced by the " jewel-like" coloring of the greatest early Flemish masters. - Like the Flemish, the Italians focused on the brilliancy of color, but could not escape dependency of browns and blacks in shadows.

At some point in time, both Vermeer and Velazquez, who both studied the Italian masters use of color, realized that the over use of the color brown in shadows, made their paintings appear dull, lifeless, heavy and dark.

It was Rubens, who in 1628 , advised Velazquez to stop using dark brown canvas preparations (primer and ground). He advised him to use white or pale colored primer/ground preparations, just as the Van Eyck's had done since the early 1400's.

Rubens, based his own color choices on the early Flemish and by studying some defects in the Venetian painters such as Tintoretto, and painted on pale colored, light gray or white colored preparations. By using thin transparent and translucent paint, with thick impasto touches, his paintings vibrate with light because the pale ground primer is reflected from beneath his colors.

ESSAY# 18: PETER PAUL RUBENS :
THIXOTROPY, BALSAMS, CHALK AND THE DE MAYERNE MSS. of 1623

For many of us that do not speak French or German......Donald Fels' in his book..on the 17th century Flemish painting methods - translated the 1623 De Mayerne Manuscript into English, (see my 2012 book's bibliography for details). This modern translation allowed English speakers to study its contents.

BRIEFLY,
Teodore De Mayerne was a French medical doctor to the rich.
He had many interests besides the Art of Painting, and he took lots of notes.
His manuscript is a disorganized jangle of notes on numerous non-art topics.
Many times the contents are written as inquiries, such as .."what would happen if I tried this?"

De Mayerne met Rubens and spoke with him, and took notes.
Sadly, De Mayerne left lots of information out. It is also clear...RUBENS did not explain all he knew nor described all the materials he used when he was interviewed by Theodore .
As one example, De Mayerne's notes do not mention Rubens used chalk.
YET, MODERN SCIENCE CLEARLY SHOWS Rubens added chalk to his paint...just as Velasquez and Rembrandt did.

BALSAM mixed with sun oil...WITH NO SOLVENTS....will mix together.
To do this place the jar ...(8 ounces. Sun oil and 1 ounce balsam) to sit out in the hot sun.....or heated in a water bath.
By doing this I found that balsam will dissolve into the oil but it must be stirred or shaken.
This mixture .is a SAFE COLD MIXTURE regardless of the Suns low heat, or the warming of the water bath.
THIS IS NOT A BOILED MIXTURE.....BOILING IS NOT SAFE FOR THE OIL.

This is not the same as MEGUILP.....NOR MAROGERS MEDIUM because both of these use leaded oil **boiled** with resin at a high unsafe temperature (Venice turpentine is a soft pine Balsam resin- not a turpentine as we know turpentine today) the Meguilp and the marogers use hard resins such as Amber or Copal , or more recently , the soft resin such as Dammar (dammar was not used until the 1800's and was unknown to the old masters).
Some writers have proposed Rubens used a MASTIC GUM...(not a resin) from the island of Chios. This in my view is not true.

RUBENS MEDIUM ALLOWED THIXOTROPY.
IT IS KNOWN RUBENS AND OTHERS ...SOMETIMES USED ...FAST DRYING... TEMPERA PAINTS IN THE UNDER LAYER. - THEY USED EITHER NON FAT MILK, OR HIDE GLUE OR EGG AS THE BINDER FOR THEIR TEMPERA PAINT.
MY BOOK ..DVDS...AND YOUTUBE VIDEOS EXPLAIN ALL OF THESE TEMPERAS.

TEMPERA paints dry in minutes if thin, or, within an hour if thick. My new creation MILK OIL PAINT is another fast dry paint. It is not a TEMPERA ... IT IS AN EMULSION OIL PAINT. Thick layers dry in an hour....thin washes dry in five minutes.

It is clear that many ancient artists did choose not to under paint in slow drying oil paints.
ARTISTS CAN USE ANY OF THE THREE ANCIENT TEMPERAS - OR THE MODERN DAY "MILK OIL PAINT" (which is an emulsion oil paint) - AS THE FIRST LAYERS OF OIL PAINTING. They save time. They create a lean layer, and they are archival.

THE WEAKNESS of the Meguilp or the Maroger's gels is that it has no sustainable body. After they dry, they slump, then over time they crack.
Chalk in oil...(CSO) ...as REMBRANDT, RUBENS Etc. found out, has a firm body that will not slump. CSO is in fact a cement of powdered stone and oil.

ESSAY # 19 : RUBENS' VARNISH AND MEDIUM

I've wondered why RUBENS' oil paintings are some of the best preserved in history . Especially since he mixed pine resin BALSAM with his oil and oil paint. In Rubens' day, they had no word for our BALSAMS. They called a balsam "TURPENTINE". They called our modern liquid distilled turpentine by the name of " OIL OF TURPENTINE".
Today we know turpentine is not an OIL but is simply a SOLVENT. It has no binding power and will evaporate. So, when you read the labels today, VENICE turpentine or Strasbourg turpentine are in fact, VENICE BALSAM and STRASBOURGH BALSAM .
Unfortunately many are confused because the ancient names have survived.

A National Gallery Technical Bulletin covering those topics.
I am prohibited by copyright laws from printing their document as it is written. Any reader can locate it online to read for themselves.
This is a very long article from the NATIONAL GALLERY IN LONDON.
MY COMMENTS ARE IN UPPERCASE CAPS.

RUBENS' MEDIUM
National Gallery Technical Bulletin Volume 7, 1983
'Samson and Delilah': Rubens and the Art and Craft of Painting on Panel
by Joyce Plesters

Introduction
Rubens' 'Samson and Delilah' was acquired by the National Gallery in 1980.
The chalk ground …is chalk calcium carbonate, with a binding medium of animal glue.
THIS WAS A STANDARD METHOD. WHATS LEFT OUT IS THAT THE SUPPORT WAS SURELY FIRST SIZED WITH TWO COATS OF HIDE GLUE TO ISOLATE THE SUPPORT. - ALL GESSOS ARE HIGHLY ABSORBENT.- FAILURE TO FIRST SEAL [size] THE SUPPORT WOULD ALLOW OIL TO DECAY THE SUPPORT AND THE OIL PAINT WOULD LOSE BINDER AND DRY MATTE.

IN 1628 RUBENS COUNSELED VELAZQUEZ TO NOT USE THE DARK GROUNDS PACHECO USED, BUT TO USE WHITE OR PALE GROUNDS. VELAZQUEZ FOLLOWED HS ADVICE and HIS PAINTINGS GAINED IN BRILLIANCY AFTER FOLLOWING RUBENS ADVICE.

ANOTHER NAME FOR" turbid effect", is " optical grays". ALL THIS MEANS IS THAT IF AN ARTIST SCRUBBED A LIGHTER OR DARKER PAINT COLOR ON A DRIED LAYER , THE OVER LAYING COLOR WOULD LOSE OPACITY, CREATING VARIOUS SHADES OR TINTS WITHOUT ANY REAL PAINT MIXTURES.

VELAZQUEZ AND TITIAN ALSO USED COARSE GROUND PIGMENTS...AT TMES FOR THIS EFFECT OF CATCHING AMBIENT LIGHT.(Rubens learned this from Titian and then Rubens mentored Velazquez).

OTHER STUDIES OF OTHER PAINTINGS SHOW RUBENS USED BOTH ....AQUEOUS AND OLEAGINOUS MEDIA FOR HIS IMPRIMATURA...

A SLIGHTLY GRAY TINTED IMPRIMATURA...DIMMED THE BRIGHT WHITE GESSO, ENOUGH SO WHITE OIL PAINT WOULD REGISTER

THERE IS TOO MUCH <u>SPECULATION</u> ON THE PAINT MEDIUM BINDER RUBENS USED, IN THIS ARTICLE, THEREFORE IT IS IGNORED.

THE ARTICLE SAYS MAX DOERNER CLAIMED THAT RUBENS MEDIUM WAS VENICE TURPENTINE [A PINE BALSAM] MIXED WITH THICKENED OIL.
-IN MY OPINION, DOERNER WAS CORRECT. - THE ARTICLE CLAIMS USE OF MODERN SYNTHETIC MEDIA CAN MATCH RUBENS PAINT EFFECTS. USE OF MODERN MATERIALS.

JACQUES MAROGER...A SCIENTIST CONSERVATIONIST AT THE LOUVRE, "SAW" A MILKY WHITE INGREDIENT IN THE PAINT......HE ERRONEOUSLY ASSUMED IT WAS WAX IN RUBENS PAINT - JUST AS HE ERRONEOUSLY THOUGHT WAX WAS IN REMBRANDTS AND VELAZQUEZ PAINT..
<u>SCIENCE HAS PROVEN HIM WRONG. THERE IS NO WAX IN THEIR PAINT.</u>
THAT MILKY TRANSLUCENT INGREDIENT MAROGER SAW IS IN FACT, CHALK MIXED WITH OIL. - CHALK MIXED WITH OIL IS 98% TRANSPARENT—GIVING IT A MILKY WAX-LIKE TRANSLUCENCY.

ART HISTORIAN EXPERT JULIUS HELD, MADE SOME NOW PROVEN TO BE, ERRONEOUS CLAIMS.
THIS TEACHES US NOT TO TRUST NOR FULLY ACCEPT EXPERTS AND THEIR OPINIONS. - DEMAYERNE NEVER WROTE DOWN THAT RUBENS USED OR ADDED CHALK TO HIS PAINT, POSSIBLY BECAUSE RUBENS NEVER DESCRIBED HIS USE OF IT. YET..SCIENCE FOUND CHALK IN RUBENS PAINT MIXTURES - RUBENS DID NOT TELL DEMAYERNE ALL.

ANOTHER ERROR..."ACQUA DE RAGIA" ...IS OUR MODERN DAY DISTILLED TURPENTINE. IT IS A SOLVENT WITH NO BINDING POWER AT ALL. THERE IS A POSSIBILITY RUBENS' SOLVENT WAS HIGHLY RESINOUS DUE TO POOR DISTILLATION. THIS WOULD EQUATE THIS LIQUID TO WHAT IS CALLED TODAY A **" SPIRIT VARNISH"**...a simple mixture of balsam and solvent = "resinous turpentine".

DE MAYERNE DID SAY RUBENS TOOK GREAT CARE NOT TO DIP HIS ENTIRE BRUSH INTO THE LIQUID...ONLY THE TIP.
I CAN SEE HIM DOING THIS AS PART OF HIS THIXOTROPIC TECHNIQUE

TURPENTINE LEAVES A RESIDUE ONLY IF THE TURPENTINE WAS RESINOUS, NOT LIKE TODAYS TRIPLE DISTILLED TYPE

THIS ARTICLE PROMOTES THE MYTH OF 'YELLOWING OIL'.
IT IS COMPLETELY FALSE. BECAUSE RUBENS USED A SUPERIOR, HIGHLY CLEANSED, FAST DRYING THICKENED SUN OIL...NOT THE LOW QUALITY, ALKALI REFINED INDUSTRIAL OIL, THAT ARTISTS BUY TODAY

HIS OIL DID NOT YELLOW. THIS ARTICLE PROMOTES THAT MYTH - THIS ERRONEOUS INFORMATION - BY A SCIENTIST THAT SHOULD KNOW BETTER...BUT DOESN'T, IS SIIMPLY RELAYING AND REPEATING THE MYTH.

IT IS TRUE THAT LINSEED OIL PAINTS LIGHTEN UP... THEY BLEACH...WHEN EXPOSED TO THE SUNS UV RAYS...WHICH BOUNCH EVERYWHERE.
ONE 20th century SCIENTIST PROVED THAT LINSEED OIL PAINT FILMS, CAN BE YELLOWED AND BLEACHED MANY TIMES, OVER AND OVER AGAIN, BY EXPOSING THEM TO DARKNESS AND THEN TO SUNLIGHTS UV RAYS.
RUBENS WAS AWARE OF THIS ACTION BY THE SUN AND WROTE IT DOWN IN ONE OF HIS LETTERS.

RUBENS DID NOT UNDERSTAND THE BLEACHING EFFECT OF UV RAYS
NO ONE ELSE OF HIS ERA KNEW WHAT ULTRA VIOLET SUN LIGHT RAYS WERE EITHER.

THIS IS MY VIEW ON HOW RUBENS VARNISHED HIS PAINTINGS.
RUBENS' LETTERS GIVE US JUST ENOUGH INFORMATION TO ARRIVE AT A LOGICAL METHOD.
WE KNOW RESIN VARNISHES DARKEN, TURN YELLOW AND CRACK.
WE KNOW RUBENS' PAINTINGS HAVE NOT DARKENED, TURNED YELLOW AND HAVE NOT CRACKED.

REMBRANDTS "NIGHT WATCH" WAS COMPLETELY DARK FROM MANY FREQUENT RESIN VARNISHES APPLIED OVER HUNDREDS OF YEARS.
ONCE THE RESIN VARNISHES WERE REMOVED..HIS COLORS GLOWED!!!!

THE NATIONAL GALLERY ARTICLE GIVES PARTIALLY TRUE FACTS, BUT, MUCH REMAINS TO BE KNOWN.

IT IS SAFE TO SAY RUBENS DID NOT APPLY A RESIN VARNISH TO HIS FINISHED OIL PAINTINGS.- THE PHYSICAL EVIDENCE LEADS US TO ACCEPT THAT HE GAVE THEM A FINAL COAT OF A FAST DRYING SUN OIL. - THIS WOULD DRY HARD IN TIME AND WOULD COVER OVER AND PROTECT THE USE OF THE SOFT PINE RESIN BALSAM OF HIS PAINT MEDIUM. - RUBENS KNEW FIRST HAND, .AFTER 9 YEARS IN ITALY STUDYING THE VENETIAN PAINTERS FROM THE CENTURY BEFORE, THAT ALL " FINAL" RESIN VARNISHES YELLOW AND CRACK. - HE THEREFORE AVOIDED THEIR USE, EXCEPT IN THE UNDER LAYERS.

I BELIEVE RUBENS MAY HAVE APPLIED A SIMPLE GLAIR APPLICATION ON TOP OF HIS SUN OIL COAT ONCE IT DRIED. A GLAIR COAT DRIES IN MINUTES, AND IT DRIES NON STICKY - A COAT OF GLAIR AVOIDS DUST ACCUMULATION.
THIS WAS A COMMON COATING USED BY THE FLEMISH PAINTERS PRIOR TO RUBENS LIFE. I ALSO BELIEVE HE MAY HAVE APPLIED AN EMULSION APPLICATION COATING, FOLLOWED BY A GLAIR APPLICATION

I HAVE READ (sorry I do not have the citation) THAT THE GLAIR COAT (used as a varnish) WAS FOUND ON A VAN EYCK PAINTING. STILL INTACT WHEN THE MODERN COATS OF RESIN VARNISHES WERE REMOVED.
.
GLAIR ..WHEN USED AS A FINAL COAT, RESULTS IN A SOFT SILKY FILM...NOT HIGH GLOSS LIKE RESIN VARNISHES. IT TAKES HEAT , OXYGEN AND MUCH TME FOR A GLAIR COATING TO BECOME CURED AND WATERPROOF.

THE ARTICLE SAYS THAT **MOST** OLD MASTER PAINTINGS…ONCE THE RESIN VARNISHES ARE REMOVED, HAVE A SPOTTY APPEARANCE. BUT THAT RUBENS' PAINTINGS HAVE A FRESH OIL PAINT APPEARANCE.
MY BELIEF IS THAT RUBENS GAVE HIS PAINTINGS A FINAL ULTRA THIN SUN THICKENED OIL COATING, AND WHEN THAT DRIED IT WAS FOLLOWED BY A GLAIR COAT

THE ARTICLE QUOTES THE DE MAYERNE MANUSCRIPT: 'Turpentine with time dries. Turpentine oil or petroleum disappear and cannot endure water. The best varnish, resisting (air, water?) is made with drying oil, very much thickened in the sun over litharge without boiling it at all.'

BECAUSE IN RUBENS TIME, A BALSAM WAS CALLED "TURPENTINE" AND OUR MODERN LIQUID DISTILLED TURPENTINE WAS CALLED " OIL OF TURPENTINE"… THIS SECTION FROM THE DE MAYERNE MANUSCRIPT SHOULD READ : "BALSAM WITH TIME DRIES...MODERN 20th CENTURY TURPENTINE OR PETROLEUM GAS EVAPORATE AND ARE NOT WATERPROOF. THE BEST COATING FOR RESISTANCE IS MADE OF DRYING OIL (his superior sun oil) MUCH THICKENED IN THE SUN (which he bought from Italy) WITH LEAD ADDED, BUT NOT BOILED."

THIS QUOTE FROM THE DEMAYERNE MANUSCRIPT LEADS US TO SEE HOW RUBENS FINISHED HIS PAINTINGS- BY APPLYING A COAT OF SUN OIL TO ACT AS A FINAL COAT .

(Note: THE FAMOUS AMERICAN ARTIST, FREDERIC TAUBES [1900-1981] stated in his book ' The Mastery of Oil Painting', that he was unable to prove that oil standing in lead had any positive or negative effect on the oil)

THE AUTHOR OF THE NATIONAL GALLERY ARTICLE MAKES "suppositions" [about Rubens NOT applying a layer of sun thickened oil, that are not true]. HERE SHE REPEATS THAT MYTH ABOUT YELLOWING OIL ONCE MORE.
RUBENS ALSO SAID..THE CURE TO REMOVE ANY YELLOWING IS EASY. SIMPLY EXPOSE IT TO THE SUN AND THE OIL BLEACHES.

THE CONCLUSION IS:
WHEN RUBENS FINISHED A PAINTING, HE APPLIED AN OVERALL FILM OF SUN THICKENED OIL. THAT WAS HIS FINAL PROTECTIVE COAT. - RUBENS DID NOT APPLY ANY RESIN VARNISHES TO HIS FINISHED OIL PAINTINGS. - ANY RESIN VARNISHES FOUND ON RUBENS PAINTINGS WERE APPLIED BY OTHERS, OVER THE NEXT 400 YEARS AFTER HIS DEATH..

ESSAY# 20: MODERN ARTISTS - THE MEANING OF ART

JEAN MICHEL BASQUIAT [1960-1988]
Was a street artist in NYC...born in NYC in 1960, he died in 1988 at age 27 from a drug overdose. He was a victim of all the worst in MODERN LIFE i.e. ART PROMOTION AND DIRTY MONEY.

I have come to appreciate the paintings of Jean Michel Basquiat. He quickly rose to stardom , and died tragically.He produced more than 1,000 paintings and over 1,000 drawings.

There is an excellent film documentary titled: 'JEAN MICHEL BASQUIAT: The radiant child'. I have seen it several times. At first sight, I rejected his doodling child like style, but no longer. Each time I view the film, I learn more and I become more understanding of what he tried to accomplish. I respect his work as being valid personal expressions of creative intuitive original art.

BASQUIAT'S PAINTING PROCEDURE
An interviewer asked Basquiat, if he began a painting with a white canvas.
Basquiat responded (paraphrased) by saying;
That he puts a lot on....and then takes a lot away.
Then puts more on......and then takes more away.
He described his painting method as requiring X a lot of editing.

BASQUIATS WORDS EXPRESS UNIVERSAL TRUTHS
He describes how all creative intuitive artists paint through a process of editing.
This is true and is also how poets and authors create their work.
Basquiat's paintings express how he viewed and experienced the WORLD...
HIS WORLD....not my world. He was a brilliant young artist.

MARK ROTHKO [1903- 1970]

Rothko committed suicide at age 66. He once said the following, as an expression of those modern evils ....".tons of verbiage and consumption". Meaning: Hyperbole promotion with money profit as the sole motive...which promoters endlessly deny.

JEAN MICHAEL BASQUIAT said it best(paraphrased) " you do not need an art critic to tell you how to paint". HE ALSO SAID (paraphrased) , " when I paint ... I paint life".

BASQUIAT'S words about painting " life", are echoed in something ROTHKO SAID:
The people who weep before my paintings are having the same religious reaction ....that I had when I painted them. In regards to what both Rothko and Basquiat said, I offer this
as my expression of " life".

I LIVE NEAR THE OCEAN. I have stood at the edge of that enormous Pacific ocean...many times. Right before sundown each day, when the weather is clear...people here in San Diego ...group near the beach...to watch the sky turn red, gold, yellow, orange... as it begins the descent......and there may be clouds waffling with touches of pure highlights...contrasting with the wide horizontal expanse of sky and ocean .

THIS MIRACLE OF HORIZONTAL ABSTRACT IMAGES.....we see at the sunset on the ocean, are things we recognize as of this world... clouds, light, ocean, declining sun... then darkness as night arrives.
BUT we see this expanse of broad abstracted patterns as something ALIVE.
Something no photograph can capture ...for lack of 3-D TEXTURES native to that flat medium, even if printed on textured papers.
But in paintings by Rembrandt where he used CSO, he captured that magic in paint.
There, we can see the 3-D PAINT TEXTURE ITSELF.

AT THE OCEAN'S EDGE....as 30 to 60 people group together ...
JUST at the moment of the Sun's descent...people yell, clap, strum guitars, scream for joy, beat drums....loudly rejoicing. THEN... within minutes, it gets dark and all goes quiet.

I myself have experienced this HUMAN REACTION to one of Nature's grand displays and phenomenon many times...this sense of a miracle happening before my eyes.
I THINK THIS IS WHAT ROTHKO was trying to capture in paint, "LIVING LIFE".
This feeling of something so extraordinary and emotionally moving, that some can perceive ....as others ignore it, or can't perceive it, nor value it..

WHAT IS IT THEY ARE REACTING TO?
Life? Our very brief transitory life? The meaning of life? Each one perceiving differently?
Religion? God? Freedom? Colors? Lights? The universe?
Each of us has our own reasons, emotions, experiences and individual search on how we perceive the world.

For me, this magic...mystery...I see in Nature, is one of the reasons I also paint.
I hope to create paintings that cause some to " weep…as they did when they stood before a Rothko painting".

ESSAY# 21: MONET'S CATARACTS

Impressionism began in France in the late 1800's as a reaction to the academic realism and the brownish colors that were prevalent at the time.

The Impressionist artists made an effort to paint "IMPRESSIONS" of nature. They did this by ridding their palettes of brown and black colors, and focusing on blues and clear colors. They made no effort to paint things as they actually appear in nature. Many of their paintings appear sketchy, unfinished, spotty, and out of focus.

One of the main artists of the Impressionist movement was Claude Monet, (1840-1926) but as he aged, his paintings became even more blurry and the colors assumed a reddish tone.
 Sometime after 1911, Monet developed cataracts that worsened as he grew older. It appears that his cataracts obscured his eyesight and impacted the clarity and how he saw the colors in nature. Medical sources state that cataracts impact how persons see color.

In 1923, Monet received an operation to remove the cataracts. It is reported that he repainted many of his paintings because after the operation he was able to see the colors better.

Some believe that Rembrandt might have encountered the same health issues as Monet. It is unfortunate he lived in an era that had no cure for cataracts.

CHAPTER THREE:

NEW DISCOVERIES AND UPGRADES TO THE 'CALCITE SUN OIL/EMULSIONS METHOD' OF OIL PAINTING

These are the advancements to the CSO Method as of August 2017.

UPDATE # 1:
CSO METHODS OF REMOVING THE MUCILAGE

When using the AIR PUMP, IT IS IMPORTANT that the Air Pump be used for a minimum period of 4 hours in hot DRY areas, or up to 24 hours in hot or cold HUMID areas. The difference in time is due to variables in Temperature and Humidity of various geographic areas. To be safe, please leave it on for a continuous 24 hour period.

My original "CSO Psyllium Husk / Alcohol method" will not use the Air pump because the mixture must stand still in the HOT DRY SUN for 10 days - while the Air Pump removes the mucilage in under 30 hours in any weather.

THE SEARCH FOR PERFECTION

Even though an Old Master once wrote that it is not possible to remove 100% of the mucilage, I have never stopped seeking a method that will remove 100% of the mucilage from the Flax-Linseed oil. However, there are too many uncontrollable variable factors that interfere with this goal becoming a reality. Even my tests of modern Alkali Refined linseed oil bought at any Art supply store, have detected some degree of mucilage in that modern product.

My original CSO method of removing the mucilage
was based on the 17th century method of Francisco Pacheco (published in 1649).
Here is Pacheco's method, word for word, as published and written in Spanish:

LIBRO TERCERO, CAP. V:
"Tomese una redoma de vidrio - y a una libra de aceite de linaza limpio y claro se le echan tres onzas de aguardiente fina, que llaman de cabeza, y dos onzas de alhucema, o espliego , en grano, y póngase al sol fuerte quience días, meneándolo dos veces cada dia, y de esta manera queda claro y purificado, y colándolo en otro vidrio …".

ENGLISH TRANSLATION:
BOOK THREE, CHAPTER FIVE
"Take a glass flask – and to a pound of linseed oil that is clean and clear, add to it three ounces of fine quality liquor spirits, that is called 'from the head', and two ounces of Lavender, in seed, and place it in very strong hot sun for fifteen days, swirling it two times each day, and by this method, it will become clear and purified, and filter it into another glass.."

EXPLANATION: It is not always possible to translate literally from Spanish to English. Research showed that a pound of oil is equivalent to our modern 16 fluid ounces. As to the oil being " clean and clear' this refers to linseed oil [which can be dark brown after pressing] that has stood still for a period of weeks to allow the dirt and particulate from the shattered seed husk to drop down by gravity. This 'clean' oil is no longer dark, but it continues to have mucilage. The term, 'from the head' refers to the stages of the distillation of the liquor. The distilled spirit is expelled from the 'Still' in sequence of strength of ethanol. First comes the 'head', followed by the 'body', and finally, the 'tail'. The 'head' has the highest percentage of Ethanol. We now know Pacheco's liquor had 87% ethanol. Pacheco says you can use either species of Lavender plant, the one called 'Alhucema Lavender' which is a short flower stock with many flower seeds - or- the 'Espliego Lavender' which is a thin long stalk with many flower seeds.. He refers to the seeds as 'Grano', to distinguish them from 'Liquid' Spike Lavender solvent.

THE THREE CSO METHODS OF MUCILAGE REMOVAL

FIRST METHOD:
The 'CSO PSYLLIUM HUSK - ALCOHOL METHOD'- [NON AIR PUMP].
This is my original method. I based it on Pacheco's method of 1649. It uses strong alcoholic liquor (87 % ethanol). I discovered and pioneered the use of Psyllium Husk for use of mucilage removal from unrefined flax-linseed oil. This method requires 10 days to remove the mucilage. **However, the 10 days is not lost because the oil stands still in the direct sun and this begins the bleaching and thickening processes.**

SECOND METHOD:
The 'CSO PSYLLIUM HUSK (Velasquez-Tavenier) AIR PUMP METHOD'.
This method was created because of the prohibitive cost of liquor in some countries.
It is an alcohol free method created by myself and Daniel Tavenier of The Netherlands in April 2015. It is the simplest method of the three and removes the mucilage within 24 to 36 hours.

THIRD METHOD
The ' CSO EGG GEL METHOD'
Full details on this method are in Volume 1, on page 42.
This is the only method that uses artificial heat. Please use all caution if this method is used. Wear Goggles to protect the eyes and use it only with a great amount of ventilation.

METHOD # 1
The "CSO PSYLLIUM HUSK-ALCOHOL METHOD"

This OLD MASTER based 17th century method does NOT use the Air Pump.
The mucilage removal takes 10 days.

The "CSO PSYLLIUM HUSK-ALCOHOL METHOD"
RECIPE:
16 fluid ounces of unrefined flax seed oil
6 fluid ounces of 80 proof liquor (do not use stronger proof).
1 volume ounce of dry psyllium HUSK

PROCEDURE

STEP ONE: VERY IMPORTANT. First mix the liquor and psyllium together.
Stir this gently for about 5 minutes so the mixture becomes like a gel.
DO NOT YET ADD THE OIL until the psyllium-liquor mixture becomes like a gel.

STEP TWO: Use a spoon to break up the gelled Psyllium. Add the oil. Cap the jar.
Shake this mixture vigorously for a minute, several times, over the next hour.
If you wish you can let it stand still overnight.

STEP THREE: If you do leave it overnight, the Psyllium settles to the bottom and forms a hard ball, You must break it up with a spoon and re shake it thoroughly until fully mixed with the oil..
If necessary, use an electric food blender at slow speed, to insure everything is fully mixed.

STEP FOUR: Pour the well mixed contents into a large aluminum disposable container.
The mixture should be about two inches high and no higher in the container.
For this stage it is preferable to use a flexible disposable aluminum baking container.

STEP FIVE: Allow this to stand uncovered in the direct HOT DRY sun for 10 days without moving. Do not stir nor move the oil. Allow it to STAND COMPLETELY STILL. If there is danger of rain or early morning moisture, cover the container with a glass sheet and place spacers to allow air to enter.

STEP SIX: After the ten day period, place the mixture in a colander, over a wide bowl to separate the Psyllium from the oil. If you wish, you can let this drip overnight because the Psyllium contains much good oil.

STEP SEVEN: Filter the drained oil through a funnel with a cotton ball. The oil will drip and filter very slowly, drop by drop. This takes several hours, possibly overnight. This cleansed oil is yellow in color, and NOT thickened, and it is very SLOW DRYING. Save some of this thin non-polymerized oil for making the 'non-viscous emulsion' and for hand-grinding oil paints

STEP EIGHT: To make the oil FAST DRYING, and BLEACHED it must be thickened, [Polymerized] See the section on THICKENING the oil. There are two safe ways to do this.

[PLEASE NOTE: IF YOU WILL BE USING THE AIR PUMP TO THICKEN YOUR OIL, FOLLOW THOSE SPECIFIC INSTRUCTIONS. READ BELOW FOR INSTRUCTIONS.

TEST THE OIL FOR CLEANLINESS
We use the same empirical observation methods the Old Masters used.

1. THE REFRIGERATOR TEST: Pour an ounce of the clean oil in a small clear glass jar. Tightly close the lid. Leave this in the refrigerator overnight [not in the freezer].
The oil MUST remain 100% transparent in the cold refrigerator. Any cloudiness indicates the oil has either moisture or mucilage. If the oil does get cloudy, add a teaspoon of dry husk to the oil. Shake hard for a couple of minutes- let this stand still about 10 minutes - and re-filter the oil through a funnel with a cotton ball. The problem with the refrigerator test is that glass jars will condense moisture inside the jar. Use only an ounce for the test.

2. THE WATER SEDIMENT TEST: Use a clear glass jar. Gently pour an ounce or two of the clean thin oil, on 4 ounces of clear distilled water. <u>DO NOT SHAKE the water and oil together.</u> The oil floats on the water. Water is polar and like a magnet, it slowly takes many days to pull any mucilage down and out of the oil. The break line between the oil and the water should remain clear after two weeks. The problem when using large amounts of oil is the issue of weight. This weight can cause a very thin emulsification at the break line. If you feel there is mucilage in the oil, you can re-filter the oil.

FILTERING: We are limited by our mechanical filters. They are not perfect. I have tested many kinds. The cotton ball is the most effective. If needed, use a double filter method.
THE DOUBLE FILTER METHOD: Place a cotton ball tightly into the neck of the funnel. Then, place two sheets of paper coffee filters over the cotton ball. Pour the oil into the coffee filters. If the dripping stops, remove one sheet of the coffee filters.
NOTE: It takes 5 to 10 minutes for the oil to begin to drip.
If needed, repeat the filtering process until the oil passes the tests

METHOD # 2:
The "CSO PSYLLIUM HUSK [Velasquez- Tavenier] AIR PUMP METHOD'

RECIPE AND PROCEDURES [Created April 2015].
This method is foolproof and simple and takes under 30 hours.
All you do is mix the psyllium with the oil and run the air pump for 24 hours
to remove the mucilage. These are the materials and procedures.

MATERIALS
Food grade, cold pressed, FLAX OIL [also called Flaxseed oil – or- Linseed oil].
(Do not use "pets" flax oil , do not use "Highest Lignans flax oil",
Do not use any Flax oil containing ANY additives.)
1 clear glass jar, 32 ounce size, with a lid
1 low cost aquarium AIR pump (not a WATER pump)
It costs about $15 at a pet store
4 feet length of plastic tubing. 1/4 inch diameter to fit onto the pump.
A medium sized fine mesh colander

RECIPE:
16 fluid ounces unrefined Flaxseed- Linseed oil
1 volume ounce of dry Psyllium HUSK, powdered or whole husk

PROCEDURE

FIRST STEP: PREPARE THE EQUIPMENT
Punch two holes the same diameter as your tube, into the lid of the jar.
One is for air release… the other is for air input, that is hooked up to the pump.
Stick the tube through the lid, to the bottom of the jar.
Use a large jar or the oil will splatter out by the force of the air pump.
Place the air pump at a level above the oil jar. This prevents back flow.
Place a clear sandwich plastic bag … loosely… over the oil jar to prevent moisture from entering the jar. Hold it with a clothespin.

SECOND STEP: MIX THE INGREDIENTS

Mix the oil and the Psyllium Husk in the jar. Cap the lid. Shake for 10 seconds.
Connect the air pump to the oil jar.
Run the air pump continuously, for 24 hours.
Keep this entire set up out of the rain. Do not let it get wet.
You can also set this up indoors.
This method works best in hot dry weather
IF YOU NEED TO SILENCE THE NOISY AIR PUMP...see YOUTUBE VIDEO
https://m.youtube.com/watch?v=4BaTCe8VqdE

AFTER THE FIRST 24 HOURS- SEPARATE ALL THE OIL FROM THE PSYLLIUM

After 24 hours pass, place a fine weave wire colander, over a wide bowl to separate the psyllium from the oil. The oil will appear very cloudy – this is normal
After all the oil drains out—discard the used psyllium [but first allow it to drain overnight].

FILTER ALL THE OIL THOUGH A FUNNEL WITH A COTTON BALL FILTER

Place a large cotton ball tightly in a funnel.
Place a funnel over a clean clear glass jar.
Pour the cloudy oil into the funnel.
NOTE: It takes more than 5 minutes for the oil to begin to drain.
The oil will drip drop by drop...very slowly...and very transparently.
This takes several hours – or overnight- for the oil to be filtered
When finished filtering DO NOT squeeze the cotton ball to try to get more oil.

SAVE SOME THIN OIL: Artists need a THIN oil as well as THICKENED oil.

Save about 6 ounces of the THIN FILTERED CLEANSED oil in a separate jar.
When finished, place the cotton and the coffee filters in a plastic sandwich bag… add water... and soak them well … this will prevent self-ignition. Seal and discard.

THICKEN THE REST OF THE OIL= USE THE AIR PUMP FOR 15 STRAIGHT DAYS,

First, pour the remaining oil into a jar
Add ½ volume ounce of dry psyllium husk
Connect the Air Pump and run it for 15 days and nights

SEPARATE THE THICKENED OIL FROM THE PSYLLIUM HUSK

After the 15 days pass , Pour the oil and husk into a colander to separate the husk from the oil. After separating the used husk, NOW place a few layers of cheese cloth, into the narrow end of the funnel ... do this firmly but not tight. Do not use the cotton ball filter because thick oil will clog it. Filtering the oil takes several hours. A warm dry room or outdoors in the sun will accelerate the filtering.

TEST THE OIL FOR CLEANLINESS
We use the same empirical observation methods the Old Masters used.

1. THE REFRIGERATOR TEST: Pour an ounce of the clean oil in a small clear glass jar. Tightly close the lid. Leave this in the refrigerator overnight [not in the freezer].
The oil MUST remain 100% transparent in the cold refrigerator. Any cloudiness indicates the oil has either moisture or mucilage. If the oil does get cloudy, add a teaspoon of dry husk to the oil. Shake hard for a couple of minutes- let this stand still about 10 minutes - and re-filter the oil through a funnel with a cotton ball.
The problem with the refrigerator test is that glass jars will condense moisture inside the jar. Use only an ounce for the test.

2. THE WATER SEDIMENT TEST: Use a clear glass jar. Gently pour an ounce or two of the clean thin oil, on 4 ounces of clear distilled water. <u>DO NOT SHAKE the water and oil together.</u> The oil floats on the water. Water is polar and like a magnet, it slowly pulls any mucilage down and out of the oil. The break line between the oil and the water should remain clear after two weeks. The problem when using large amounts of oil is the issue of weight. This weight can cause a very thin emulsification at the break line. If you feel there is mucilage in the oil, you can re-filter the oil.

FILTERING: We are limited by our mechanical filters. They are not perfect. I have tested many kinds. The cotton ball is the most effective. If needed, use a double filter method.
THE DOUBLE FILTER METHOD: Place a cotton ball tightly into the neck of the funnel. Then, place two sheets of paper coffee filters over the cotton ball. Pour the oil into the coffee filters. If the dripping stops, remove one sheet of the coffee filters. NOTE: It takes 5 to 10 minutes for the oil to begin to drip. If needed, repeat the filtering process until the oil passes the tests

----

METHOD # 3:
The 'CSO GEL METHOD'
The full instructions are in my book, Volume 1, on page 42.

BLANK PAGE FOR NOTES

BLANK PAGE FOR NOTES

UPDATE # 2:
THICKENING THE OIL SO IT DRIES FASTER

There are two safe ways to thicken [polymerize] the cleansed oil.
ONE: The Traditional Old Master Method that takes between 15 to 60 days.
TWO: The modern Air Pump method that thickens the oil in 15 days.
NOTE- CAUTION: Heating the oil with fire is hazardous and not recommended.

THE OLD MASTER METHOD OF SUN THICKENING THE OIL

The traditional Old Master method makes a beautiful, viscous faster drying oil.
It can take between 15 to 60 days, depending on how hot and dry your summer weather is.

PROCEDURE:

Use a white opaque glassware container like those used in baking. This type container accelerates the thickening 2X faster than a clear glass container.
Expose the mucilage-free, cleansed oil, to the direct sun rays of hot dry summer weather for between 15 to 60 days, depending on how hot and dry it is in your area.
Stir the oil 2X each day for one minute. Do this thing in the morning and last thing in the evening. In extreme hot areas stir the oil more times each day, to prevent skinning of the oil. Protect the oil from rain or moisture. Place a clear glass sheet over the container with spacers to allow air to circulate.

BLEACHED COLOR

Within 2 weeks the oil begins to become bleached. With more time it will become water clear in color. This color is temporary, because when the oil is removed and placed indoors it will become a very pale straw color. However, this color is deceiving because you are seeing it in concentration in the jar. To test the actual color, place one drop on a pure white glazed ceramic plate and rub it in. You will see it is fully transparent and colorless like glass.

TEST THE OIL FOR DRYING RATE AND VISCOSITY

The oil is ready when it meets your needs.
Some artists prefer a thick very fast drying viscous oil, and others prefer a less viscous slower drying oil. Periodically take a few drops and mix it with a small amount of oil paint, then, smear it on a piece of glazed tile or a ceramic plate to see how fast it will dry. Do two tests. One with tube oil paint, and one with dry powdered pigment colors. Be aware that all colors dry at different rates. Umber dries within 6 to 10 hours, and white tube oil paint can dry very slow because many are manufactured with slow drying poppy oil.

FILTERING THE FINISHED OIL
The Old Master method requires a final filtering of the oil to remove bugs, dirt, dust and leaves. These are easily removed. Use a plastic funnel and place a wad of cheese cloth , loosely into the neck. Place the funnel over a clean jar and pour the oil into the funnel. Allow several hours for the oil to drain.

STORAGE OF THE OIL
Store your oil in tall thin clear glass jars. Tighten the lid tightly, then loosen the lid 1/4 turn to allow expansion air release. Keep the extra stored jars full of oil. The oil in Half full jars will continue to thicken because of the air. Place the oil jars in a window to get light. It does not have to have direct sun rays.

THE MODERN METHOD TO THICKEN THE OIL WITH THE AIR PUMP
This method takes 15 days.

PROCEDURE [for 16 fluid ounces of oil- or less]
1. After the cleansing of the oil is completed, we thicken the oil so it dries faster..
2. Place the cleansed oil in a clean jar and add **1/2 volume ounce of dry psyllium husk** to the oil. This will capture any moisture pumped in by the air pump. Do not add psyllium SEEDS.
Use only psyllium HUSKS.
3. Connect the air pump again and run it for 10 days minimum but not more than 18 days.
A total of 15 days is recommended.
4. After the 15 days, use the colander again, to separate the oil from the husk.
5. Filter the oil with the funnel and the cotton ball. Filtering is slow and may take several hours or even overnight. Be patient. It may take several minutes to begin the filtering draining of the oil. The draining is drop by drop. If the oil stops draining completely, because the oil has become too viscous, use another funnel, **but instead of a cotton ball**, use a few layers of **cheesecloth as the filter**. Cheesecloth can be purchased at a grocery store in the Baking section.
6. The oil thickened by the Air Pump is not as viscous as the oil thickened out in the sun.

USE OF FIRE HEAT TO THICKEN THE OIL
IS NOT RECOMMENDED
Some Old Masters living in northern snow country would heat their oil slowly and at very low temperatures over a fire. I do not recommend using artificial heat to thicken the oil. The oil can catch fire and is highly dangerous. Also, heated oil emits hazardous toxic fumes that can damage your eyes. The Old Masters warned, " Heating oil inside can burn your house down".
Some artists living in cold northern areas are using heat lamps normally used in Reptile care..

----------.

REMINDER: USE OF A SUBSTITUTE OIL:
Those artists that are new to CSO, can use the substitute Alkali refined art store oils, as they wait and begin to process their own Superior Oil at home.
Just be aware that the Art store oils are very slow to dry.
When you do have the Superior oils you will see they are much faster drying.
By using the instructions in this book, even with the substitute oil, you can immediately eliminate ALL hazardous Solvents, Resins, Varnishes and Driers from your oil painting.

UPDATE # 3:
A NEW OIL PAINT:
"THE THICKENED EMULSION OIL PAINT"
The next entries explain a new development in oil painting.

TWO TYPES OF GLAIR - THIN GLAIR AND THICK GLAIR
In the past when I prepared my GLAIR, I would make more than I needed. I kept this in a tightly closed jar and in the refrigerator to stop decomposition. Fresh Glair is 85% water! so I believe this condensation does not negatively impact the Glair, like it does an Emulsion of mixed Glair and Oil. The refrigeration kept the GLAIR fresh for weeks.

One day I left the GLAIR jar without its lid, outside of the refrigerator for a few days.
I saw that the Glair had thickened and had become more viscous. This happened because some of the water portion of the glair had evaporated.

WARNING: The longer the unrefrigerated GLAIR is left exposed to air, the thicker and more viscous it becomes. If the THICK GLAIR is left out for too many days, it will eventually dry out and crystalize and crack. Do not use this crystallized glair because the hard small crystals are brittle and of no value.

These developments taught me there are TWO consistencies of GLAIR
These are important for making unique new EMULSIONS for oil painting.
The FRESH GLAIR is very THIN because it contains 85% water.
The THICK GLAIR is very viscous because much of the water has evaporated.
Both contain the same original 15% of sticky Albumen.

EXPLAINING THE NEW 'THICKENED EMULSION OIL PAINT '

The THICK GLAIR is mixed with the THICK OIL,
This creates the new THICK EMULSION

THE THICK EMULSION is mixed with DRY CHALK
This creates the THICK EMULSION PASTE

The THICK EMULSION PASTE
Is mixed with Tube Oil Paint or Dry pigments

This creates the new 'THICKENED EMULSION OIL PAINT'

THE 'THICKENED EMULSION OIL PAINT'
is only one more option for painting with oil paint.
IT DOES NOT REPLACE THE ORIGINAL CSO MIXTURE
which is: CSO MIXED WITH TUBE OIL PAINT

THE ORIGINAL CSO MIXTURE, continues to offer the oil painter
the control for complete mastery of the oil paint medium.

WORKING WITH THE NEW 'THICKENED EMULSION OIL PAINT'

STEP ONE:
1. Create THICK GLAIR by allowing it to thicken by standing exposed to oxygen
2. Mix two spoons of THICK GLAIR with 3 spoons of THICK FLAX-LINSEED OIL
3. This mixture is called the THICK EMULSION
4. Add enough dry chalk to the THICK EMULSION to make a thick mixture
5. This thick mixture is called the THICK EMULSION PASTE

STEP TWO: HOW TO MAKE THE 'THICKENED EMULSION OIL PAINT'
1. Add enough of the THICK EMULSION PASTE to some tube oil paint (or dry pigment) Each color requires a different amount. Add only enough to make a firm oil paint that holds its shape and does not drip or spread out.
2. You can add more or less dry chalk, or THICK EMULSION, to change the consistency of the oil paint mixture to suit your needs (thinner or thicker).

STEP THREE: PROPER MIXING
1. Do the grinding only with a palette knife. This insures an evenly mixed mixture.
2. Do not dip your brush into the emulsion or the paste to swirl it with the tube oil paint. Mixing with the brush causes an uneven distribution of the paint mixtures.

STEP FOUR: 'OIL OUT' THE SURFACE
1. You can ignore applying an 'oil out', or you can apply one.
2. If you do apply an 'oil out' to the support, use the ORIGINAL VE or the ORIGINAL NVE. This lubricates the support and aids adhesion.
2. The 'oil out' MUST be applied correctly. See the correct procedure below.

STEP FIVE: PAINTING
1. You will find that the THICKENED EMULSION OIL PAINT mixture does not dry as fast as does the ORIGINAL CSO MIXTURE.
2. Normally, no further thinning of the THICKENED EMULSION OIL PAINT is needed as you paint during the day. If thinning is desired, try different mixtures to suit your need.
You can experiment with adding one or more drops of the VE or the NVE.

CHARACTERISTICS OF THE NEW 'THICKENED EMULSION OIL PAINT'

1. The THICKENED EMULSION OIL PAINT is stiffer than the ORIGINAL CSO OIL PAINT

2. This paint can be made even stiffer by increasing the amount of dry chalk.
This new mixture lends itself to creating higher impasto effects.

3. The THICK EMULSION PASTE (the mixture of thick glair, thick oil and dry chalk) must be used the same day it is mixed. Within several hours, it will dry on the palette and will become useless. It must be mixed with tube oil paints or dry pigments, the same day to be of use.

4. When the THICKENED EMULSION OIL PAINT mixture begins to get firm on the palette, use the palette knife to add one or two drops of the THICK EMULSION or one drop of oil, and grind well with a palette knife. This extends the use of the mixture.

UPDATE # 4:
THE 'BLUE COLORED CSO'

In recent years I studied the latest technical information on studies of Vermeer's paintings and his mixtures of ultramarine blue. Technical studies by the London National Gallery show Vermeer mixed varying amounts of ultramarine blue with almost all of his colors.
Vermeer thus created a "bluish appearance" to his paintings that simulate atmospheric effects. This is how he created his "magical light".

These observations led me to testing a 'BLUE COLORED CSO'. It is a simple mixture of CSO mixed with ultramarine blue Tube oil paint. This blue color CSO is used as a way of creating a sense of "atmosphere", to subsequent layers of paint.
I tested this concept out in painting a small portrait described here next.

STEP BY STEP - PORTRAIT PAINTING OF A WOMAN
This is an example of a painting painted with the BLUE CSO and the THICKENED EMULSION OIL PAINT

1-The raw wood panel was sealed with two coats of hide glue. No primer and no oil out were applied.
2. A bristle brush and umber were used to outline the portrait face with CSO umber brown oil paint.
3. The " BLUE COLORED CSO" was applied with a flat blade palette knife.
It was scraped thinly on the surface, over the wet brown outline painted image .

NEXT
The palette knife was also used to remove and scrape away most of the wet blue CSO, leaving a thin, even wet film that has "body". The wet brown image under the blue CSO remained clearly visible without the brown outline being smeared.

NOTE: Do not try to spread an even coat of the blue COLORED CSO with your fingers or it will smear and lift the wet brown oil paint.

NEXT
Into this damp COLORED CSO blue paint film......a grisaille was painted using a "round" soft haired natural hog hair bristle brush and a limited palette of black, white, ochre, sienna. Wet into wet paint produced an extraordinary number of beautiful grays resulting from the blended mixtures. The grisaille was then allowed to dry.

NEXT
Once the grisaille was dry, an "oil out" was applied using the
"THICK EMULSION" (a mixture of 3 parts thick oil and 2 parts thick Glair).
All excess emulsion was removed by patting with a dry paper towel...not rubbing.

NEXT
I mixed the THICK EMULSION with DRY CHALK , to make the "THICK EMULSION PASTE" and mixed it with tube colors 50/50 to make the" THICKENED EMULSION OIL PAINT".

I finished the painting alla prima in a few hours.
The palette was of bright colors. Bright red, yellow, blue, Etc. plus brown, black, white.
I painted Alla Prima with all the local colors, white and black.

STEP-BY-STEP PAINTING: A PORTRAIT OF A MAN
Painted with the BLUE CSO and the THICKENED EMULSION OIL PAINT
Date painted: 8/25/2015 Wood panel 12" x 9 " inches.

SUPPORT PREPARATION
The raw wood was sealed with two coats of hide glue (ratio is 1 vol. Ounce dry hide glue granules and 10 fluid ounces water. (Please disregard the recipe calling for 23 fluid ounces of water per 1 ounce of dry glue, as advertised by some manufacturers. I have tested it and it fails to seal the support). I applied the 2 coats of the hide glue several days ago to 6 panels, all on the same day.

I DID NOT APPLY A PRIMER ONTO THE GLUE SURFACE.
THERE IS NO VALID REQUIREMENT TO APPLY GESSO OR WHITE OIL PAINT AS A GROUND OR PRIMER.
One can paint directly on the glue sealed non-absorbent surface of the support.

The reasons for applying a primer or a ground (they are synonymous) by the Old Masters, was for special reasons.
(1) To create a smooth surface
(2) To create a pure white surface (Flemish method) that would create reflective light from beneath to increase coloristic beauty of thin glazes.
(3) To create a colored ground in preparation for a GRISAILLE or for direct ALLA PRIMA methods.

PROCEDURE FOR THIS PAINTING

I began to paint on the glue surface layer.
I DID NOT apply an 'oil out' for this painting.
My next step was to scrape and apply a thin film of 'BLUE COLORED CSO' with a palette knife. I did not make a preparatory outline of the face.
I then painted a GRISAILLE into the wet blue CSO color, using few colors...black, white, umber, sienna, ochre.

I mixed the THICK EMULSION PASTE with tube oil paint in a 50/50 ratio with the tube paint to create THICKENED EMULSION OIL PAINT - it becomes flowing and easy to brush on.

The THICKENED EMULSION OIL PAINT, made with the THICK EMULSION PASTE still remains more stiff than tube oil paint mixed with the original CSO.

The THICKENED EMULSION OIL PAINT also dries faster, and creates a higher impasto and because of the THICK GLAIR in the mixture, the impasto will not wrinkle.

When the paint begins to stiffen on the palette, use the palette knife to grind one or two drops of the emulsion paste , OR oil, into the stiffening paint.

BENEFITS OF THE "THICKENED EMULSION OIL PAINT"
For a modernist painter, the bold effects are useful. An artist can creatively pursue this abstracted quality. For a painter wishing more realistic images, the stiff paint is easily blended, but only for the next six hours or more. I blended with a natural hair hog bristle, round ferrule brush. The tips of Natural hog hairs separate [bifurcate] and have a very soft tip. I use the brush tip as a dry brush and I repeatedly wipe away any paint build up as I blend.

THE NEXT DAY the paint was firm and touch dry in all areas.

UPDATE# 5:
COMPARING 'ESPESO OIL PAINT' AND 'CSO OIL PAINT'

I created ESPESO, after I completed my studies of the methods of Peter Paul Rubens in which Rubens effectively used THIXOTROPIC PAINT.

THIXOTROPIC PAINT allows the artist to paint layers of wet paint---on top of wet paint—without drastically smearing the lower layer of wet paint.
My full length Rubens DVD is free on YouTube.
To locate the video type in the words: CSO VELASQUEZ.

This information clarifies the difference between ESPESO OIL PAINT as compared to using the CSO OIL PAINT.

THE CSO OIL PAINT
CSO is a mixture made of 3 parts chalk and 1 part thick sun oil.
CSO is added 50/50 to tube oil paint, and mixed together well.
CSO mixed with tube oil paint is called CSO OIL PAINT
CSO OIL PAINT is viscous, sticky and firm.
CSO OIL PAINT should not be thinned (if thinning is desired, add only one drop of (VE)
CSO OIL PAINT is painted into a damp correctly applied OIL OUT film of the Viscous Emulsion (VE)

THE ESPESO OIL PAINT
ESPESO is a mixture of the Viscous Emulsion (VE) and Chalk
ESPESO is made to be a thick paste (the ingredients ratio can vary)
ESPESO is mixed well with tube oil paints, this creates ESPESO OIL PAINT
ESPESO OIL PAINT can be made to any desired consistency by varying the ratios
ESPESO OIL PAINT is made thinner by adding more VE
ESPESO OIL PAINT is made thicker by adding more dry chalk
ESPESO OIL PAINT is painted into a damp correctly applied OIL OUT film of the Viscous Emulsion (VE)

UPDATE #6 :
THE MATH BEHIND FRANCISCO PACHECO'S LIQUOR : AND ITS IMPACT ON THE CSO METHOD OF MUCILAGE REMOVAL

When I first studied Pacheco's method, I was unaware of the ETHANOL content of his liquor. Unaware of how powerful Pacheco's liquor was, I fumbled with what I thought would be appropriate. I subsequently learned Pacheco's liquor had a very high content of ethanol:
174 proof = 87% ethanol and 13% water.
The amount of liquor he prescribed became important to the updated recipe of the CSO method

FRANCISCO PACHECO'S RECIPE [from 1649]
16 fluid ounces oil
2 Volume ounces of Lavendar flower buds.
3 fluid ounces of liquor (174 proof = 87% ethanol and 13% water)
For those three ounces of liquor this is equivalent to :
2.61 fluid ounces Ethanol AND .39 fluid ounces of water

THE PREVIOUS CSO PSYLLIUM HUSK- ALCOHOL METHOD [now outdated]
(my original recipe was based on Pacheco's recipe)
16 fluid ounces of oil
2 volume ounces of dry Psyllium husk
3 fluid ounces of 80 proof liquor [80 Proof is 40% Ethanol and 60% water]
This is equivalent to 1.20 fluid ounces of Ethanol , and, 1.80 fluid ounces of water

Over time I learned that the husk needed more water to function at its optimal level. I determined it needs approximately 3 fluid ounces per 1 volume ounce of the dry husk. I learned that the amount of Ethanol in my CSO method needed to be increased.

THE UPDATED RECIPE: CSO PSYLLIUM HUSK- ALCOHOL METHOD
(updated 2015)
I increased the amount of the liquor and decreased the amount of psyllium husk
16 fluid ounces oil
1 volume ounce of dry psyllium husk
6 fluid ounces of 80 proof liquor
This is equivalent to 2.40 fluid ounces of Ethanol , and 3.60 fluid ounces of water

BENEFITS FOR THE UPDATE TO MY CSO METHOD
The CSO method recipe now contains 2.40 ounces Ethanol
compared to Pacheco's 2.61 ounces Ethanol for 16 fluid ounces of oil

And includes 3.60 fluid ounces of water [contained in the liquor]
which satisfies the water need so the Psyllium husk will function more effectively

----

UPDATE# 7:
CAS VAN DER SLUIJS, EXPERIMENTS IN MUCILAGE REMOVAL

I have met many wonderfully gifted artists over the last 15 years of CSO. Some of them also are born researchers and have always stimulated and inspired me with their intellect.
Cas Van Der Sluijs , a resident of The Netherlands is one of those persons.

Well over a year ago he wrote to me with his experiments. His experiments are very valuable and must be included here for those persons who can follow up on his experiments. I myself have been testing and experimenting with the removal of the mucilage for too many years. I think it is time for new thinkers to work on the issue. I need to get back to my own paintings.

I am proud and happy that he gave me permission to include it - in his own words - here in my book.
Thank you , CAS.
Here follows his letter with my response letter I sent him.

CAS VAN DER SLUIJS
MY ANALYSIS OF HIS TESTING
Dear friends, I was so happy to receive CAS' letter of his experiments.
They are valuable tests. I had to digest the information and offer this as my viewpoint.
Thanks to each of you, especially Cas Van Der Sluijs

I WRITE IN CAPS.
CAS WRITES IN LOWERCASE.

Anyway this is a good time to share with you my own findings of the past 2 years experimenting with your system. Reluctant to do so earlier, because of the stream of alternative methods from your part and insufficient experience with my own adaptations, I feel now confident enough to say that it works for me. Barleans is very hard to get in The Netherlands and very expensive, so I'm using a organic cold pressed flax oil without additives. I

It is mechanically filtered before bottling and not cooled during storage afterwards.
The presumed shelf-life of the bottled produce is 9 months.
The brand name is Ekoplaza and their flax is grown in Kazakhstan.

1. I found that the oil will not bleach significantly faster under UV-light

THIS IS TO SAY, THAT UV LIGHT WILL ALSO BLEACH THE OIL. THE TRADITIONAL OLD MASTER METHOD WAS EXPOSURE TO HOT DIRECT SUN FROM 15 TO 60 DAYS , DEPENDING ON HEAT DEGREE. IN ADDITION, LONGER DAYS WILL THICKEN THE OIL SO IT BECOMES VISCOUS. THE SUNS UV RAYS AND DAILY STIRRING, WILL BLEACH THE OIL IN ABOUT 3 WEEKS. USE OF THE AIR PUMP WILL CAUSE THE OIL TO BLEACH WITHIN 2 WEEKS

2. and will even bleach in pitch darkness in a heat stove at 50° C. within 18-24 days.

50 CELSIUS IS 122 FAHRENHEIT. A FEW YEARS AGO, AN ARTIST WROTE ME WITH THE IDEA OF USING A FOOD DEHYDRATOR. I MADE TESTS USING A LOW COST FOOD DEHYDRATOR, I FOUND THAT IF THERE WAS CIRCULATING HOT AIR HEAT SOURCE (a fan and a heat element) THE OIL CAN BE BLEACHED IN TOTAL DARKNESS. BACK THEN, I WROTE (it's in my book) THAT THIS EXPERIMENT POINTED OUT THAT THE UNIVERSALLY HELD BELIEF THAT LINSEED OIL PAINTINGS DARKEN IN THE DARK, WAS POSSIBLY WRONG.
MY DEHYDRATOR WAS SET AT ABOUT 120 DEGREES FAHRENHEIT. I FORGET THE NUMBER OF DAYS NEEDED.

3. This is with the air pump method and a controlled air input of 40° rH air at room temperature using a dehumidifier in combination with a hygrometer switch, with the air pump inlet connected to the dehumidifier outlet. The switch is not really necessary, but helps in measuring and saves on electricity and wear.

THIS IS A SIMILAR SETUP OF HOW A DEHYDRATOR DRIES OUT MOISTURE FROM FRUIT AND MEATS, BY BLOWING ...MOVING HOT AIR .

4. In the warmer stove environment the air output from the oil results in 20° rH (or less). The temperature, INPUT humidity and measured OUTPUT humidity are at the edge of the capacity of the devices used.

5. All devices use energy-saving peltier-element technique. The stove can be reversed to a fridge. I also use a regulator valve on the air pump. It is set to keep the oil in motion to promote moisture release at the "oil-air interface" and to prevent splattering.

THE FOOD DEHYDRATOR I USED WAS A LOW COST ELECTRICAL UNIT THAT RAN CONTINUOUSLY FOR SEVERAL DAYS. I DID NOTE THAT FOR MY SET UP TO BLEACH THE OIL...THE OIL HAD TO BE VERY THIN IN THE JAR..ABOUT 1/4 INCH, OR IT WOULD NOT BLEACH WELL. I STOPPED MY TESTING AFTER THAT. I DID NOT MAKE A DRYING TESTS.

6. First I used this method in combination with the CSO gel method and it worked fine. I tested the end result in the fridge every time and it stayed crystal clear for a couple of weeks, but eventually a small amount of clustered mucilage would be visible in the cleansed oil. This was then easily removed by filtering through a paper coffee filter.

CAS' RESULT SHOWS THAT A SECOND FILTERING WITH A PAPER COFFEE FILTER..REMOVED "LEFT OVER " MUCILAGE. PROOF THAT ONE OF OUR MAIN PROBLEMS IS OUR FILTERING MECHANISM. IT APPEARS THAT THE SECOND FILTERING WAS EFFECTIVE.
I TOO HAVE ALWAYS ADVOCATED A DOUBLE FILTERING OF THE CLEANSED OIL, BUT LEFT THAT CHOICE TO THE ARTIST, SINCE THE SUBSEQUENT ACCUMULATION WAS SO VERY MINOR. (THE METHOD OF TESTING FOR " LEFT OVER" MUCILAGE, WAS BY PLACING SEVERAL INCHES OF CLEANSED OIL TO

REST (not shaken) QUIETLY ON SEVERAL INCHES OF WATER, WITH THE JAR UNCAPPED. WE KNOW THAT WATER IS POLAR AND ACTS LIKE A MAGNET, SLOWLY DRAWING DOWN ANY MOISTURE INGREDIENTS (mucilage) THAT IS IN THE OIL.

This got me thinking…If cold is so good in driving mucilage out of suspension in already cleansed oil, could it be used as an equally effective cleansing method by itself?

THIS IS CAS' HYPOTHESIS
1. Mucilage in oil absorbs water from the oil/air that slows the polymerization of the oil.
2. In warm oil, the microscopic mucilage is mostly in suspension and invisible.
3. In cold oil the watermolecules become denser and will be pulled closer together, making the waterlogged mucilage flocculate and become heavier. This will promote precipitation of the mucilage in the oil and make filtration more effective.
4. As water meets its highest density round 4°C this will be the most effective temperature to test this phenomenon.

(NOTE: 4 CELSIUS IS 39.2 FAHRENHEIT)

THIS IS CAS' EXPERIMENT
1. I kept my bought oil in the fridge for three days (set at high cooling wich resulted in a 4°C. temperature), before filtering it through a single (sturdy, unbleached) paper coffee filter WHILE IN THE FRIDGE.
2. I split the result in half, and repeated the filtering with one half.
3. Then I processed both batches in the stove as mentioned above.

CAS' EXPERIMENT OF FILTERING THE OIL INSIDE A REFRIGERATOR, IS AN EXCITING NEW IDEA. SINCE 2014, WHEN I BEGAN EFFORTS TO TRY AND FIND A NON-ALCOHOL MUCILAGE REMOVAL METHOD, I TOO MADE TESTS
WITH " CHILLING" THE OIL IN MY REFRIGERATOR AT APPROXIMATELY 40F.
I THEN FILTERED IMMEDIATELY WITH THE OIL STILL COLD. THIS APPEARED TO OFFER A BENEFIT. THANKS TO CAS FOR EDUCATING ME THAT THE WATER MOLECULES BECAME HEAVER AT 40F. (4C) , THEREBY EXPLAINING THE SCIENCE BEHIND THE RESULT

THIS IS CAS' RESULT
The result was a bleached, fast drying oil in 18 days. I've repeated this process several times now, with consistent results. The once filtered oil had a very thin non-continuous (scattered) break layer, the twice filtered oil none at all and with a water test in the fridge the latter started drying at the water interface first.

THIS SPEAKS TO THE EFFICIENCY OF THE SECOND FILTERING
IN COMPARISON: THE " CSO PSYLLIUM HUSK- AIR PUMP (VELASQUEZ - TAVENIER) METHOD" WILL REMOVE THE MUCILAGE IN A 24 HOUR PERIOD, AND ONCE THE HUSK IS FILTERED OUT, (a second filtering is recommended) THEN REAPPLYING THE AIR PUMP FOR ANOTHER 10 TO 15 DAYS , WILL CREATE A FAST DRYING OIL. HOWEVER, IF THE SET UP IS KEPT IN THE SHADE, THE OIL WIL NOT BLEACH. AND, IF THE SETUP IS IN THE DIRECT SUN, THE OIL WILL BLEACH.

To be sure, I shared my findings with my painting friend Erik van Elven, who made a similar set-up, but with a heat-mat under a cardboard pyramid instead of a €150,- brood stove. It works fine as well, but I understood it costs more time (a month), due to a lower temperature (35° C) before the oil is bleached. The resulting product worked just as well.

(NOTE: 35 CELSIUS IS 95 FAHRENHEIT). IN THE PAST I HAVE EXPERIMENTED WITH HEATING THE OIL ON AN ELECTRIC GRIDDLE AT 120F. THIS METHOD CAUSES THE OIL TO BECOME A VERY BRIGHT YELLOW AND TAKES SEVERAL DAYS TO BEGIN POLYMERIZATION. IN ONE TEST, I PUT A JAR OF PREVIOUSLY WATER CLEAR SUN BLEACHED OIL ON THE ELECTRIC GRIDDLE AND THE OIL BECAME BRIGHT YELLOW . I CANNOT EXPLAIN THIS PHENOMENON.

The merit of this procedure is that it can be fulfilled independent of the weather in an indoor environment. All parameters can be controlled and experimented with. An accidental higher temperature due to a UV lamp in the oil container showed to speed up the bleaching, but promoted wrinkling of the drying paint layer. (Putting the light 2" higher above the oil and improving ventilation cancelled out the speeding up).

THE AIR PUMP METHOD CAN BE DONE INDOORS IN COLD GEOGRAPHIC AREAS. DANIEL TAVENIER , AN ARTIST IN HOLLAND CAME UP WITH THE IDEA OF REMOVING THE HUMID AIR BY ADDING DRY PSYLLIUM HUSK TO THE JAR OF CLEANSED OIL AS THE AIR PUMP BLEW HUMID AIR THROUGH THE OIL.
I MODIFIED HIS IDEA TO USE IT AS A MUCILAGE REMOVER . IT DID THIS IN 24 HOURS, INDOORS OR OUTDOORS.

THIS IS CAS' CONCLUSION
My conclusion is that warmth in combination with dry air contact is sufficient to bleach the oil, makes it dry faster and slightly thickens it. More thickening occurs automatically in time when the oil is exposed to air, e.g. In a half full pot or one with a slightly opened lid. No UV-, or sunlight is needed for this process. The resulting oil stays clear with a light straw color, even after being kept in the dark for several weeks.

MY FINDINGS OVER MANY YEARS, IS THAT OIL NOT EXPOSED TO UV RAYS... WHETHER DIRECT OR INDIRECT....WILL NOT BLEACH.

I am curious if this works as well with your barleans oil and what temperatures you would measure in the pot in full sun (greenhouse effect). Would they exceed 50° C. ? What would be the difference with the night temperature of the oil (heat retention)?

DEAR CAS, YOU ASK QUESTIONS THAT WOULD REQUIRE TOO MUCH TIME FOR ME TO FOLLOW UP ON. IF I WERE AGE 30 (again) I WOULD FOLLOW THE LEAD. HOWEVER. I LIVE IN SAN DIEGO CALIFORNIA AND MY HOME IS 5 MILES FROM THE BALMY PACIFIC OCEAN. SAN DIEGO'S WEATHER IS MOSTLY BEAUTIFUL ALL YEAR ROUND WITH USUALLY 70 DEGREE FAHRENHEIT TEMPERATURES (near the ocean edge) . WHEN IT GETS HOT..ITS ABOUT 80 to 85 FAHRENHEIT. BUT, JUST A 20 MINURE DRIVE INLAND, THE TEMPERATURES WILL BE 10 TO 20 DEGREES HIGHER, AND A ONE HOUR DRIVE WILL GET EVEN HOTTER BECAUSE WE HAVE HOT DESERTS NEARBY.
HAVING SAID THAT. IVE MADE TESTS WITH THERMOMETERS. EXAMPLE, THE OUTSIDE TEMPERATURE MIGHT BE 80 F. BUT THE OIL INSIDE THE OPAQUE WHITE GLASS CONTAINER , THE TEMPERATURE WAS UP TO ABOUT 120 F. ADDITIONALLY, THE TEST REVEALED THAT THE THREE DIFFERENT BRANDS OF WHITE GLASS CONTAINERS...CAUSED THE OIL TO VARY IN TEMPERATURE. ALSO, BECAUSE I LIVE NEAR THE OCEAN, THE NIGHT AIR AND EARLY MORNING AIR IS COOL AND HUMID. I USED TO COVER MY OIL WITH GLASS SHEETS...BUT ID FIND MOISTURE CONDENSATION UNDER THE GLASS. I THEN SWITCHED TO COVERING MY OIL WITH PIECES OF PLYWOOD.

Every answer will create new questions and I hope this will not add to the confusion...
I hope you can use this information for your own benefit or that of your adepts in less favourable climates. Feel free to share this information, your platform is larger than mine.

I FOUND YOUR TESTS TO BE A CHALLENGE TO ALL OF US WHO CARE ENOUGH TO SEARCH, RESEARCH AND TO USE TECHNOLOGY THE OLD MASTERS NEVER HAD. THERE IS STILL MUCH TO LEARN. MY RECENT TESTS OF USE OF SODIUM POLYCRYLATE TO ABSORB THE WATERY MUCILAGE ...PROVED IT TO NOT BE USABLE BY MY EFFORTS. POLYACRYLATE IS THE SUBSTANCE USED IN BABY DIAPERS TO ABSORB URINE.

Keep up the good work, kind regards,

THANK YOU CAS, FOR YOUR SUPPORT AND YOUR TESTS

Cas van der Sluijs.
LOUIS R. VELASQUEZ

DEAR ARTIST FIENDS,
HERE IS CAS' SECOND LETTER ...IN RESPONSE TO THE ANALYSIS LETTER I JUST SENT HIM. HIS EXPERIMENTS ARE FAR REACHING AND VALUABLE FOR ALL PERSONS INTERESTED IN THAT WONDERFUL MIRACLE OIL WE USE.
I READ HIS RECENT LETTER WITH GREAT INTEREST
BEST...LOUIS.

Hi Louis,
Thanks for your enthusiastic and quick first response. Feel free to use and share the letter(s) as you please. I also read your comments in your second mail. You are right not spending valuable time to test temperatures in your set up. I was just curious and maybe others will take up the task. As far as the dehydrator test is concerned: I think it only worked in a thin layer, because the oil was not stirred? The dry air has to make contact with the whole volume of oil. In my set up the air pump takes care of that. Not only with the air bubbles, but because of the circulation of the oil in the glass container. I processed 3-4 inches at a time and it worked. I used 3 air outlets in a 6 inch wide container to have optimal circulation.

For the UV test I used different (A,B and C type) UV compact flouresent lamps in a lightproof container. The lamps which are made with uv-transmitting quartz glass were positioned above the oil, without regular glass (because about 25% of the UV-a rays would be blocked and the UV-b and UV-c rays would be blocked out completely)in between. Given the same temperature, the oil bleached in the light proof container with or without UV light equally fast.

Therefore I think it is mainly the IR-spectrum light, which contains most of the heat of the sun, that does the work. This is pure radiation heat and putting the set up in the shade removes this source of heat. This also explains the variation in the different white containers you used for testing: open glass will not absorb much heat, but earthenware of different thickness and compactness will do so in different amounts. This heat is released again when the heat source (sun) is gone. An interesting test would be to use brown and/or black earthenware containers and see if it makes a difference in bleaching rate and temperatures compared to the white ones.

So maybe it is the exact opposite of the sunlight spectrum that does the job and this can easily be replaced by alternative (low) heat sources. The yellow coloring of the heated oil on a stove might be due to higher temperatures at the heat-transfer point in relation to the set or measured temperatures in the body of oil. I encountered a similar problem in experimenting with heating a large batch of cso-gel mixture in an electric frying pan with the thermostat set to 50° C. : it turned bright yellow and stuck to the heating elements in an instant... Although the heating lasted only a couple of minutes, the color change was permanent and it couldn't be undone with subsequent low heat cleaning and bleaching procedures.

The color changes that I observed in my brood stove set up are very sudden and around day 18 or 19. They happen most overnight, with a slight improvement in clarity the next day. Then I turn down the air supply a bit to prevent foaming and leave the oil in the stove for another 3 days and this gives me a non-wrinkling, fast drying and slightly polymerized oil.

These conclusions are just alternative ones derived from the same observations and I hope this does not make it more complex. I am very intrigued by the observed phenomena and try to make sense of them. This explanation would cover your, as well as my observations. Ofcourse this is not necessary at all to enjoy the fantastic CSO system and any procedure that gives the required result in terms of effectiveness and efficiency is a valid one, no matter the explanation. It is good to have choices to suit the different circumstances.

I hope to welcome you someday in The Netherlands,
Kind Regards,
Cas

UPDATE # 8: RECOMENDED READING

This old book from the 1970's is worth reading. It discusses the YELLOWING AND BLEACHING OF DRYING OILS TESTS

http://cool.conservation-us.org/jaic/articles/jaic24-02-002.html

Artists' pigments: Lightfastness tests and ratings : the permanency of artists' colors and an evaluation of modern pigments Paperback – 1976 by **Henry W Levison**

UPDATE # 9:
DO NOT REFRIGERATE THE EMULSIONS

When I first created the recipe of the CSO EMULSIONS I would refrigerate them. Over time, I observed that refrigeration caused the glass jar to condense moisture. Added moisture is not good for the Emulsion, so I stopped refrigerating the Emulsion jar. I would tighten the lid and place it in a shady cool part of the studio.

UPDATE # 10:
CRACKING OF CSO EGG TEMPERA

When using CSO EGG GESSO, we should not be concerned with a few hairline cracks. The chalk we use in the CSO EGG TEMPERA-GESSO mixture, is POWDERED STONE.....and the CSO EGG TEMPERA-GESSO is a form of plaster.

In my book, I describe how I created the procedures for applying the CSO EGG GESSO. I relate that many years ago I watched a masonry worker plaster the exterior of my new room addition to my home. He began with a very thick rough application of plaster called, " the brown coat". After it dried it was full of large cracks. The brown coat was followed by the " scratch coat". It dried and it had lots of thin cracks .Then other thinner coats of liquid plaster were applied after each coat dried. Eventually, each successive layer filled in the cracks. These cracks are normal and are caused by expansion as the water content evaporates.

WHAT IS IMPORTANT TO US ARTISTS IS THIS.
When the masonry worker applied the several coats of plaster -- each coat was allowed to dry thoroughly -- to allow the moisture to evaporate. After each coat dried well for a few days...it was full of cracks ..some quite large, some very thin.

Also, each subsequent coat he applied, dried and cracked...and each subsequent mixture of his plaster was increasingly thinner and more liquid . Each new layer filled in the cracks.

When the FINAL FINISH coat of VERY fine liquid plaster was applied ...and had DRIED, I noted it had no cracks.

ALL THE CRACKING IN THE LOWER LAYERS IS DUE TO expansion during drying, and IS NOT A DEFECT. Each subsequent coat of plaster fills in any cracks of the previous coat.The construction process is fully permanent and not defective.

Once finished with the plastering, the masonry worker then applied a coat of paint to FINISH THE JOB. The actual FINAL coat to the entire process, is the FLUID PAINT that is applied to the plaster. The final paint filled in any final hairline cracks.

DO NOT WORRY WHEN YOU SEE FINE HAIRLINE CRACKS IN THE CSO EGG GESSO
It is simply from water evaporation and expansion. Each subsequent layer of CSO EGG TEMPERA-GESSO PAINT will correct the cracking.
The final PAINT LAYER , be it Egg Tempera or Oil Paint covers any hair line cracks.

UPDATE# 11:
CSO EGG GESSO- AN ERROR IN MY BOOK
There is an error in my book (Vol. 1- Dec.2012) in the application of the CSO EGG GESSO, that is contradicted by the instructions in the CSO EGG TEMPERA DVD.

THE ERROR IN THE BOOK (page 217)SAYS THIS:
If the "GESSOED" board has been allowed to dry hard for several days... you may experience difficulty and resistance in applying the CSO EGG GESSO.

THE CORRECT INFORMATION SHOULD SAY THIS:
If the "GLUE SEALED" board has been allowed to dry hard for several days ..you may experience difficulty and resistance in applying the CSO EGG GESSO.

(On the same page of the book I continue with the erroneous information by saying) You may find the CSO EGG GESSO will not adhere, it will curl up, and resist any texturing with combs. I then give the erroneous instruction that the correction is to apply a thin coat of vinegar.
This is incorrect.
There is no need to apply vinegar to any gesso surface.
Because a gesso surface will not resist CSO EGG GESSO.

But if the surface was prepared ONLY with HIDE GLUE (no chalk) as shown in the DVD, and allowed to dry hard for a few days....then there will a resist...Because if the glue is allowed to sit for several days, the glue hardens to a glass like hardness. Then, vinegar is needed to soften and "etch" the glue so the gesso can adhere to it.

IN THE BOOK ON PAGE 213
(This is what caused me to make the error)
In the book, I instruct how to prepare the raw wood board. We know raw wood is highly absorbent and (if we will use oil paints at some stage) it must FIRST be sealed so it is completely non absorbent. The Old Masters did this by applying at least 2 coats of animal hide glue.

IN THE BOOK : I relate how over time, I learned that if NOTHING is added to the glue , it will seal the wood. However, if ANYTHING (especially chalk) Is added to the glue, the glue remains porous , and does not seal the wood. If you decide to not over paint with oil paint, then you do not have to first seal the wood with glue all you need do is apply a gesso . If you will use oil paints on top of the tempera paints, then you MUST first seal the raw wood with glue .

IN THE BOOK: I state that after the wood board is sealed with two coats of hide glue, the next step us to apply one thin coat of hide glue mixed with chalk. This coat will be porous. I then say that this porosity is important so the CSO EGG GESSO will adhere correctly.
IN THE DVD: I forgot to use that thin coat of gesso, of chalk mixed with glue. The reason is that i focused on the process of " etching" (softening) the dry glue coat, with vinegar .

CORRECT METHODS
1. One can apply a thin coat of glue mixed with chalk on the surface having the glue , before applying the CSO EGG GESSO.
2. One can apply the CSO EGG GESSO directly on the surface having the glue, after applying the vinegar to etch the glue...IF the glue surface dried so hard ..that it resists .

IN THE DVD: I demonstrate the application of the CSO EGG GESSO, on the board that was first prepared with two coats of the hide glue only...with no chalk added.
The glue dried so hard, it resisted the CSO EGG GESSO.
IN THE DVD, I demonstrate the corrective step is to apply a thin layer of common vinegar . This will " etch" the glazed, hard dried glue. As soon as the vinegar evaporates, one can apply the fresh CSO EGG GESSO. It will adhere correctly.

CHAPTER FOUR

ESSAYS ON VARIOUS TOPICS

ESSAY# 1: The movie titled "Tim's Vermeer"

Tim did not prove that Vermeer used anything remotely like Tim's "comparator mirror" to paint. In fact, the movie shows Tim's method of oil painting – which is a basic Alla Prima daubing method- contrary to Vermeer's traditional method of the 17th century. Vermeer used the same method used by all the artists of that era. This alone actually DISPROVES Tim's hypothesis.

The movie is not an academic documentary by any means. It is a Hollywood/ Las Vegas production meant to ENTERTAIN those persons who have little knowledge of Vermeer's working methods, who are easily fooled and easily entertained. These are those who write a 5 star review. I posted my 'one star' REVIEW on Amazon.

I saw the movie at the Theaters, but one cannot really analyze it there because the editors made it change scenes too fast. Mr. Tim Jenison's personal friends are two famous Las Vegas magicians. They know how to 'fool the eye" of the observers. They left out crucial scenes so the viewer could not understand how this copy painting was made.

To understand what was left out, I downloaded the Digital version onto my Ipad,
Here I was able to stop the movie frame by frame. That is how I was able to see the withheld information. I was able to see – frame by frame- that some facts were left out or muddled and some truths were found out that disprove the hypothesis.

I later had an online conversation with the creator [and Artist] in the movie, Mr. Tim Jennison. He is a fine family man. I respect what he did and I view it as a scientific experiment, not as a factual Old Master method of creative Fine art.

MY CRITICAL REVIEW OF THE MOVIE "TIMS VERMEER"
posted on AMAZON REVIEWS on July 1, 2014   [1 star rating]

Hello.

By viewing the movie on an IPAD, one can stop the film frame by frame to examine it. These are the key points proving Vermeer did not use Tim's gadget to paint with.

1. Tim and Penn state that Vermeer drew no lines and that x-rays prove no lines are under the oil paint. Scientific x-rays confirm this. YET...an extensive outline drawing is on the Masonite wood panel before Tim begins to paint. This outline drawing depicts the architecture of the room, the mirror and painting on the back wall, windows and their glass design, the virginal, floor tiles, furniture, rug, plus many other things. At no time in the film, is there an explanation WHY the under drawing was put there, nor does the film show HOW the drawing was done. It appears to be a tracing from a color reproduction of a color photograph. We simply do not know! But we do know Vermeer did NOT draw any lines.....SO....why did Tim?

2. The Van Eycks were born 200 years before Vermeer, and their paintings are even more photo realistic than those of Vermeer. In 2001, David Hockney's book " secret knowledge" eloquently proved they did this by using simple "projection " optical lenses and mirrors. Vermeer did not discover this knowledge ...he learned it from the long tradition of their use ...and he used it. There is NO Vermeer secret.

3. Tim is an expert in VIDEO graphics. Video graphics do not use paint colors....they use colored light. Vermeer and the Old Masters had very few colored paints, but by a sophisticated method of applying and overlaying the paint, they painted highly realistic and photographic-like images. Modern video graphics have an unending number of colors. Tim's COMPARATOR device can match COLORS that DO NOT MOVE, but it cannot match nature's colors that are in constant change, like nature's natural living changing light and colors.

Vermeer used an ancient artist's VALUE FINDER to match the gradations of values and colors. It is simple to make. You draw ten squares in a line. Place pure black paint in the first square and at the other end you put pure white paint. Then you carefully mix each square so it shows the subtle gradations of the grays (values). Every Old Master knew how to use it. It is as effective as a modern light meter.

4. Tim and his gadget could never paint a 21st century view of Delft with its ships, people, clouds with light and shades CONSTANTLY MOVING. . Try to imagine Tim's Texas high tech studio in place. His trusty gadget in his hand, Hockney and Steadman are by his side. Overhead the North Sea winds blow dark clouds over the city of Delft! The church steeple INSTANTLY turns dark black, covered with shadows… but seconds later it is gleaming in brilliant light shafts......The people on the shore are walking to and fro, busy with their lives. Just as we see in Vermeer's masterpiece. Suddenly, the ships hoist their anchors, the sails billow out with air, and the ships float away!!!!What will Tim do? An artist using Tim's gadget gizmo cannot copy the rapidly changing colors and lights we see in nature!

5. At the beginning of the movie, the video camera zooms in within an inch of Vermeer's original paintings. We see the great Master's beautiful and sophisticated application of layers of the oil paint. Vermeer's paintings are truly stunning! It leaves us breathless and spellbound! At the end of the movie, the film makers DO NOT DARE zoom in on the surface of Tim's finished painting. They SHOULD have - and COULD have - placed magnified zoom details of both paintings side by side so you could COMPARE the Vermeer masterpiece with the "Tim-piece".

SUMMARY
Tim did NOT discover Vermeer's secret because there is NO secret on how Vermeer painted his pictures. Vermeer's paintings are the result of hard work combined with his genius. Vermeer used optical tools to help him with TRACING space, and perspective and verisimilitude....but he changed the colors and he changed the lights, and rearranged the furniture in the buildings and made up extra things to put in the composition.

Vermeer created photographic looking paintings. BUT, Vermeer did not COPY what his optical tools projected. Only a modern camera can take a picture of a FROZEN instant of time. If you Google (images) of "Monet's Haystacks", series, you will see the profound nuances of nature's living changing colors and light.

Beginning at sunrise Monet painted the same haystack throughout one day. Each hour he changed the canvas. Note how the colors, lighting, and the shadows change. Daybreak colors are muted and cool, early morning they become brighter and warm, at noon the colors are stark bright with dark shadow contrasts, early afternoon colors become romantic, late afternoon they become bluish. Mother Nature holds still for no man ....and for no "comparator" gadget.

To see how Vermeer really painted , see the Youtube film TITLED: The madness of Vermeer: Secret lives of the artists. This video on Youtube is a scholarly documentary by the BBC. The information in this documentary PROVES Vermeer did not use
a " comparator mirror" device to " color swatch match" the constantly changing and profound colors and lights of Mother Nature. Tim's movie reinforces that proof.

THANK YOU
Cordially, Louis R. Velasquez; Professional artist, age 70 , retired art teacher, publisher of books and DVDS on the methods and materials of the Old Masters.
PS: Several readers have encouraged the writing of my comments. I hope my comments are of help to others. I wish Tim, Penn, and Teller and their families the very best in life.
7-1-2014 posted on AMAZON REVIEWS

POSTSCRIPT:
SEPT 2014
Tim Jenison and I had a civil discussion about his movie: Go to www.essentialvermeer.com
CLICK on the BLOG- then on the section: "FROM A PAINTERS POINT OF VIEW".
Then scroll way way down to Tim and I. You will enjoy the conversation.
He is a Gentleman. Go to my Page REMBRANDT VERMEER to see a caricature
painting I painted of Tim Jenison. I gifted him the original.

ESSAY # 2: FALSE VERMEER THEORIES

Vermeer did not use Tim Jenison's " small comparator mirror" to paint his pictures.
TIM's movie demonstrated a method TO COPY a still life in nature. Any artist using Tim's "small mirror" could never paint REAL LIFE because real life is made of constantly changing lighting conditions and constant movement of subjects.
No artist, not even VERMEER could paint so fast as to paint a REAL LIFE image in a second. A modern camera can take a picture in an instant. But, it is not a creative artwork. The modern camera takes a still photo, without regard to human creative choices of the FORMAL aesthetics of art making.

Vermeer also did not use the double mirror set up as Nigel Konstam's 2 part Youtube video indicates, and I will support my opinion below. In part two of Nigel's video, Nigel uses an accomplished painter to demonstrate how- he believes- Vermeer used the double mirror method.

Nigel makes several accurate observations about Vermeer's optic tools. The first is that if an artist looks at REAL nature, the brightest light and the darkest dark, CANNOT be duplicated by oil paints. This us because the range of Natures light and darks are simply much to great.Nigel accurately recognizes this very important observation.

He then accurately explains how mirrors of Vermeer's day were created using SILVER as the reflective coating. He accurately explains how each time the REAL image is reflected by one mirror it loses 30% of the actual light of nature. He then accurately explains how use of two mirrors, creates the loss of a total of 60% of the actual bright light of nature. This resulted in Vermeer looking at the REAL image through two mirrors. Now, his oil paints CAN DUPLICATE the range of values from light to dark.

Another accurate observation Nigel points out is that the first mirror creates a reversed image of the REAL image , and the second mirror CORRECTS that mirror reversed image . We can see that Vermeer's images are NOT mirror reversed images. In many of Franz Hals' paintings, everybody is a left handed person. This is because Hals used a lens in a Camara Obscura to project , without use of a second mirror, to correct the reversed image.

Nigel's observations to some extent, are accurate, and I believe it was the way Vermeer used his two flat mirrors. I believe I can demonstrate why Nigel's theory is NOT complete. He is accurate to a certain degree, but is not complete.

Nigel agrees that Professor Philip Steadman's book from 2000, undoubtedly proves that Vermeer did use the Camara Obscura to some degree. I agree with Steadman, but having read Steadman's book, I think Steadman has left out important information on how Vermeer actually did use the Camara Obscura.

In my opinion, Part two of Nigel's theory, in which he uses the lady painter, is wrong.

First, she uses a wire eyepiece to align her view of the reflection on the mirror, and DRAWS/COPIES the image on the surface of the mirror. In my opinion it is unnecessary to use an eyepiece, and not necessary to draw on the mirror as she has done. I will explain below.

Secondly, after drawing on the mirror, she uses translucent tracing paper to TRACE the image she previously drew on the mirror. This is unnecessary as I will explain below.

Third, after finishing the tracing with tracing paper, now, she had to TRANSFER the image from the tracing paper to the canvas support. This adds up to having drawn the image three times, and each time it was done with a pencil. Scientific X-ray examinations of Vermeer's paintings show there are NO PENCIL lines under Vermeer's paint layer.
This evidence alone disproves Nigel's theory as demonstrated by the lady artist.

MY STUDIES OF VERMEER'S METHOD
I believe Vermeer had to use the Camara Obscura (as proven by Steadman) in order to accurately record the extraordinary amount of visual detail.

Contrary to Nigel's theory, Vermeer used the Camara Obscura to accurately TRACE the projected image DIRECTLY onto the canvas. Vermeer only had to trace the projected image one time, not three times.

The Camara Obscura works like this:
A glass lens is placed on the vertical wall of a Dark Room. The Latin word, 'Camara Obscura' means ' Dark Room'. The glass lens projects a full color, accurate, image of whatever subject is placed in front of the lens outside of the dark room. There are two technical problems with this projection.
First, the image is projected upside down.
Second , the image is projected reversed.
Professor Steadman admits he could not solve either problem,
even after more than 20 years of study.

The solution is actually very, very simple.
Professor Steadman actually knew, and in his book he writes of the ACTUAL solution. But he refuses to accept it because it CONTRADICTS his theory of 6 of Vermeer's paintings matching up exactly in size, on the VERTICAL rear wall of the Camara Obscura darkened room.

Here is HOW Vermeer solved both technical problems.
Inside the Camara Obscura, Vermeer placed a flat mirror at a 45 degree angle to the lens. This causes the projected image to be BOUNCED downwards to a horizontal surface ... which is the canvas ...which is placed horizontal on a table . This BOUNCE causes the image to be mirror corrected and it is NOT upside down, because it is flat on a horizontal table. Vermeer could now sit down in a chair, and paint the MONOTONE brown paint tracing, while comfortably sitting down, just as if he were writing a letter.

Professor Steadman said he could not figure out how Vermeer painted IN THE DARK.

The simple fact is, VERMEER did NOT paint in the dark, not with COLORS because no one can do that.
Vermeer did paint in the darkened room, with brown paint and with a very fine haired brush to TRACE the projected image.This projection ILLUMINATES the darkened room sufficient to be able to paint with a dark colored paint to trace! Vermeer's use of paint - instead of a pencil as Nigel's theory claims- explains why there are NO PENCIL LINES under the paint layers as science proves. Also, the DARK room is not pitch dark black with no light. It is in fact just a shaded room. My experiments demonstrate one can paint easily with any dark paint in the darkened, shaded, room. Also, the projected image is a light filled full color image that is projected on the canvas that is on the table.

VERMEER'S NEXT STEP
Once the brown monotone was completed inside the darkened room, Vermeer did the following. Vermeer DID IN FACT...OUTSIDE OF THE DARK ROOM—AND IN THE LIGHTED ART STUDIO- and did place two flat mirrors, just as Nigel explained, in such a position so as to allow VERMEER to SEE the muted second reflection in the second mirror. Vermeer then placed his finished brown monotone traced image, NEXT TO AND RIGHT ALONGSIDE the second mirror (having a corrected reflection, not the reversed image of the first flat mirror).

VERMEER'S ONE CLOSED EYE, TO SEE AND MATCH COLOR VALUES
Vermeer recognized that human sight has two eyes that rotate individually in a normal sighted person. Vermeer also recognized that because our eyesight has 180 degrees of peripheral vision, there are NO BORDERS and our normal eyesight allows us to see DEPTH. This ability gives roundness to what we look at. The frame of the mirror creates a border that allows us to FLATTEN the image being reflected and looked at.

To counter the roundness of reality, Vermeer could close one eye to accurately see the FLAT COLOR VALUES. Vermeer looked at the VALUES in the REFLECTION HE SAW IN A MIRROR to guide him as he painted.

Vermeer was then able to use two ancient artist's tools to copy EXACTLY the colors and values he saw in the second mirror. This is called a VALUE FINDER. Simply, it is a premixed value range of black to white oil paints, in as many gradations as the artist wishes. This Value Finder tool is created in a wet and a dry model. The dry model is placed alongside the image in the mirror to compare and match. He then used the VALUE FINDER wet oil paint to paint with. Leonardo Da Vinci wrote about this method over 100 years before Vermeer's birth. Theophilus Presbyter wrote about it in the 1100's, 500 years before Vermeer's birth.

HOWEVER, Vermeer was no slave to optical reality.
Like all great masters, he painted with his creative intuitive aesthetic sense to guide him. He MODIFIED the values and colors seen in the mirror, as he desired. The tools he used...were just a start to achieve the paintings we see today. They are his personal expression, and NOT A COPY LIKE A MODERN STILL PHOTOGRAPH. [see page 149- Essay #17]

Please see my Youtube videos on Vermeer's methods.
To locate them, type in: CSO VELASQUEZ

ESSAY # 3 : MONA LISA'S HANDS
...WHAT DID THEY REALLY LOOK LIKE?

Mona Lisa's hands have been called the most beautiful in all art history. BUT, They are not real. What we see is Leonardo's "creative construct".. A wonder filled expression from the mind of an ARTISTIC AND SCIENTIFIC genius. Mona Lisa's hands are His personal aesthetic sensibility in paint, design, color and light values . Photographic Reality.. Mona Lisa is not!

This is the same Leonardo who spoke of placing the finished painting right alongside a large flat mirror...a mirror that was reflecting the true image of...let us use MONA LISA......so that the artist , by comparison, could see differences in colors, lights and shading. Obviously, Leo's painting is not photographically accurate, nor close to a true mirror reflection of the real Mona Lisa looked like.

So what did Leonardo mean? He meant to say that we can learn from nature's examples. THATS all...he of all artists would never lavishly COPY, MATCH, TRACE, DUPLICATE colors or values or contours or anything else of what he saw in a mirror or from direct observation.

Leonardo was a "creative" artist...and his use of a mirror, is only a guide to help. It was a beacon light, .a crutch, so the artist can use that "information" seen by his TWO GOOD EYES, to creatively, adapt, modify, delete and to CREATE.

The author of the "Tim's Vermeer " movie –in my opinion- does not understand that difference between ART and SCIENCE. Of course artists use technology and all the tools. To COPY lavishly is to DIE creatively! None of the greatest masters...including Vermeer were lavish "copy cats" of whatever it was they saw in nature...or in a mirror.

Look at Mona Lisa's background landscape...it is pure imagination. But what great imagination ...it has several perspective viewpoints...contradicting nature....But creatively it is a mass of swirls, that conform to the elements and principles of FORMAL ABSTRACT DESIGN, with its use of negative and positive spaces.

Yes, Mona Lisa's hands are not real...not photographic ...but mother nature guided Leonardo's observations of sfumato, roundness, softness , exquisite shadows and lighting. They are a poetic rendition of Mons Lisa's real hands. Still, I would like to see a real photo of MONA LISA ...I think we would all be very surprised at what she really looked like.

ESSAY # 4: THE EXPERIMENT of "TIM'S VERMEER".

The author made a SCIENTIFIC experiment. He did NOT create a work of ART. NO one disagrees that artists have used all the technological advances since the last 6,000 years. Painting with wax? The Egyptians did that. Then egg, milk, oil, now acrylics.. Every tool is a form of technology. Brushes, collapsible tubes for oil paints. There is nothing wrong with using them...and OPTICS,...since the 1400's....all perfectly appropriate, and wise ...to use in art creations. None of these tools create great art...it is the person wielding the tool that creates great art. Like Leonardo! Van Eyck, Vermeer, others.

WHAT FUTURE FOR THE VERMEER EXPERIMENT?
I would like to see the Smithsonian Museum take the original Texas Warehouse set-up and place it in the Scientific wing of the museum. It would be an educational tool for kids, ..and artists and art historians. The museum theater could show the movie endlessly. The bookstore could sell his book, a true scholarly book to offset that misleading magic trick, Hollywood entertainment film. An academic scholarly book with all the technical data, and reams of photos. Books, DVDS , and lenses could be sold for all to enjoy...and to take home and do their own scientific experiments.

None of this is in jest. Tim's idea really deserves to be critically evaluated...as a science experiment...not as a method to create art. The museum scenario would keep his experiment alive...until the end of time....to continue the discussion of the relationship between ART and SCIENCE TECHNOLOGY.

We know there is a real relationship, but give future generations the choice to make up their own minds....as to what are the real differences between CREATIVE GENIUS ARTISTS ...like LEONARDO...and geniuses like EINSTEIN.

ESSAY # 5 : ANTHONY VAN LEUWENHOECK
FATHER OF THE MICROSCOPE

Antony Van Leuwenhoeck and Jan Vermeer were neighbors. Forget the scholars who say ... we can't prove any communication between them. Vermeer no doubt used lenses for his Camara Obscura. Who better than to talk with than his neighbor?

In my Youtube video..." Tim's Vermeer, why the movie failed", I show my cardboard DAYLIGHT camera...it is simple. A stationary lens, a flat mirror and a FOCUS LENS to bring the projected image into sharp detail. It was a creative solution to a problem of solving a dim image It works well. It's based on a telescope. You move the FOCUS lens in and out to focus. Simple. Steadman is on film saying the short barrel telescope was not invented until the 17th century, after Vermeer died. Wikipedia disagrees with Steadman, stating that in the early 1600's a Dutchman filed a claim in the Legal courts of The Netherlands, of copyright infringement on his telescope he invented. **Sadly, sometimes the biases of scholars limits their own ability to see clearly....or, to admit they simply do not know everything.**

ESSAY# 6: A FALSE THEORY THAT REMBRANDT USED MIRRORS: TO PROJECT AND TRACE HIS SELF PORTRAITS.

IN July, 2016 two independent researchers [I purposefully ignore their names] published a research paper in England. Their hypothetical theory had two components.

The first part was that it was POSSIBLE that Rembrandt might have used the then known projection mirrors of his time in order to create his self-portraits in paint, drawing and etching.

The second part was that IF part one was true, then it was PROBABLE that Rembrandt did project and trace his facial image to create his many self-portraits.

The two researchers were an artist and a physicist in optics.
I had known the artist since 2010 when he acquired my books and DVDS on the methods and materials of the Old Masters. Over those 8 years he and I exchanged numerous letters regarding oil painting. As of this date, I have never previously met nor corresponded with the physicist.

IT MUST BE NOTED that the artist researcher never once made a studio art test to demonstrate whether or not the hypothetical theory could be workable.
The artist never made any painting, drawing, or etching to demonstrate and prove his theory worked or not.

ON September 9, 2016, over a two day period of several hours, I tested the theory out in my art studio. It failed to produce a projected image onto a canvas.
I determined that part one of the theory was false. This fact automatically makes part two of the theory false.

THE TESTS AND ASSOCIATED EVIDENCE I COLLECTED ARE ON MY WEBSITE.
I concluded that Rembrandt did not use projections to trace his face in the making of his self-portraits. The evidence clearly shows that Rembrandt, like all masters, copied his facial features by looking at himself in a flat plane mirror.

A VIDEO SHOWING DRAWING A SELF PORTRAIT FROM A FLAT MIRROR. ADDITIONAL FACTS PROVING THE REMBRANDT THEORY IS FALSE

https://m.youtube.com/watch?v=UL4TqQV7r4A

This video is 8 minutes long. IT IS ABSOLUTE PROOF that a professional artist can accurately draw his own face [self portrait] by looking at his reflection in a flat mirror.
Please NOTE that in the final finished drawing....the EYES OF THE ARTIST ....are looking SIDEWAYS, LATERALLY....and not STRAIGHT AHEAD
as that author of the false theory claims self portraiture from a flat mirror will appear.
This is just one more bit of evidence proving the theory is completely false .

ESSAY # 7: THIS IS HOW REMBRANDT PAINTED HIS SELF PORTRAITS

Rembrandt is one of the world's greatest geniuses and is equal to Da Vinci, Michelangelo, Einstein, Mozart, Shakespeare and other great minds.
Besides being considered the greatest masterful oil painter...he is also considered to be the greatest etcher...and the greatest draughtsman. The false theorist has failed in trying to reduce Rembrandt's formidable genius down to his own common level.

Quite simply, Rembrandt painted his self-portraits by looking at himself in a flat mirror. This ancient method has yielded the greatest self-portraits of all the great Old Masters throughout history. With the invention of modern photography in the early 1800's, today's artists can use digital photographs, electric projectors and all manner of modern technology if they wish to paint accurate images of themselves. None of these tools were available to Rembrandt. .

If Rembrandt had wanted to experiment with optics, he had a choice of two commonly available crude "projection" tools. One is the concave mirror and the other is the glass lens. The clarity of a projection by a concave mirror depends on the surface it is projected onto. When projected onto a shiny metallic surface the image is highly detailed and in full color. When projected onto paper or canvas, the image is blurry and indistinct. The subject must be highly illuminated for a projection to be possible.

IN CONTRAST, A FLAT MIRROR can be used in ANY lighting situation.
No special tools, arrangements, nor outside assistance are required. There are easy ways to use a flat mirror to assist the placement of the facial features. The various Old Master artists used different methods to place their features accurately...but they all used the same flat mirror to see their face for self-portraiture.

For an artist to paint or draw his/her facial features from looking in a flat mirror the challenge is keeping one's head still. It can be done. Rembrandt did it throughout his life. The reason the 3/4 view is the position MOST represented is because Rembrandt only had to move his eyes and NOT his head between the mirror reflection and the canvas that were placed side by side.

ESSAY # 8 :POETIC LIGHTING

I happened to turn on the TV and saw Boggie and Hepburn in an old movie, " The African Queen". The lighting on their faces was simply magical. I was reminded of the poetic lighting in some of Thomas Lawrence's finest portraits of British children.

Several jungle river scenes of Bogart and Hepburn faces seen together, show a masterful use of studio lighting by the movie technicians. Certainly, several electric lights of various intensity and shade screens were used together to create the poetic lighting effects. Light, as related to shade, is the magical ingredient to creating visual poetry.

Like the movie lighting technician, the painter controls the lighting and is not subservient to " how light is in seen in nature". A painter can creatively illuminate or darken any area of the painting as desired without criticism. Rembrandt was a master of creative lighting and his most successful paintings fool our logical thoughts.
The lighting "looks real", but, it is not.

ESSAY # 9: POETRY AND PAINTING

One day in January 2013, I was awaken at about 4 AM with a poem running through my brain. I had to get up and I wrote it down. I went back to sleep, and the next morning I edited the poem. The next day the same thing happened, but with a new poem. This procedure continued each day, for two and a half years. Then, one day, the poems stopped waking me up. There were no longer any poems.

During that period of two years, when I would accumulate about 40 poems, I would self-publish them. An idea came to me one day that it would be interesting to connect one of my poems with one of my old paintings...some being over 50 years old.

So I did it and I published 2 digital poetry books. These are illustrated with my paintings. They are at **Amazon.com**. One is titled ' American Boy', the other is ' American Girl'. To locate them on the Amazon website search under books… then enter my name. Here one can see about 50 of my paintings that span the years from 1957 through today.

ESSAY # 10 : VINCENT VAN GOGH : A LETTER HE WROTE TO THEO on 9 January, 1889

In the letter he says he suffers from Insomnia. He says that to be able to sleep he puts a strong amount of Camphor on his pillow and mattress.

I looked Camphor up on Wikipedia. It appears Vincent may have suffered from Camphor poisoning, causing him to be placed in a mental health asylum for a short period. I wonder if medical doctors ever looked into this as the possible cause of Vincent's erratic behavior and serious mental issues.

These words are cited on Wikipedia:
Camphor produces symptoms of irritability, disorientation … convulsions, and seizures.

ESSAY # 11: PETER BRUEGHEL and THE IMPORTANCE OF DESIGN

Numerous books have been written about the importance of Design in ALL art forms, not only in the visual arts. - I have read and studied the academic lessons BUT in my art creations I trust and rely on my intuition.

When I taught High School Art classes, teaching the Principals and the Elements of Design was obligatory. It was important for students to learn a new vocabulary. This new vocabulary allowed them to express their opinions in written and verbal communication as they evaluated an art piece. The listeners, who also learned the new vocabulary, were able to comprehend better.

'HUNTERS IN THE SNOW', a painting by Peter Breughel (1525-1569) is one of my all-time favorites ever since I saw it in a book as a kid. I did not know anything about how the force of Design would cause a reaction on my aesthetic emotions.

RECENTLY I WAS MARVELING AS I STUDIED JUST ONE SMALL AREA.
This is a brief comment on how Brueghel used five small black colored birds to lead our eye through the geometric design.

As I looked at the five birds in the tree, I saw each is a simple black flat design.
The bird on my right is the flying bird and its shape looks like an X .
The body is a long thin straight line...at an approximate 30 degree angle to horizontal... and is placed right at the opposing angle of the mountain snow line. The vertical line in the wings is another directional line that directs your eye downwards, past the skaters, to the dark clumps of trees . These trees are also placed at the same 30 degree angle as that of the flying bird's thin body. Together they form a set of parallel lines.

The flying bird, when visually connected with two of the birds perched in the tree, forms a directional line with the farthest bird ....which is placed.....facing away to my left. This facing towards my left makes me look in the direction it is facing. It is placed right before a tall vertical tree. My eye then follows the face of the bird to the tree...then straight down along the tree to the hunters in the snow.

REFOCUSING on the other two tiny birds perched in the tree..
Beginning with the highest bird on top, then looking to the two below it, together they create a strong curved line that connects to the direction of the flying bird. One could continue and explore the ingenious abstract design in all parts of this painting.

YEARS AGO, I STUDIED AN ORIGINAL BRUEGHEL AT THE NYC MET.
The subject is the harvesting of wheat. The colors are bright and clear with lots of ochre yellow. I inspected the painting up close. I saw lots of pencil lines on the white gesso that outline and draw the forms. Also, there were lots of thinly smudged and rubbed charcoal areas to create shadows. These had to be set firm with a fixative to hold and not smear. Then I saw lots of gray colored washes. These three "under work" techniques, pencil, charcoal and washes, created the monochromatic STRUCTURE. On top of this structure, the bright colors of "watercolor thin" transparent oil paint glazes were applied. These were followed by touches of thin impasto of opaque colors.

CONCLUSION
I am amazed at the awareness in the 1500's, of the power of "placement"(design) of flat patterns representing real objects ....arranged within the 2-D space of the painting's surface to create an aesthetic emotional response in us humans 500 years after it was painted.

ESSAY # 12 : THE CREATIVE IMAGINATION

I would like to tell you how I use my imagination to create my paintings.

REMBRANDT'S DRAWINGS show the variety of his methods of drawing. One is Rembrandt's iconic world famous lion drawing. On Google are many lion drawings...I did not know he made so many, until today. WHY OF COURSE!!!!! REMBRANDT would not have made only one drawing of this exotic very rare animal to Europeans. He made many.

Rembrandt also walked and drew the countryside. These drawings do not look like the art school realism drawings of classic studies of light and shade that art students make.
What excites me is Rembrandt's direct power of sketchy scratches and the suggestion of realism by economic means. He uses fine lines mixed with broad swatches...made with a goose quill or a reed...or a brush.

Just as important, I see in his drawings...his concern with Design, Organization, Balance and Structure ....we sometimes call this **"composition".**
He intuitively does this as he draws the beauty and variety of natural ...or man- made forms.

Drawing from our imagination is different from copying nature's actual appearance. That is magical. Our imagination is connected to our subconscious mind. It's the storehouse of everything we have experienced with our five human senses. We access that great storehouse by way of a **STIMULUS.** Something to trigger the imagination, so it can be used.

Looking at clouds is one way to trigger the imagination.
Da Vinci is said to have tossed a jar of ink at a wall.to then "see" ('timulate' his imagination) images that he could then draw.

My granddaughter was age 2 when she saw a scary image in the concrete.
I was holding her hand walking in our patio, she was looking down.....all of a sudden she screamed a cry of fear. Being like her... or her being like me....I looked at what she was looking at . There in the concrete were three irregular jagged holes.
I immediately saw what she was "visualizing" and seeing. It was THE FACE OF AN ANGRY MONKEY WITH TEETH. I knew it was nothing more than three holes in the concrete...that APPEARED...TO A CREATIVE MIND...to be the face of a fierce animal.

Another time, I was walking on the pier with a friend....I stopped and asked ...do you see a figure of JESUS kneeling and praying...made up by all those scuff marks ?
He said ... NO. I took out a black marker and connected the dots. To his amazement, he could now see what I had "seen" by use of my creative imagination.
Had I wished, I could have drawn it on paper and then painted it later.

THUMBNAIL SKETCHES
Almost all of my paintings begin with small drawings. Maybe 3 x 4 inches in size as I work out the DESIGN....Position...structure of the subject that I am creating.
This has nothing to do with the lighting, shading, coloring ...as those decisions come later.
We artists paint... ideas.
The focus is about putting the IDEA on paper.
This composition sketch is not set in concrete.....it remains fluid I change things as I work.
The perimeter lines change too....bigger or smaller...wider ...narrower.
It's all very messy...but this method works for me.
It worked for REMBRANDT too.

ESSAY# 13: BOOK REVIEW
Title: THE SECRET OF THE OLD MASTERS
Author: ALBERT ABENSCHEIN
Date published :1906

The title of this book published over 100 years ago, immediately draws one's attention. After studying it, I offer today's oil painters my review of its contents. There is some interesting historical information on various master artists, but there is much erroneous and misleading information.

Today's scientific knowledge allows us to understand Mr. Abenschein's basic ignorance of the qualities and properties of linseed oil (flax seed oil) especially as used by the greatest Old Master painters.

IN THE FIRST FEW CHAPTERS
The author , Mr. Abenschein, discusses his lifelong search for the "secret" methods and materials of the Old Masters, the foundation of their extraordinary oil paintings.
He discusses his own life long failed technical efforts and the failures of many other artists, with special emphasis on the failed experiments by Sir Joshua Reynolds (1723-1792). Mr. Abenschein's sincerity is notable but not helpful.

Page 36.
In his search for the "secret", the author focuses on the oil the Old Masters used. He says that if the seeds are 'GENTLY pressed' to extract the oil ... as the Old Masters did it....the oil is better than the oil extracted by modern hydraulic machine pressers. His claim is that the HARD pressing of the seeds by modern pressers, produces a poor quality oil that is the real cause of the browning and darkening of oil paintings.
This erroneous claim exposes the author's ignorance, and the remainder of his book rests on this false premise.

Mr. Abenschein is COMPLETELY unaware of the existence of the mucilage in the oil, and he does not know it is the mucilage that causes the browning and darkening of the colors of oil paints. Nowhere in his book does he even mention the word MUCILAGE, nor does he display knowledge of any methods the Old Masters used to cleanse and remove the mucilage from their oil.

My own tests show how the mucilage....will turn dark umber brown within a year. If the artist uses unclean oil containing mucilage, to make his paints, the oil paint colors will gradually become darker and browner as years pass. Mr. Abenschein is completely unaware of this fact.

Mr. Abenschein has no awareness on how to remove (cleanse) the mucilage from the oil. The author describes how artists ....of his time blamed the browning of oil paintings on the " OIL MEDIUM" itself.....that is, of using oil to paint with.

TODAY'S SCIENCE
Today's science supports our observations, proving that the mucilage is on the outside of the seed. Linseed oil is pressed from Flax seeds which are very tiny . The seed shells are very hard and require great pressure to pulverize and extract the tiny amount of oil inside each seed. When pressing the seed to break it open - no matter how GENTLY or how HARD - the pressing will unavoidably incorporate the mucilage with the oil.

This mucilage will remain in full suspension in the oil until the artists removes it. The Old Masters knew of the irrevocable damaging effects of the mucilage, and developed simple ways to remove the mucilage. I assure the reader that removal of the mucilage is one of the true 'secrets of the Old Masters'. In my books I call the mucilage cleansed linseed/flax oil, " The Superior Oil of the Old Masters". Without it one cannot achieve the coloristic beauty and archival durability they achieved.

20th CENTURY SCIENTIFIC BOOKS

Recent 20th century scientific conservation books have described the ignorance of the era in which Mr. Abenschein and his contemporary artists lived in. As our modern books state.....the ignorance of those earlier artists could not explain how the Van Eyck oil paintings from the 1400's that were in their museums had not darkened and had not become brown. Mr. Abenschein and his colleagues simply did not understand this basic issue that unclean oil containing mucilage was the real cause of darkening and browning of oil paints.

THE USE OF EGG IN OIL PAINTING

Mr. Abenschein makes a tragic mistake in blaming egg as also causing the browning of oil paintings. He says that if egg is added to oil it will cause the oil painting to turn brown over time. Once again, he has no idea that the eventual darkening and browning of the finished oil painting is being caused by the USE OF UNCLEANSED OIL CONTAINING MUCILAGE, and is not caused by the addition of egg. Modern science has found the use of egg protein additives in Velazquez' and Rembrandt's paintings, thus, disproving Mr. Abenschein's claim.

MR. ABENSCHEIN IS UNAWARE OF EGG WHITE GLAIR

The author has no idea -and makes no mention - that the white of the egg (called GLAIR) is the part of the egg that is important and usable for oil painting.

Mr. Abenschein cites the use of egg YOLK as a dangerous additive to oil paint. In my books I have made it very clear that egg YOLK has no place in oil painting. My books contain the tests and reasons why egg YOLK should not be used. The egg white, called GLAIR, contains no egg oil. GLAIR is safe to use with oil paints and is a necessary ingredient that creates a perfect EMULSION when mixed with the linseed-flax oil.

THERE IS SOME HELPFUL INFORMATION IN THE BOOK

The author has expended a great deal of time and effort in studying literary research of letters and notes of important older artists such as Titian, Veronese, and Reynolds. This information is combined with his on site evaluation of many unfinished and finished original Master paintings in museums. His observations are well expressed and are interesting to read. They teach the successes and failures of many painting methods that today's artists can learn to avoid.

OLD ENGLISH VOCABULARY

The author uses outdated, old English vocabulary that can mislead today's readers.
EXAMPLES:
(1) He uses the term " penciling" to mean " brushing" , as when today one is applying paint with a brush.
(2) He uses the word" crayon" to mean any " dry drawing tools" , such as charcoal or our modern lead pencils.
(3) His use of the word ' modem' is confusing, but appears to mean ' modern'...as in describing the contemporary 'modern art' of his period.

144-146 . The author makes an erroneous claim that the thick foundational under paint layer of the oil painting needs to be " burned out" " and "bleached to a firm sold state", by use of direct hot sunlight " to " effectively reduce the quantity of oil", to make sure the under layer of oil is fully dry, before applying a new layer. He claims that by this method, the Old Masters prevented the discoloration and browning of the oil paint.
His claim is in error.

Page 146 The author offers his theory on why " resin varnish" should not be mixed with oil paints. He claims that the resin and the oil do not fully intermix and that the resin eventually rises while the oil drops. Then, once the varnish dries it stops the natural process of oxygen entering into the lower layers of oil. He claims this is one of the causes of darkening of oil paints.

In my studies I have made a similar point , if an oil is mixed with a resin it will not fully fuse. As resins dry out, they become brittle and crack. The forces of nature are such that the oil under the thin cracked thin film of resin will eventually receive sufficient oxygen to cure correctly. I myself cannot say if the resin added to oil paint, will eventually add to the darkening and browning of the oil paint colors over time. I would need a lifetime of 100 years to make observations. However there is no doubt that UNCLEANSED oil containing mucilage WILL cause the oil paint colors to darken and become brown over time.

Page 146: The author continues to say that the " burning out" of any excess oil in the oil paint, by placing the oil painting in hot direct sun , is the only way to achieve the transparent lasting colors of the Old Masters. ..adding that " It is not otherwise attainable ". The author's claims are erroneous.

I will remind the reader that the real reason older paintings by the masters have become darkened is not for the reasons this author claims. The very best example is Rembrandt's painting "The Militia company of Capt. Cocq", painted in 1642. By the time Joshua Reynolds (1723-1792) saw it , it was so darkened that it was called " The Night Watch". Modern day conservators removed the numerous layers of DARKENED resin varnishes and saw that the painting represented an afternoon scene, and all of Rembrandt's natural colors became visible once the numerous layers of dark resin varnishes had been removed.

Page 155: The author provides misleading information in order to prove his theory of the sunlight " burning out" of the excess oil, the author quotes a letter by Rubens, in which Rubens tells a client to expose the painting to the sun if it had yellowed or darkened. The author calls the " fierce white light and heat of the sun as being the magician".

I will point out to the reader that Rubens' famous well known letter cited here, refers to a painting that Rubens sent rolled up, and that remained rolled up for quite some time during the shipment. Today's modern science has proven through varied tests that linseed oil paintings will slightly yellow when kept in darkness for long periods of time , but will bleach when exposed to the UV rays of sunlight.

Page 162: The author states the SECRET OF THE OLD MASTERS is exposure of the painting, to hot direct sunlight during the various painting of layers to include the completed painting. This exposure to hot direct sunlight , he says, will insure color depth, transparency, solidity of body .

Page 190. The author claims that using resin varnishes , whether in between layers or as a final coating, stops the breathing of the dried oil paint (preventing solidification), and cites a supposed statement that Rubens only allowed " sun thickened linseed oil " as the final coating to his finished oil paintings.

A 20th century technical report by the National Gallery of London agrees that Rubens did not apply a final resin varnish, and the extraordinary fine preservation of his paintings lend credence to the report. I do not recommend use of any resin varnishes
(retouch resin varnishes) to be used at any step of the painting process, nor as a final coat.

IN CONCLUSION

I have paraphrased the author's final words in the book. He recommends for archival oil painting, that the artist paint on a white ground, use light-fast colors, use a fine oil and expose the painting to the hot direct rays of the sun. This is his " Secret of the Old Masters"

- Louis R. Velasquez,

ESSAY# 14: HISTORICAL FACTS ON HOW THE AIR PUMP WAS INVENTED FOR CLEANSING AND THICKENING THE OIL

This essay details the development of the AIR PUMP METHOD for the purpose of mucilage removal from the unrefined Flax Linseed oil. I begin with my history of mucilage removal.

It was Francisco Pacheco's method from 1649, that guided me to create the 'CSO PSYLLIUM HUSK- ALCOHOL METHOD' of removing the mucilage from the oil.
Even though my CSO method is highly effective, I continued experimenting and searching for other methods.

THE FIRST TIME I heard about the idea of using an air pump to thicken the cleansed oil was prior to 2010 and it was from my friend Mr. Maurice Garson.

THEN In 2010, a lady artist wrote to me with her idea of thickening the oil with the air pump
The reason I ignored her suggestion was because I had learned in the 1960's that OIL PUMPED WITH HOT AIR...was called " Blown OIL", and it had the reputation of wrinkling and yellowing badly.

My mistake was that this 1950's AIR PUMPED OIL " Blown Oil", was low grade INDUSTRIAL linseed oil processed for house painting. I made a mistake because I neglected to see that my own Superior Oil of the Old Masters would not have the defects of that cheap oil.

In 2012 I received a letter about an AIR PUMP experiment by Mr. René Benvenutti, a very fine artist residing in Puerto Rico.
In June 2012 I began testing the air pump. The initial tests were a resounding success.

PLEASE SEE MY YOUTUBE VIDEOS
THAT DISCUSSES THE DEVELOPMENT OF THE AIR PUMP METHOD :
PART ONE: https://m.youtube.com/watch?v=Dx_xT69MSg0
PART TWO: https://m.youtube.com/watch?v=I3b-6-qxXAk

THEN QUITE QUICKLY, THE DEFECTS OF THE AIR PUMP BECAME KNOWN.
DEFECT # 1: Wet humid air will pump water from the air into the oil. This causes the oil to become a very slow drying oil.
DEFECT # 2: It matters not if the outside temperature is either HOT muggy weather like in Florida's hot summer ...or ... COLD wet weather as in Washington or Oregon.
IF the air is HUMID where you live, then the air pump will blow water into the oil.

THEN in April 2015, my friend from The Netherlands, Mr. Daniel Tavenier thought of the idea to add dry psyllium husk to the oil being treated by the air pump. His brilliant idea was that any moisture would be intercepted by the Psyllium Husk. After testing, his idea it was determined to be effective.

THEN IN 2016, my friend Mr. Mohamed Tawfik, a resident of Egypt, came up with the idea of using PSYLLIUM SEEDS...instead of PSYLLIUM HUSK as the main ingredient for mucilage removal. His experiments appeared to be successful but I had to test his hypothesis.
IN OCTOBER 2016 I began to test Mr. Tawfik's idea of using seeds instead of husk.
I found them both to be of equal value.:

ESSAY# 15: POLYMER-SODIUM POLYACRYLATE - A NEW IDEA FOR MUCILAGE REMOVAL

Since antiquity, artists knew by direct observation and traditions, that the Mucilage had to be removed from the FLAX SEED OIL. They learned that the mucilage, if left in the oil, it would ferment, decompose and turn dark brown. This then, over many years, would turn all the beautiful colors a permanent irreversible brown color.

A new ingredient was brought to my attention.

An artist wrote to inform me of a powder called POLYMER-SODIUM POLYACRYLATE.

It is used in baby diapers to hold the urine

DESCRIPTION: Super absorbent Polymer - sodium polyacrylate, Non-Toxic, 100% biodegradable, 1 oz can absorb 100 oz of water or more.

I tested it for mucilage removal and it failed the tests.

ESSAY # 16: MODERN INDUSTRIAL OIL PRESSING FLOW CHART

The first three steps shown are standard, and used for centuries
1. Cleaning..... Mechanical sifting to remove organic material clinging to the seeds
2. Pressing... The Old Masters used screw presses (with loss of up to 60% oil) modern hydraulic presses lose less. If the oil is for human consumption, it is now labeled as " flax oil" and uses no additional steps. If the oil is for Industrial use, such as modern commercial tube oil paints, it is now labeled as "linseed oil" and uses solvents and steam heat to remove almost all the oil from the crushed seeds (known as 'cake').
3. Filtration... This is a mechanical process of removing husk particulate and debris from the oil, to make the oil "clear"... But the oil is not yet "cleansed of mucilage".

WHAT FOLLOWS IS THE PROCESSING: The oil for industrial construction such as painting houses and fences or for making linoleum, is now treated very differently, sometimes boiling, and adding metallic driers. If processed for artists use, it is treated with caustic lye to remove the mucilage. This treatment is damaging in that it removes the iodine which is necessary for drying. Artists oil that is not thickened is bottled. If desired to be viscous, it is BOILED without oxygen and is labeled "Stand Oil". Both are slow drying oils.

THIS FLOW CHART : THE TERM PURIFICATION
Not to confuse the issue. There is a SWEDISH company named: ALLBACK, that produces linseed oil for house painting. It uses the very same term "PURIFICATION".
As best as I can tell, (I have written to them with questions with no answers other than to say their methods are ' proprietary'). Their website says they allow their oil to lie fallow, to allow cleansing to happen by natural gravity. However, it can be proven that gravity does not remove the mucilage no matter how long the oil is allowed to stand (my test photos are on my website). The Old Masters knew of one natural method, which takes a great amount of time , months and months, and certainly not of use for modern mass production for retail profit driven sales.......it is this: placing raw unrefined oil on water....not shaking with water...just placing the two together in a container. The oil floats. The water is ' polar' acting like a magnet. The mucilage is microscopic , very complex, and contains water. Over much time, the mucilage drops. Then cleansed oil can be withdrawn carefully.

THE FLOW CHART: PURIFICATION MEANS WHAT?
Lists the next step as PURIFICATION .
They include a blend of secret ABSORBENTS.
Obviously now...oil producers are aware of the "aqueous" content make-up of mucilage. They are using methods to withdraw the mucilage via use of ABSORBENTS.

In the early 2000's, discovered on my own, that Psylluum husk is an extraordinary absorbent of water/ aqueous ingredients. Psylluum husk was never identified either in ancient or modern literature. I discovered this husk because my doctor recommended I use a common laxative named METAMUSIL . This laxative is nothing more than ...Psyllium husk...with flavoring and sugar. One day I saw that a teaspoon of METAMUSIL absorbed a tremendous amount of water. BINGO! From that information, I created the CSO method of removing the mucilage, combining the husk with Pacheco's use of liquor . PACHECO did not know of Psyllium husk ...he used lavender flower buds.

THE FLOW CHART : TESTING THE RESULTS
I guess if the "blend of absorbents" they use is ' proprietory ' secret, they will not release that information. Nature has many absorbent materials. They claim metals and organic contaminants are removed in their purification process.. The ' purity' of their oil would be easy to test.

TEST 1. Tighten the lid on the jar with CLEANSED OIL and place it in the refrigerator. Oil that has mucilage will come cloudy when cold. Oil cleansed of mucilage remains clear. Oil with extra moisture/water, from the environment will also get cloudy.

TEST 2 : Place 2 fluid ounces of oil on 4 ounces of water. Don't shake it. REMOVE the lid and let it stand two weeks or more in a dry environment, indoors or outdoors. Because water is POLAR, much of the mucilage will drop to the break line of oil and water.

TEST 3: Fill a jar ½ full of oil, leaving oxygen in the jar. Tighten the lid and shake the jar vigorously. If the oil is cleansed, the oil will get full of air bubbles but the oil will remain transparent. If the oil has mucilage or water, the air mixes with it and the oil becomes cloudy.

THE FLOW CHART
The next step is lab analysis....and drumming [storage?].
I am not familiar with the term of drumming, other than that it is stored in huge metal drums.

ESSAY # 17: VERMEER'S "MIRROR REFLECTION" PAINTINGS

This essay presents information that hopes to explain HOW VERMEER viewed Nature's colors and values, that he then painted in his paintings. My view is based on what I propose was his use of flattening images - that he then saw in nature.

To explain this, I must present a very brief overview of his paintings created with the 17th century methods, materials and traditions he was born into, was taught, and used. His paintings are 17th century paintings - they are NOT 21st century duplications or reproductions that do not follow the 17th century norms and steps of paint application.

THE 17th CENTURY LENSES AND MIRRORS
Compared to the highest quality of today's optical lenses and mirrors, Vermeer's lenses and mirrors can be judged as sub-standard. However, his paintings prove that he was able to make full use of them, and even argue that today's superior optical equipment would not have improved the quality of his paintings.

Science tells us that mirrors in Vermeer's day - being glass backed by silver- were impacted by oxidation of silver's darkening. This caused the mirrors to be reflective of less light and brightness than non-oxidizing modern mirrors.

MR. Nigel Konstam (in his YouTube videos) has accurately stated that because of the " reduced light-dark values" reflected in Vermeer's lower quality mirrors, he did not have to accurately MATCH the unmatchable range of values of darks to lights caused by nature's pure white light.

THE 21st CENTURY
First we must recognize what Vermeer's paintings tell us today - keeping in mind how 300 years of aging (slow decomposition of color changes) have changed how those paintings look today.

By evaluating Vermeer's paintings, we can argue convincingly that the vast majority of Vermeer's personal aesthetic sense of color and light that we can still see in his paintings - is still IN TACT, as he intended.

THE HUMAN EYES
Human eyes focus on one area at a time. The use of two eyes allows humans to see roundness and depth perception.

Artists know this and do several things to "flatten" the roundness and depth perception of reality - in order to "SEE" the artistically important ABSTRACT SHAPES OF NATURE.

The great beauty of all masterpieces regardless of "style" is not, whether it is realistic or not. It is in fact, the underlying foundation of ABSTRACT SHAPES and ABSTRACT COLORS and its LIGHT AND DARK VALUES that move our aesthetic emotional response.

In order for artists to better SEE the SPATIAL ABSTRACTION OF NATURES BEAUTY, they do one or all of these things (1) They squint their eyes (2) They purposefully un-focus their "minds eyesight" - like one does when viewing a stereogram graphic in order to see the hidden 3-D image (3) They cover ONE EYE (4) OR THEY LOOK AT A REFLECTION IN A MIRROR.

All of these methods are effective to FLATTEN the roundness and depth of how the human eye sees reality - and it is done for the artist's benefit of creating SPATIAL and COLOR-VALUES, and ABSTRACT DESIGN.

VERMEER'S USE OF MIRRORS

Undoubtedly, Vermeer experimented with all the optical tools (lenses and mirrors) that were well known and well understood hundreds of years before his lifetime. Undoubtedly, Vermeer's paintings are the proof of that.

I agree with Nigel Konstam, that Vermeer used two flat mirrors to create his paintings in order to capture that special quality of light they possess. One flat mirror was used to reflect the image, but this image would be mirror reversed. The second flat mirror was used as a corrective action , to reflect and correct the reversed image in the first flat mirror.

As I have previously stated, Vermeer TRACED the carefully arranged "scene" that was projected into his camera obscura - with dark brown paint. This monotone thinly applied paint was a simple FLAT image with no realistic coloring. Non-artists do not know that a great variety of OPTICAL VALUES of lights and darks are easily obtained by use of only ONE DARK BROWN color. To achieve this, one applies the paint thinly or thickly on an OCHRE colored, " colored imprimatura". This brown monotone paint layer was painted with BOTH EYES OPEN.

Once this BROWN MONOTONE painting was completed, it was removed from the dark room Camara Obscura, and placed vertically on an easel in bright clear studio natural daylight lighting. VERMEER was able to MATCH colors and values by viewing the reflections of the two FLAT PLANE mirrors. As I have previously said, one FLAT PLANE MIRROR was placed alongside and RIGHT NEXT TO, the brown monotone painting on the easel.

IT WAS AT THIS POINT that Vermeer CLOSED OR COVERED ONE EYE.
Two factors came into use: The mirror's reflection by its nature flattened the reflected image and the closing of one eye further flattened the image.

Under these conditions, Vermeer was able to use the DRY VALUE FINDER and the WET PAINT PALETTE to achieve that "photographic" appearance we can still see in his paintings. Once can say with a certainty, that VERMEER'S PAINTINGS LOOK LIKE A REFLECTION IN A FLAT MIRROR.

CHAPTER FIVE:
REVIEW OF FREQUENT PROCEDURES

This chapter covers many topics that I frequently get questions to clarify or explain. The topics are not in any order.

REVIEW # 1: BASIC CSO PROCEDURE

1. For archival painting, Oil paint must be painted on a non- absorbent surface that has a tooth. This tooth can be visible to the eye, or even microscopic in size and is called a ' mechanical lock'. Examples of "tooth" are the visible weave of a canvas, or the microscopic texture caused by sand papering a gesso surface

2. All gesso surfaces are HIGHLY absorbent, be it modern acrylic gesso, or traditional Old Master glue-chalk gesso. Before applying oil paint, they must be rendered non- absorbent for archival purposes. My book , Volume 1 has a section on sealing the canvas or wood support.

STEP ONE : PREPARE THE CSO
On your grinding table ...(a 12"x12" glazed floor tile),
use a palette knife with a six inch flat blade and
MIX 3 spoons of dry chalk with 1 spoon of the thickened oil
Take your time mixing the oil and chalk. It takes a minute.

Once you MIX it...now ..GRIND it......use the same palette knife to grind.
This means you must put pressure on the blade as you go in small circles
It takes only one minute to grind the ingredients together to make the CSO.

Next, mix and grind ... equal amounts of tube oil paint and the CSO.
This creates CSO PAINT and it is thick, flowing and viscous.
Do not thin this paint , except as will be later instructed.

STEP TWO: MAKE AND APPLY THE ' OIL OUT' MEDIUM
Before beginning to paint you must apply an "oil out" to the entire surface of the canvas or the panel. The easiest medium to use is the AGUADO "oil out"out medium

CSO has 4 "oil out" mediums........3 are an EMULSION.
You can read all about them in my book volume 1, and the CSO Oil Painting DVD explains it

The AGUADO medium is not an Emulsion and is the simplest to make and use.
Get a small jar and put in 1 spoon of oil (thickened oil or thin oil) and 1 &1/2 spoons of chalk.
 Stir them well. You will note that the AGUADO is very soupy, and the CSO is very thick and viscous.

Use a flat brush to apply the AGUADO ...thinly......all over the surface.
IT IS NOW IMPORTANT TO WIPE MOST OF THE AGUADO OFF!!!
USE a dry paper kitchen napkin and gently wipe the excess AGUADO off.
DO NOT WIPE IT COMPLETELY OFF... Just gently blot and remove all the excess.

Once you do that ... use the Palm of your bare hand and rub it in.
If your hand is skimming across the surface ... you still have too much.
Use a dry napkin and dry off your hand and gently wipe the surface again.

Repeat the rubbing with your dried Palm of your hand
THE GOAL IS AN ULTRA THIN FILM.

Once the AGUADO is applied on correctly, we paint into the damp film of AGUADO

REVIEW # 2: THE CSO EMULSIONS

My study of the 15th century Flemish paintings of the Van Eycks led to my creation of two Emulsions for oil painting. They are the VE (viscous emulsion) and the NVE (non viscous emulsion).

When I initially created CSO, I created 3 EMULSION mixtures containing Glair
and 1 mixture without Glair which is called AGUADO.
Each mixture has a reason and a purpose.

The VE (viscous emulsion) is a mixture of 3 spoons of thickened oil and 2 spoons of glair (use any same sized spoon). When applied as an "oil out" it requires to be rubbed in by hand only- not with a brush.

2. **The NVE** (non viscous emulsion) is the same recipe as the VE except that thin oil is used instead of thickened oil. Read my book for reasons of when to use one or the other. When applied as an "oil out" it requires to be rubbed in by hand only- not with a brush. .

3. **The ESPESO** is the same as the VE with some dry chalk added. When applied as an " oil out", it requires no rubbing but it must be a thin film.

4. **The AGUADO** is not an Emulsion. It is a simple very soupy mixture of dry chalk and either a thin oil or a thick oil. When it is used as an "oil out" it requires no rubbing but it must be a thin film.

WHEN USED AS AN 'OIL OUT', THE 'VE' AND THE 'NVE' EMULSIONS REQUIRE RUBBING BY HAND ONLY. I CANNOT STRESS THE IMPORTANCE OF MIXING THE RATIO CORRECTLY... AND THE IMPORTANCE OF APPLYING IT CORRECTLY.

REVIEW # 3:
THE 'OIL OUT' APPLICATION PROCEDURE

1. Apply the VE or the NVE emulsion all over the surface with a wide flat brush.

2. Gently use a soft paper towel to remove all excess. Do not rub, just BLOT off the excess.

3. Rub the Emulsion with the BARE HAND ONLY ... Using only with the bare hand ... begin to rub the wet surface with vigor ..pressing down and moving the emulsion in circles. If your hand is moving effortlessly, easily sliding across the surface, you have too much emulsion. Use a dry paper towel and dry your hands off. Then gently BLOT off some more of the emulsion from the surface. Repeat the vigorous rubbing with the bare hand. If your hand continues to effortlessly slide around...repeat the hand drying and the BLOTTING.

4. The goal is to rub until you feel a TUG....a resistance ... to the rubbing.
On a wood panel, this happens quite soon. On a canvas, depending on how coarse the weave is, this can take several minutes. You might even feel it can't be done. This happens because the canvas weave holds the wet emulsion in the weave pockets. Blotting with a dry paper towel helps , as does the rubbing.

It is crucial that the final damp film of the emulsion MUST be an ultra thin film.
You then paint your oil paint into this damp film.
VERY IMPORTANT : Please use only the bare hand only. Do not use a rag, brush, etc. Rubbing creates friction...friction creates heat...heat evaporates moisture. This insures adhesion.

REVIEW # 4:
THE EASY WAY TO MAKE AND APPLY HIDE GLUE
[also called Rabbit Skin glue]

1. Boil 12 fluid ounces of water in a pot
2. Pour the boiling water into a large heat resistant 16 ounce jar ..that has a lid
3. As you stir the boiling water...slowly pour into it...1 volume ounce of dry hide glue granules. Stirring the water....helps prevent globs from forming.
NOTE: Some manufacturers recommend a ratio of 1 volume ounce of the dry glue with 23 fluid ounces of water. My tests show this ratio to be ineffective.

4. Cap the jar....then gently shake the jar until all the granules are dissolved.
5. With a wide flat brush ...apply one LIBERAL coat on all sides of the dry unprimed wood or unprimed canvas. Keep the surface vertical to avoid puddles....let this dry
6. When the first coat is dry, ..apply one liberal coat to the front surface
Keep the surface vertical.
7. Let this dry. For oil painting there is no valid need to apply a primer or a ground. You can paint directly on the sealed glue surface with oil paints. If you wish, apply either a gesso ground or an oil ground/ primer. (both words – ground or primer- mean the same).
8 if you want to paint ONLY with any tempera....egg, ..glue ..milk casein...do not primer/ ground with oil. Instead, primer/ ground with glue chalk gesso.
9. If you want to under paint with tempera....WITH THE GOAL of over painting with oils. You must seal/ isolate the finished tempera painting with hide glue, ..or you can seal the tempera with a coat of sun oil. Let it dry.
10. Before oil painting, apply an 'oil out'...with any of...the CSO. oil out mediums.

NEXT ... ADD CHALK TO MAKE GESSO
1. Gesso is an ancient archival primer ground for Temperas or oils.
2. Easy to make. Prepare the hide glue as before. As it is hot...pour in as much of the calcium carbonate chalk as you want....keep it loose and easy to brush.
One can add some white powdered .titanium dioxide if you wish. There is no need to measure any of this...do it by feel and eye
3. Put the canvas or panel surface vertical.....apply with a wide flat brush ...brushes leave bubbles...so use the palm of your hand to smooth the gesso down.
4. Apply as many layers as you want. Sand between layers if you wish. It is not needed.
5. Try the CSO EGG TEMPERA GESSO. see the DVD for instructions
6. If you will paint with oils, seal the gesso first with one coat of glue with no chalk..

REVIEW # 5
HOW TO MAKE YOUR OIL PAINTINGS DRY FASTER.
and safely without solvents or driers
Many artists dislike using oil paint because it dries too slowly
Sir ARTHUR H. CHURCH (chemist and artist) in his book of 1909
gives the 3 stages of hardening of non-viscous oil paint
Stage 1: Remains wet for several days
Stage 2: Rapidly hardens to the touch by the crosslinking of molecules
Stage 3: Needs 300 years to dry fully hard

These are practical matters artists can use to make their oil paints dry faster.

1. OIL: use viscous, pre polymerized flax linseed oil, such as Sun thickened, or, Air Pump thickened. Avoid tube paints made with slow drying oils such as Poppy, Walnut, Safflower.
2. PIGMENT: Each pigment dries at different rates. Under paint with fastest drying colors, like Umber (manganese is a natural drier). Overpaint with slower drying colors
3. THICKNESS: under paint with thin layers. Overpaint with thicker paint
4. WEATHER: Oil paints dry fastest in hot, dry air. Humid air, regardless of hot or cold, slows down drying.
5. VENTILATION: Moving air dries oil paint faster. Stagnant air slows it down . Use a fan indoors, or place the painting outdoors overnight in warm dry weather.
6. SURFACE: If you want archival oil paint, paint only on fully NON absorbent surfaces. Absorbent surfaces dry paint faster but absorb binder out of the paint, weakening it.
7. MIXED MEDIA: Begin with any tempera paint; Egg, Casein, Glue. They dry in minutes. Apply tempera paint to canvas thinly. Over paint in oils almost immediately.
8. HAND GROUND DRY PIGMENTS: Hand grind your own paint using Pre polymerized oil and DRY pigments for the underpainting. Use slow drying tube oil paints in the over painting.
9. CSO (CALCITE SUN OIL): Make CSO , a mixture of one part pre polymerized oil and three parts of calcium carbonate chalk. Grind this well, into tube oil paints, 50/50 ratio.
10. REMOVE PAINT: At the end of the day, use a palette knife and scrape off all unsatisfactory painted areas.

NOTE: Many oil paint companies add hazardous driers to their paints, especially walnut oil paints.

REVIEW # 6
THE IMPORTANCE OF EGG GLAIR
IN ARCHIVAL ART MAKING
A Dutch artist sent me thus excellent research paper on the subject of medieval illumination, With focus on binders, and materials, it deals strongly with egg white glair....
Glair, is used of course in the CSO METHODS
THIS SCHOLARLY ARTICLE IS EXCELLENT!
Don't be fooled by the first paragraph written in GREEK

http://revistadehistoriadaarte.files.wordpress.com/2011/09/art08.pdf

CHAPTER SIX : WEBSITE DATA

INFORMATION FROM MY WEBSITE

I know that one day my website will one day cease to exist. In preparation for that date I wish to preserve for future generations some of that information. I feel it is important to preserve this information in book form, even though the information is found in other parts of my books and DVDS.

There is NO special organization of the information in this chapter. When I first read the Theodore De Mayerne manuscript, written in the 1620's, I judged it to be a mish-mash of seemingly unstructured notes, thoughts and incomplete ideas that he thought he could try out and test later as experiments. In this regard, I feel a kinship with his book.

When I became a certified teacher at the University, I was taught that REPETITION of important facts - is a valuable tool in teaching. With this in mind, I have included these summaries here.

WEBSITE 1
THE TEN BENEFITS of " CALCITE SUN OIL" / EMULSIONS
DRYING is accelerated without driers -
ADHESION, without drips and beading
BLENDING is facilitated -
TRANSLUCENCY is increased
BODY of Impasto or Glazes -
COLOR DEPTH and LUSTER is increased
MICRO-FINE LINES and DETAILS are allowed
THIXOTROPIC quality is promoted
SUEDE EFFECT of Tube Oil Paints is eliminated
WRINKLING of impasto is eliminated

WEBSITE 2
The SUPERIOR OIL of the Old Masters is :
UNREFINED COLD PRESSED FLAX OIL
that has been organically cleansed of its mucilage and slowly Sun
Thickened I created the term "SUPERIOR LINSEED/FLAX OIL", out of necessity,
to avoid confusing it with industrial processed 'linseed oils' or
mediums used by artists today.

The importance of the SUPERIOR FLAX SEED OIL [Linseed oil] used by the Old Masters is supported by TWO IRREFUTABLE FACTS that are documented by clear EVIDENCE which CANNOT be denied, disproved or misrepresented by any well paid Scientist, Media Advertising Director, Attorney, or other controlled employees of Linseed oil manufacturers, oil paint makers, and sellers.

THE FIRST IRREFUTABLE FACT ARE THE 600 YEAR OLD OIL PAINTINGS PAINTED BY THE VAN EYCK BROTHERS WHICH ARE IN AN EXCELLENT STATE OF PRESERVATION.

THE SECOND IRREFUTABLE FACT IS THAT THE VAN EYCK PAINTINGS WERE NOT PAINTED WITH MODERN INDUSTRIAL, CAUSTIC CHEMICAL CLEANSED, BOILED 'STAND' LINSEED OIL USED BY ARTISTS TODAY AND SINCE THE 19TH CENTURY INDUSTRIAL ERA. but were painted with THE UNREFINED SUPERIOR FLAX OIL DESCRIBED IN MY BOOK AND ON MY WEBSITE.

My CSO patent was approved by the US Patent and Trade Mark Office in November 2006. See patent # 7141109. Now, in 2014, I allowed my patent to expire and it now is available for use by anyone.

WEBSITE 3
THE FINEST RAW OIL FOR ARTISTS IS LABELED FLAX OIL- NOT LINSEED OIL:
If the label says FLAX OIL or FLAX SEED OIL.. it is THE oil the Old Masters used.
BUT, it has to be cleansed of its mucilage. This easy process is described in my book and DVD.
I have used human grade flax seed oil for many years . It is high quality. There are several sellers of FLAX OIL. DO NOT buy FLAX OIL containing any anti-oxidant additives.
Antioxidants stop the oil from drying [hardening]. Simply, it will not dry. Commom anti-oxidants are vitamins E or C , or Rosemary, or tocopherols or polypherols.

THERE ARE NO ' LIN" SEEDS IN NATURE
LINSEED OIL and FLAX SEED OIL are pressed from the same seed--the FLAX SEED.
FLAX OIL is pressed cold and without any solvents or extra heat or lye caustic chemicals.
Humans can safely eat FLAX SEED OIL.
IF the oil is labeled LINSEED OIL, it has been pressed and exposed to caustic lye chemicals and or solvents. HUMANS cannot safely eat LINSEED OIL.

PLEASE NOTE: The only exception to this is [possibly], the 'OLD HOLLAND' brand of UNREFINED COLD PRESSED LINSEED OIL from The Netherlands.

WEBSITE 4
DAVID HOCKNEY'S BOOK, " SECRET KNOWLEDGE"
HAS INVESTIGATED IN DEPTH THE USE OF MIRRORS AND LENSES
by some of THE OLD MASTERS
SEE MY YOUTUBE VIDEO ON THIS SUBJECT
It is controversial but I accept David Hockney's belief that beginning in about 1420, many of the Old Masters [but NOT ALL OF THEM] used Mirrors, Lenses, the Camera Lucida, the Camara Obscura and any other means to TRACE an image of PROJECTED practice...to save time AND TO GET RESULTS not possible BY ANY OTHER MEANS.
To locate all my Youtube videos. Search for : **CSO VELASQUEZ**

Grandma Moses, began to paint at age 81 and died at age 101.
She could not draw well. So she would CUT OUT photos from magazines---move them around on the canvas to get a nice design composition.....tape them down.... use a TRANSFER PAPER... then would transfer the image by outlining the images with a pen.
THEN, she would ' COLOR IN" the outlined images with oil paint. It is basically the same as a child's coloring book, and is what VERMEER DID... but VERMEER had no modern photos to trace, so he projected the images with a lens, and traced them.
Neither she nor Vermeer left any drawings.

WEBSITE 5
IMPORTANT MUSEUM STUDIES SINCE 1988 SHOW REMBRANDT AND VELAZQUEZ USED SIMPLE ADDITIVES TO THEIR PAINT
Velazquez' paintings were studied by the Prado Museum. Results published in 1992 show he added large amounts of Calcium Carbonate (Calcite AND Chalk)) to ALL his colors not just the White, and in all layers of his paintings. This addition gives the paint great translucency, body and sumptuous textures not achieved by other means. Calcium Carbonate has a cement-like quality that improves adhesion to the support. Also, his paint includes an addition of a protein which creates an Emulsion. This protein additive gives great control to the viscous leveling linseed oil, allowing a great variety of application methods and visual effects.

Rembrandt's paintings were scientifically examined by the National Gallery London. Results published in 1988 show he used Calcium Carbonate Chalk and a protein additive to create an Emulsion that in turn allows the extraordinary ' paint quality' that is a trademark of his work. Rembrandt did NOT use resins but his followers and students did. The protein additive replaces the resin and is superior to it because it becomes one with the oil ageing together, while the resins simply co mingle and age at different rates. Resins turn yellow and brittle over time. The emulsion does not.

WEBSITE 6
The " WONDER MEDIUM" of two EXTRAORDINARY EMULSIONS

Contemporary artists and those of past centuries have studied the paintings of the Van Eycks. Numerous Old and Modern books give uncounted Emulsion or Medium recipes, each with FAULTY complex mixtures of solvents, varnishes, balsams, resins, water and other ingredients.

These FAILED MIXTURES have been TRIED and REPEATED by each subsequent generation since the 1800's ...and today...various websites continue the FAILURES.
I developed two SAFE and PERMANENT Emulsions, using two SIMPLE ancient time-tested ingredients available to the Van Eycks, Velazquez and Rembrandt:

The specific MIXING method, the specific RATIO of the mixtures, and ESPECIALLY the specific APPLICATION procedures ARE IMPORTANT TO THEIR SUCCESS. Lack of this information leads to failure. The EMULSIONS are the "paint thinner". They insure adhesion of layers -They eliminate wrinkling - They allow painting of micro-fine details -They allow the creation of Impasto - They eliminate drip and spread -They control the behavior of the viscous oil - They have no toxic fumes, or objectionable odors, and are 100% safe. -They are simple to make, easily and quickly made.

WEBSITE 7
MY WEBSITE HAS THREE PRIMARY OBJECTIVES:
1. SAFETY FOR THE HEALTH OF THE OIL PAINTER
2. PERMANENCE OF THE OIL PAINTING
3. TEACHING OIL PAINTERS AND TEMPERA PAINTERS TO UNDERSTAND THEIR CRAFT

Since 2000 I have achieved these objectives by discovering mixtures and procedures in the development of a safe method of oil painting, and now, egg tempera painting, allowing elimination of hazardous materials. The CSO METHOD and the rebirth of the SUPERIOR oil of the Old Masters is far superior to the currently taught " resin-solvent-varnish-drier method". I am happy to have the free time to have corresponded one-on-one with artists all over the globe.

WEBSITE 8
HISTORY OF THE 'CALCITE SUN OIL/EMULSIONS' METHOD OF OIL PAINTING [CSO].

2000: After 40 years of oil painting with Solvents, resins, varnishes, driers and alkali refined linseed oil I began this work which resulted in the creation of the Calcite Sun Oil / Emulsions method of oil painting [abbreviated as CSO]. Over the next few years I made additional discoveries and developments which I have shared with artists across the globe.

2000: My identification of the superior UNREFINED FLAX OIL used by the Old Masters. This very important development is named ' The Rebirth of the Old Masters' Superior Oil'.This extraordinary oil is the foundation of the 'Calcite Sun Oil' method of Oil Painting and without it, the CSO method could not exist.

2000-2009 : Sustained research with creation of several new cleansing methods of cleansing the UNREFINED FLAX OIL, with my identification of Psyllium Husk as an important ingredient for mucilage removal.

2000: Creation of ' Calcite Sun Oil', a modern grinding oil, based on published reports of scientific examination of microscopic sized paint samples of Rembrandt's and Velazquez' paintings by important scholars - with my creation of three additional mixture variations.

2000: Creation of two Emulsions used in conjunction with CSO; the 'Viscous emulsion' , and the ' Non viscous emulsion'. Including my discovery of the crucial application method of the two emulsions and their uses in oil painting, which I believe to be part of the lost Van Eyck method. The two emulsions used with CSO allows the artist of today to achieve the paint quality and permanence of the Old

Masters with complete control and safety.

2004 : Published and sold across the globe, the first edition of my book containing the CSO/EMULSIONS method of oil painting. The first book to be published with ratio mixtures of calcium carbonate powder and oil as an oil painting method.

2004: Applied for a provisional patent with the US Patent Office for CSO, with approval in 2006.

2005: Establishment of the CALCITE SUN OIL website.

2008: Published the current revised edition of my book, (2012) sold globally though online bookstores.

2009: Developed the 'CSO-FIXATIVE' method of fixing a charcoal drawing without aerosol sprays

2009: Developed the ' CSO/AGUADO' method , the first expansion of the original CSO/EMULSIONS method of oil painting, allowing artists to work on large sized paintings with speed and efficiency. These advancements are described in my book and on this website.

2009: Developed the "CSO-EGG TEMPERA" medium. A fast drying medium for under painting of oil paints.

2010 : Developed CSO-EGG GESSO" . A cold gesso using basic archival ancient artists materials = wood, egg, chalk

2010: Published the book: CSO-EGG TEMPERA, and the two DVD's OIL PAINTING WITH CALCITE SUN OIL, and, CSO-EGG TEMPERA PAINTING
2010: Developed CSO-CASEIN TEMPERA . A NEW look at an ancient medium
2010: Posted my research on RUBENS' THIXOTROPIC METHOD and his use of CHALK, EMULSIONS, and PINE TREE TAR
2010: Development of a thixotropic new OIL OUT medium, named 'ESPESO'
2011: CREATION of a NEW MILK OIL PAINT for Art School Classes . New mixtures and new application procedures. SEE THE DVD: Oil Painting with MILK
Safety for New Painters and School Art Classes ALSO THE NEW 2011 DVD: THE NEW MILK OIL PAINT AND THE VAN EYCK SECRET MEDIUM
2012- Publication of the book " OIL PAINTING LESSONS WITH REMBRANDT AND CALCITE SUN OIL"", a collection of all my studies,
2013: Published the BEGINNERS BOOK : Velasquez' Safe Oil Painting' for Beginners and Art Teachers"
2016: MY NEW BOOK - VOLUME TWO - WILL BE PUBLISHED WITH NEW DISCOVERIES AND UPDATED INFORMATION.

I have summarized my accomplishments because there are two persons on the web who in late 2006 began to experiment with mixtures of calcium carbonate and oil.
One of these has embarrassed HIMSELF by name calling and insinuating I am lying regarding my warnings of NOT TO USE ALLBACK Swedish linseed oil for fine art painting.
The behavior of this one person is unfortunate .... and exposes him as being very jealous of my accomplishments.

True academics do not engage in name calling ... but engage in civil dialogue to question decisions by others. I will continue to work with truth and integrity for the safety of the artists and permanence of the artworks and I am always willing to assist artists and to explain my postings by responding to email inquiries. My studies of Allback Linseed oil posted on my site explain why I warn fine artists of using this oil.

My discoveries and contributions to oil painting are supported by dated publications, dated applications and approval of a US patent, several registered US letters, and testimonials from artists across the globe.

WEBSITE 9
ACADEMIC TERMINOLOGY IN FINE ART PAINTING

The Art of Painting is noble and deserving of respect. Slang terms have no place in naming the mixtures of ingredients the Master painters used in painting their Masterpieces. The Old Masters used various Ochres and Umbers.
We call them, 'Earths" ...... not, Dirt, nor Mud, nor Muck.

The name, 'Calcite Sun Oil", honors its archival ingredients. As others experiment with mixtures like CSO, they use slang terms such as, ' GUNK', 'GOOP',
and 'PUTTY''. These slang terms denigrate Painting. GUNK collects in auto radiators, GOOP is sticky like a glue, and PUTTY is used by plumbers as a water sealant. The word PUTTY has a negative reference in describing the Masters' work.

WINDOW PUTTY, is a mixture of boiled leaded linseed oil mixed with calcium carbonate. It has a life span of under 50 years .
Modern mixtures use silicone. = 'SILLY PUTTY', is sometimes known as SILICONE BOUNCING PUTTY. = 'GOOFY PUTTY :Read the entire article and see
how to make it. http://www.worsleyschoolnet/science/files/silly/putty.html = 'GOOP PUTTY::See the recipe to make it= http://www.worsleyschool.
net/science/files/goop/page.html
'SLIMY PUTTY' View a video on making : http://www.wonderhowto.com/how-to/video/how-to-make-slimy-silly-putty-with-glue-and-borax-130536

In 2004, I sent Tad Spurgeon a copy of my 2004 published book describing my development of ' Calcite Sun Oil', the two Emulsions, and the new methods I developed in cleansing the Unrefined Cold Pressed Flax oil as I identified the Superior oil of the Old Masters.
I did this because his website showed he knew nothing about these Revolutionary new developments I was working on, and I saw he was still using Solvents, Resins and Varnishes. Three years later—in 2007 – Tad's website reported that he began his experiments into the knowledge of mixing calcium carbonate with oil (this information was contained in my 2004 book I sent him). I am happy for Tad and I support his research. I believe my book has inspired many artists to learn this revolutionary new yet ancient information.
In 2004 I also sent copies of my book to others I thought needed some guidance.

The formulas and application methods described in my book, website and now DVD'S make it possible for all oil painters today to, "Achieve the Old Masters' Paint Quality" with SAFETY and PERMANENCE"

WEBSITE 10
WARNING !.. French chalk!!! ..not the same as " chalk from Champagne France !

AS THE PATENT HOLDER OF "CALCITE SUN OIL" MIXTURE, I RECOMMEND ONLY CALCIUM CARBONATE that is true ...CHALK FROM CHAMPAGNE FRANCE for making CSO.

The German based company, KREMER-PIGMENTE KREMER sells this chalk and has worldwide distribution . Look at their URL for a site nearest you.
http://kremer-pigmente.de/en/Laeden/Distributors-worldwide KREMER'S ID # for this item is # 58000 and is listed as: Chalk from Champagne, France. It
is true , very fine, natural Calcium Carbonate.

IN THE PAST, I used to purchase my CHALK FROM CHAMPAGNE FRANCE/ CALCIUM CARBONATE from SINOPIA, a Fine Art Supply store in San
Francisco, California. As of this writing, December 2008, they no longer carry this item. They do list an item they call FRENCH CHALK. Several respected
Academic sources state that the term, FRENCH CHALK is a common name used to describe TALC, and TALC is hydrated magnesium silicate with the
chemical formula $H2Mg3(SiO3)4$ or $Mg3Si4O10(OH)2$.
GO TO http://en.wikipedia.org/wiki/Talc to read the hazard FRENCH CHALK/TALC may present to humans and use it at your own risk.

Sinopia states their FRENCH CHALK is not a TALC, but is a CALCIUM CARBONATE. I purchased their FRENCH CHALK, and found it to be inferior for
making "CALCITE SUN OIL" as per my patented formula because their FRENCH CHALK lacks the great adhesiveness of the CHALK FROM
CHAMPAGNE FRANCE CALCIUM CARBONATE, and it separates while in storage from the oil. Therefore, I do not recommend the item named FRENCH
CHALK. For other Fine Art Supplies, SINOPIA remains an excellent source and it has always been one of my favorite art supply stores.

I hope SINOPIA will carry Chalk from Champagne France, in the future. As of this listing, I am not aware they now do. If they do, I offer them my gratitude. They are indeed an excellent Art Supply store.

WEBSITE 11
THE TERM.... "OIL OUT"

It is abbreviated for... " OIL rubbed in and oil wiped OUT" : which is the procedure by guiding artists in a specific GOAL ORIENTED AND INSTRUCTIVE procedure.
The term ' OIL OUT" tells the artist that for the EMULSION OIL OUT to be effective, the Emulsion must BE APPLIED CORRECTLY-- OR--IT FAILS.

SEE MY OIL PAINTING DVD to see exactly how to correctly apply the OIL OUT to create the IDEAL condition for the subsequent oil paint application to achieve the Old Masters paint effects..

SOME misguided English speaking artists use the English word COUCH. In English, a COUCH is a SOFA. FRENCH artists call the OIL OUT a 'COUCHE' .
This translates as ' A THIN FILM OF OIL OR PAINT". Other equally misguided English speaking artists use the word CUSHION. A CUSHION is a PILLOW.

NEITHER 'couch' nor, ' cushion' are INSTRUCTIVE NOR GOAL ORIENTED. This leads to a common problem AN INAPPROPRIATELY APPLIED " OIL OUT" will FAIL to achieve the desired effect. The Emulsion OIL OUT must be applied with the bare hand only- then rubbed, then wiped. IT MUST NEVER BE APPLIED WITH A BRUSH
Read my book to understand why JACQUES MAROGER'S emulsion formula FAILED

WEBSITE 12
VARIOUS TOPICS FOR SUCCESSFUL ARCHIVAL SAFE OIL PAINTING

1. THE OIL OUT: The emulsion "oil out" must be applied ONLY BY HAND !--never with a brush--and it must be wiped down to remove all excess--then rubbed in BY HAND!--or it will FAIL!

2. FINAL OIL OUT: IF using the ' viscous emulsion' as the FINAL 'varnish' for a completed oil painting--to equalize the entire surface--IT MUST BE APPLIED as an "OIL OUT" --again--- wipe off all excess--then rub into an ULTRA THIN film. IF you do not do this--you will have discolored areas. SEE my photo on my website showing the viscous emulsion in a jar. NOTE how the ultra thin area is COLORLESS and how the thick emulsion is yellowish.

3 The FIRST STEP in preparing canvas or wood--is to apply two liberal coats of HIDE GLUE or--acrylic varnish [its a glue]--THEN apply the gesso--
NOTE: ALL gessos are absorbent and must be sealed with two coats of HIDE GLUE before oil painting… or--if using acrylic gesso--use acrylic varnish / gloss or matte

4. SEE MY THREE BRIEF YOUTUBE VIDEOS ON " AIR PUMP OIL"
Know the issues involved!!!type in...CSO VELASQUEZ

WEBSITE 13
EMULSIONS:
The Emulsions have VERY important uses and functions. My book will guide you on the CORRECT application method and the correct ratio mixtures. The Emulsion MUST be applied correctly, IF it is NOT applied correctly, the Emulsion "oil out" will fail. The book explains how to easily make and use the two Emulsions. Each emulsion has a purpose.

The Emulsion is truly a WONDER MEDIUM.
It is safe, easy to make in 5 minutes. (note: Oil paint made with the superior oil will dry within 30 hours or less, without use of any driers, solvents, resins or varnishes)

Many artists are concerned with FAST DRYING. Titian and the old masters solved this problem by working on several paintings at once.
On day one you can start a painting and work all day on it.
On day two you start another painting and work all day on it.
On day three you start the third painting and work all day on it.
On day four, you work on the first painting, and so on.
The superior oil I describe dries within 30 hours if thin paint is used.
So, if you use paint with more impasto, the extra day of drying allows it to set and be ready for a next layer.

WEBSITE 14
WARNING - ON THE OIL YOU USE
The Old Masters did not have to deal with a very important modern evil -- additives of antioxidants to their oil by well-meaning manufacturers.

READ MORE AT WIKIPEDIA: http://en.wikipedia.org/wiki/Antioxidants

DEGRADED LINSEED OIL CARELESSNESS AND IGNORANCE

Many websites and books on oil painting promote use of
DEGRADED Linseed oil.
THEY IGNORE THE SAFE HEATING TEMPERATURE OF
THE OIL. The oil begins DECOMPOSING at 230 degrees Celsius.
Modern Stand Linseed oil is cooked to 288 degrees Celsius.
Burnt Plate Oil is the most decomposed of all , reaching above 400 C.

Many websites "experiment" with time proven FAILED methods of processing the oil and continue repeating the failures.
They ignore the basic fundamental rule: DO NOT OVER HEAT THE OIL.

Their mixtures to create 'painting mediums', oil varnishes, and other experiments include a dash of this, a bit of that, some of that, shake and bake ..
and hope for the best.

WEBSITE 15
FRANK COVINO'S "CONTROLLED PALETTE" IS HOW THE OLD MASTERS
JUDGED THE GRADATIONS OF LIGHT VALUES AND COLORS.
SEE this YOUTUBE video: Titled "Sherry Hunting Studio: Frank Covino Workshop :
FRANK COVINO EXPLAINS HIS CONTROLLED PALETTE AT 03:29 OF THE VIDEO

PLEASE READ AN EXCELLENT TIMELESS ESSAY BY FRANK COVINO
ON MY FRONT PAGE MENU ---Click on my page ... STUDY WITH LOUIS

TO LOCATE ALL MY BRIEF VIDEOS ON YOUTUBE, ...TYPE IN .... CSO VELASQUEZ
TWO OF MY FULL LENGTH VIDEOS ARE AVAILABLE FREE ON YOUTUBE.
" Rubens methods and materials" - and- "Milk oil paint for beginners"

WEBSITE 16
CSO-EGG TEMPERA"
A NEW 21ST CENTURY EGG TEMPERA PAINTING

HISTORY
Before the Van Eycks' perfected the oil paint medium, they and all the painters painted with EGG TEMPERA. They drew a careful ink drawing on a brilliant white gesso board and then applied thin layers of transparent egg tempera paint. The egg tempera paint dries instantly. Blending is not allowed. All blending is done with thin hatching strokes in a variety of value changes. This method is also painstaking, and paintings are normally small [exceptions to everything exist].
Since the Medieval and Renaissance periods -- among many, this has been
and continues to be today --the ONLY WAY to paint with egg tempera.
IMPORTANTLY: Impasto is not allowed as it will crack and peel off.

THE FLEMISH METHOD OF OIL PAINTING: Late 1300's
In the 14th- 15th Century, Jan Van Eyck and the Flemish masters perfected a method of oil painting where they layered thin transparent glazes of color on a careful constructed ink outline drawing made on a PURE WHITE GESSO board. This brilliant white gesso gave the thin color glazes an inner light that gave the appearance of jewels. This method was slow and painstaking.

THE ITALIAN RENAISSANCE METHOD : 1400-1500's
The Flemish oil method arrived in Italy where Titian and other masters MODIFIED the method to allow larger sized paintings and faster finishing. To do this they painted with an OPAQUE GRISAILLE, of mixtures of white, black and brown. They used THICK brilliant white paint to create the under painting. They then applied thin color glazes on top of these thick brilliant white under painting areas. By doing this, they achieved the same vibrant transparent jewel-like colors as Jan Van Eyck and the Flemish masters. They were able to create large sized paintings and used virtuoso brush strokes for their aesthetic value.

MY 21ST CENTURY EGG TEMPERA DEVELOPMENT
I added chalk --not to the yolk- but to the egg white and by doing so, I created an opaque egg tempera that allows the same freedom with EGG TEMPERA that TITIAN developed with OIL PAINT.

I know painters everywhere will find this to be a boon and a wonderful advancement for Egg Tempera painters and by oil painters who will use it as the fastest drying thickened medium available for under painting for oil paints.

POSITIVE FACTS ABOUT THIS NEW MEDIUM
* It is a Safe and Permanent fast drying aqueous medium
* It replaces modern synthetic paints containing hazardous chemicals
* It is compatible with the traditional Egg Tempera medium
* Egg is a proven archival ancient binding medium
* It is inexpensive, using chalk, eggs, vinegar and dry pigments
* A vast variety of application methods are possible including impasto
* Scratching and raised textural effects are possible
* A variety of application tools can be used, brushes, palette knives, fingers
* Application can be broad, fluid, free and spontaneous or controlled
* Over paints, corrections or changes have no time limits or precautions
* The medium can be used alone or as a fast drying under painting for oil paints
* It mixes easily with colored dry pigments to instantly create paint
* The Medium is also a Gesso - that requires no heating for application
* The mixture of Glair and Chalk dries to a hard cement-like material
* The adhesiveness of the medium and gesso is exceptionally strong
* The gesso can be made ivory smooth or scratched with cloth weave patterns

WEBSITE 17
THE DVD " THE NEW MILK OIL PAINT and THE VAN EYCK SECRET MEDIUM"
Available on AMAZON.COM

Ancient artists learned of milk's natural adhesive property. Paint made from milk is called CASEIN TEMPERA PAINT. The DVD, offers artists NEW 21st century DEVELOPMENTS of the ancient CASEIN medium.

Artists throughout art history have used CASEIN MILK PAINT because it is inexpensive, fully archival, and easy to apply. Like all aqueous media, it is difficult to achieve the 'REALISM" offered by easier blending oil paint, yet, it remains an outstanding paint. Andrew Wyeth and many others of our modern era have solely used a TEMPERA aqueous medium in creating realist style paintings.

For the modern artist of today, who may be more concerned with AESTHETIC FORM rather than visual reality, the NEW CSO-CASEIN TEMPERA PAINT will expand the visual expression of today's artists.

WEBSITE 18
DEVELOPMENT OF THE CSO-EGG TEMPERA MEDIUM

I studied the past to develop an effective FAST DRYING modern medium using ancient archival materials. My research sought out information on cave paintings far older than those of the Renaissance. Some cave paintings have been tested to be 40,000 years old. The Van Eyck paintings are only 700 years old.

The oldest binders of paint are MILK, EGG, GLUE, and natural tree exudates such as BALSAMS, GUMS and RESINS, as well as GLUES from boiling animal skins. Any sticky substance, that can be mixed with powders creates a PAINT and can be applied to a wall or almost any absorbent surface.

Because oil paints dry relatively slowly, Renaissance artists of the 14th through the 16th centuries sought a faster drying medium. A tempera paint is the fastest drying ancient medium but Realism is difficult to obtain with tempera. Some artists of the period combined egg or milk with an oil into am Emulsion, or, under painted in tempera and overpainted in oils. Modern artists of today have the same needs and concerns. Modern artists frequently use acrylics as ancient artists used Temperas.

The real issue of any paint is its PERMANENCE. Unfortunately, I was informed by an expert [see below] that modern science has done little to analyze the binders used in the Cave paintings. The few published results are debatable or inconclusive. Some contemporary artists have made many tests with a variety of binders. I do not have faith in test results or theories from recent testing of a few years time.

No one knows the changing conditions of these caves over a 40,000 year time period. Yet, modern theories are interesting. One artist believes human urine (Uric acid) was one possible binder. Another artist believes cave water rich in calcium carbonate was also used. Historians tell us the cave painting were not done by one artist but evolved over thousands of years with frequent over paints on existing paintings. This leads us to believe the binders were of many kinds. 40,000 years is quite a long time to try to reconstruct any paint layer.

We do know LIMESTONE CAVES are calcium carbonate. The CSO oil painting method uses calcium carbonate powder as an important component that guarantees permanence. My previous creation and formulation of CALCITE SUN OIL, provided me with new ideas as I experimented in developing a FAST DRYING UNDERPAINTING MEDIUM FOR OIL PAINTING. This led to a new discoveries.

WEBSITE 19
'CSO-EGG GESSO' - A NEW 21st CENTURY GESSO

DO NOT USE ACRYLIC GESSO WITH THE CSO-EGG TEMPERA MEDIUM
Like most oil painters I have used acrylic gesso because it is convenient. It is not GENUINE traditional gesso like that of the Old Masters that has proven archival for more than 600 years. We do not know the permanence of ACRYLIC gesso. But it is inexpensive and convenient and it can be applied to walls, canvas and wood panels. Acrylic gesso is made of modern synthetic emulsion glue mixed with one or more of a variety of dry powders such as marble dust. It dries by evaporation of its water content and when dry can be brilliantly white.

I did not make traditional Gesso panels like the Old Masters until late in life. Many recipes can be found and they vary little. Basically it is a hot animal skin glue mixed with Calcium Carbonate Chalk, or Gypsum. The 15 century master Cennini gave detailed instructions on how to gesso a wood panel. Later artists made changes to his recipe. Cennini's procedure was labor and time consuming. One reason was because he did not have modern flat plywood like we do, nor did he have electric planers to quickly smooth out the wood surface.

Even with modern materials, my gesso panels have not turned out perfectly. I cut corners to speed up the finish. My research found the scientific analysis of one Rembrandt painting on wood. He first applied a glue to seal the wood again the oil paint. He then applied ONE thin gesso layer to cover the brown wood and to create a brilliant white surface. He then applied a single thin coat of oil paint made of some black some lead white and umber [umber accelerates the drying]. This pale translucent warm gray oil layer was applied thinly.

It served as a sealant to the very thin white very absorbent gesso. On this simple preparation, Rembrandt painted that painting. One thing you frequently see in Old Master paintings, IF they used a thin gesso, is the grain of the wood.

I believed that if Rembrandt could deviate from Cennini's laborious multi layered gesso panels, I could too. As much as I dislike applying the gesso, I dislike the dry powder dust from sanding even more. So I do not sand. Therefore I settle for a mildly textured gesso as the primer coat for my oil paintings.

Development of the CSO-EGG TEMPERA medium led me to develop the CSO-EGG GESSO, based on egg and not glue.

Years ago, an experienced masonry worker taught me how to apply stucco on my home so it would be permanent. The first requirement is to create a waterproof barrier so moisture will not enter the home. Second, a wire mesh is attached, so the wet stucco has a place to grab onto. The first coat of the stucco is made very very thick and it is applied roughly with a trowel.

On drying, it cracks, splits and breaks.

The next coat of plaster is almost as thick and is called the ' scratch' coat. It too is applied with a trowel but it is made more smooth and level. While this coat is wet, it is scratched with a tool that looks like a comb to create ridges that will hold the next coat. After the 'scratch' coat dries a thinner stucco is applied smoothly. Note that all the coats are allowed to dry hard..and that all will crack. When the last coat is dried...and cracked...a liquid thin layer of fine stucco is brushed on with a wide bristle brush. This fills any fine fissures and is the final coat before the house paint is applied.

My creation of CSO GESSO and CSO EGG TEMPERA follows the same logical procedure! Apply- Dry- Crack- Paint.

THE DVD WILL GIVE DETAILED INSTRUCTIONS WITH DEMONSTRATION IN LIVE FILM. Contents of the DVD:

STEP ONE: MILK CHOICES

STEP TWO: CHOICES ON HOW TO CURDLE THE MILK
THE TRADITIONAL METHOD
NEW METHODS TO CURD THE NON FAT MILK
THE 'CSO- CHAMPAGNE INSTANT CURD METHOD'
THE 'CSO-TONIC WATER METHOD'

STEP THREE: MAKING "CSO-CASEIN" PASTE

STEP FOUR: MAKING "CSO-CASEIN" MEDIUM

STEP FIVE : MAKING ' CSO-CASEIN' PAINT

STEP SIX: PREPARING THE SUPPORT WITH 'CSO-CASEIN GESSO'

STEP SEVEN: DRAW FIRST- THEN SEAL THE GESSO WITH MILK

STEP EIGHT : PAINT THE PICTURE WITH THE CSO-CASEIN PAINT

STEP NINE : OPTIONAL 'CSO-CASEIN' PAINT AS AN UNDERPAINTING FOR OIL PAINTS

WEBSITE 20
CAVE PAINTINGS OF ALTAMIRA AND LASCAUX AND
THEIR IMPACT ON MODERN OIL PAINTING - PART ONE
In Spain one finds the cave paintings of Altamira http://www.thenagain. info/Webchron/World/Altamira.html and nor far away, those of Lascaux in France http://www.lascaux.culture.fr/#/en/00.xml.

Scientists estimate them to be between 15,000 and 40,000 years old and older. The 600 year old Van Eyck paintings pale in comparison in regards to age. The paint is made of colored natural earth pigments but the binders used are unknown or the results of tests are debatable or inconclusive.

My research shows very little has been done by modern scientists to determine the binders used and the reasons given are many. We do know the most common ancient paint binders are egg, milk, glues, oils, gums and resins and any sticky substance, or mixtures of these simple ingredients. However, no synthetic acrylics, liquin, nor modern alkali refined linseed oil, nor mixtures of synthetic mediums were ever used in the cave paintings.

It is these basics that I write about here.
The cave painters of old, did not employ the refined Renaissance technique taught in Ms. Schadler's book. Anyone who has left egg yolk on a plate after breakfast, and has returned hours later to wash it off the non-absorbent glass plate, must scrub hard. Adding hot water only increases the resistance of its removal. The extremely strong adhesion of the yolk is extraordinary. Not only that, but it dries hard within minutes, though time is required for final curing. The yolk and the egg clear are both very complex.

In the Calcite Sun Oil method of oil painting, I found the NON VISCOUS limpid thin egg white, once converted to GLAIR, to be ideal for mixing with VISCOUS thick sun thickened flax oil into an extraordinary "wonder" emulsion. Yes, I did test the yolk and found it to be not advantageous for mixing with sun oil as sun oil is sufficiently viscous. The egg yolk contains a great amount of egg oil, and the egg clear hardly none.

RESEARCH OF CAVE ART : PART TWO

{LETTER FROM PhD. DR. PAUL BAHN }
Dear Mr. Velasquez, the best way to answer your question is to send you the relevant text from my 1997 book "Journey Through the Ice Age" (Weidenfeld & Nicolson: London / Univ. of California Press: Berkeley), as far as I am aware, nothing new has been published on this subject since then.
Best wishes, Paul Bahn.

[Excerpts from Dr. Bahn's letter and book]
In the past it was often assumed that some form of fatty animal product was used for the binder; ... 205 experiments in two caves was carried out by Claude Couraud, involving a variety of pigments and binding substances (including fish glue, Arabic gum, gelatin, egg white, bovine blood, and urine), and a range of wall- types and degrees of humidity.

Observation over three years led him
to the conclusion that fatty and organic substances were totally unsuitable binding agents, and fail to adhere well to humid walls... the only substance which seemed to be good at fixing and preserving the pigments on the rockface was water -- especially cave-water, which is rich in calcium carbonate, and which was probably used at Lascaux .... pigments adhered better if they had been finely ground.

In 1978, Cabrera Garrido's analyses at Altamira led him to suggest the possible use here of powdered fossil amber as a binder. In some Ariège caves, recent analyses of paints, using gas chromatography and mass spectrometry, have detected traces of what are thought to be oils of animal or plant origin, presumably used as a binder. On art from Enlène and at Trois Frères it seems to be a plant oil, whereas figure at Fontanet seem to contain an animal oil. Other sites such as the Réseau Clastres have no trace of any binder, as at Lascaux.

WEBSITE 21
THE VAN EYCK SECRET MEDIUM :
I am convinced the Van Eyck secret medium was in fact TWO separate considerations.
1. A very simple Emulsion . 2. A crucial application method.
My experience with formulating emulsions, and formulating the ' calcite sun oil' grinding oil, has given me intimate insight into how Emulsions work .
I believe the secret medium of the Van Eycks did not include use of solvents, resins, varnishes or driers...because there is NO NEED for them.
Since my [2012]book goes into this in great detail, I will skip explaining myself in any detail, on why I believe this.

The two extraordinary Emulsions I formulated are extraordinarily simple,
but very profound in their foundation. This also is explained clearly in my book.
If one does not know the crucial method of application, the medium itself FAILS.
If one uses the unique method of application I developed, the result is ASTONISHING.
My book clearly describes that application method and explains why it is important
for it to be applied correctly.

I believe I am the first to make this claim. Of course we will never know what the
' secret medium' of the Van Eycks was, unless one day a document from them or their students is discovered.

WEBSITE 22
GIORGIO VASARI and the VAN EYCK SECRET MEDIUM
In the year 1550, Giorgio Vasari (1511-1574) first published his multi-volume book," Lives of the Most Eminent Italian Architects, Painters and Sculptors". In book Eight, titled, " Antonello Da Messina ...", Vasari wrote that John of Bruges (Jan Van Eyck) had invented painting with oils.
Modern scholarship shows oil painting is an ancient art, existing centuries before the Van Eycks. It is clear Vasari meant to say, Jan Van Eyck 'perfected' oil painting. 100 years after the death of Van Eyck, Vasari accurately wrote that Van Eyck's oil paintings far exceeded the quality of the paintings of his (Vasari's)day.

In book eight, Vasari says the following , (paraphrased in brief):
Before Van Eyck, artists used 'distemper' [a glue or egg Tempera medium]. Many artists all over Europe tried to find a way to paint more realistically. They tried different liquid varnishes and colors but did not succeed. Jan Van Eyck made a secret varnish that he would not share. The full story from the actual text is available at the Internet Medieval Sourcebook, www.fordham.edu

Not only does the quality of the Van Eyck's paintings stand out amongst those of their era (1385-1441) (there were two brothers) but when compared to paintings of recent centuries and of today, the Van Eyck paintings are held by conservators as being in the most
remarkable condition. Frequently they are referred to as being "jewel-like". The radiant colors and the micro-fine details causes one to ask,
"What medium did the Van Eycks use to do this"?

That is the subject of this essay:
The "secret" medium the Van Eycks used that allows full control of the paint, allowing the painting of sharply defined micro-fine details and lines, with hard lustrous paint and great depth of brilliant color. I believe the methods and materials described in
my book will shed light on the issue.
QUESTIONS and ANSWERS

Since Vasari did not know the 'secret medium", what oil painting method did Vasari and his peers use?
Vasari and his colleagues used a method of oil painting still in use today and taught at the highest and lowest academic levels around the world.

Was the Linseed oil the Van Eycks different from the linseed oil of today?
Yes, The Van Eyck's oil was different from today's oil in that they had. the Van Eyck's used ancient press equipment that extracted the oil.

Did Vasari have access to the same linseed oil used by Van Eyck?
Yes, Vasari and his colleagues did have the same SUPERIOR oil that was commonly available to the Van Eycks.

Do today's artists have access to Van Eyck's superior linseed oil?
Yes, it is abundantly available, and it is LESS expensive than the linseed oil sold in art stores.

Do you think Alkali Refined Linseed oil and the tube oil paints made with it should be discarded?
No. Alkali Refined linseed oil and modern tube paints are here to stay…they have an important place in classes of beginning oil painting, and for many hobby oil painters.

Do some art stores sell Unrefined, Cold Pressed linseed oil?
Yes, some art stores do sell Unrefined Cold Pressed linseed oil, but one should buy FLAX OIL from a health food store because it has not been refined nor pressed with heat, steam, or solvents.

How is the Van Eyck 'Secret" medium made?
We will ever know EXACTLY. They did not leave a document with their recipe. I believe their secret involves two separate steps. One, is a simple emulsion. The other is a unique application method. Both are well described in my books and DVDs.

What is an Emulsion and how is it made?
An Emulsion is the mixing of two liquids, one being aqueous, the other being oleaginous. An emulsion is a miracle of nature.

Is the Van Eyck method of oil painting of value to modern artists of today?
Yes it is, for these reasons. Our world is very different from the world of the Van Eycks. We live in a fast paced, scientific, technological age. Our age is characterized by a demand for instant gratification, intolerance of anything that 'wastes' (requires) our time, and accustomed to using disposable items.
Modern styles of painting reflect this energized anxiety, with splashes, drips, and broad wet-in-wet painting methods that are 'best' done within a few hours.

What are you offering today's oil painters?
In two words: SAFETY and PERMANENCE. Sharing knowledge, facts and accurate information with artists is important to me so they can make wise choices. I also offer my invention, 'Calcite Sun Oil", and the emulsions, which changes and improves modern tube oil paint giving it the properties and control, like that of the Old Masters' paint. My "Calcite Sun Oil formula was patented by the US Patent and
Trademark Office in November 2006. It is patent # 7141109. My book also discuss the important uses of the "wonder medium" of Emulsions in oil painting which allows us to eliminate ALL hazardous Solvents, Resins, Varnishes and Driers, and gives us full control of the oil paint.

What is 'Calcite Sun Oil"?
I call it 'CSO' for short. It is a carefully measured mixture of two ancient, archival ingredients used for centuries: a superior oil and calcium carbonate powdered stone.

You mentioned SLOWLY sun thickening the oil. Why is it important to do it slowly?
Linseed oil can be thickened indoors or outdoors. I have now created a new method jointly with a friend (Daniel Tavenier, from the Netherlands) that uses an Air Pump.

Did the Van Eycks use mixtures of Calcium Carbonate with their oil paint?
I have read that some Aragonite, which is a calcium carbonate powder, was found in their paint. I do not have the source citation.
-. End of Essay copyright 2007

WEBSITE 23
FRESH CLEANSED OIL IS CALLED 'THIN' OIL

Once the oil is cleansed of its damaging mucilage, it can be used for several important tasks in the 'Calcite Sun Oil / Emulsions' method of oil painting.

1. TTHIN OIL: Before the oil is thickened, it is limpid and yellow. It is used to make the simple ' Non Viscous' Emulsion" described in my book. The Non Viscous Emulsion serves important tasks not offered by the Viscous Emulsion. If not applied correctly, the Emulsions will fail. Application procedures are in the book.
2. THICKENED OIL:.Sun thickening takes 15-60 days depending on geographical area and season. This process produces the VERY FINEST OIL or oil painting. FAR SUPERIOR to walnut, poppy, or any other oils used by some. This is the PREMIER oil used by the greatest European Old Masters, the one spoken of by the Renaissance master, Cennino Cennini.
Once this oil is thickened, it is viscous and bleached.
It is then used to make the' Viscous Emulsion". Both emulsions are made within 30 seconds if the glair is available. Glair takes 5 minutes to make.
Both EMULSIONS are crucial to oil painting without solvents, resins and varnishes or driers.

WEBSITE 24

THE MAGIC OF PSYLLIUM HUSK FOR REMOVING THE MUCILAGE

THERE DOES NOT EXIST ....IN ANY ANCIENT TREATISE NOR IN ANY MODERN TEXT ....ANY MENTION OF PSYLLIUM HUSK AS AN INGREDIENT
TO REMOVE THE MUCILAGE FROM THE UNREFINED FLAX LINSEED OIL
Psyllium husk was completely unknown to all the Old Masters , and remained unknown to all subsequent theorists, artists , conservators and writers, including the artist-theorists of today.

THIS IS HOW I DISCOVERED THE USE OF PSYLLIUM HUSK FOR REMOVAL OF THE MUCILAGE FROM THE OIL.
My CSO methods are based on the 17th century method of Francisco Pacheco. But, Pacheco did not know about psyllium husk. He used dried lavender flower buds combined with alcoholic liquor of 87 % ethanol and 13 % water. This left spike solvent in the oil ('spike oil' us not an oil-it is a solvent). In my search for non-solvent oil painting, I had to eliminate the lavender flower buds but I did not know how I could do this at that time..

THEN THE UNPREDICTABLE HAPPENED. My doctor recommended I drink Metamucil for irregularity. Metamusil is the brand name for a high fiber laxative and it is pure Psyllium Husk. One teaspoon in an 8 ounce glass of water quickly expands to four times it's size because it absorbs the water. This gave me the idea to use it as a " mucilage remover" because mucilage is an aqueous ingredient .

To our benefit, It worked! PSYLLIUM HUSK is extraordinary and I believe it will make all other methods of Mucilage removal obsolete.

WEBSITE 25
THE OLD MASTER METHOD OF SUN THICKENING THE OIL

The traditional Old Master method makes a beautiful, viscous faster drying oil

PROCEDURE:
Use a white opaque glassware container like those used in baking. This type container accelerates the thickening 2X faster than a clear glass container.
Expose the oil to the direct sun rays of hot dry summer weather for between 15 to 60 days, depending on how hot and dry it is in your area.
Stir the oil 2X each day for one minute. Do this thing in the morning and last thing in the evening. In extreme hot areas stir the oil more times each day, to
prevent skinning of the oil.
Protect the oil from rain or moisture. Place a clear glass sheet over the container with spacers to allow air to circulate.

BLEACHED COLOR
Within 2 weeks the oil begins to become bleached. With more time it will become water clear in color. This color is temporary, because when the oil is removed and placed indoors it will become a very pale straw color. However, this color is deceiving because you are seeing it in concentration in the jar. To test the actual color, place one drop on a pure white glazed ceramic plate and rub it in. You will see it is fully transparent and colorless like glass.

TEST THE OIL FOR DRYING RATE AND VISCOSITY
The oil is ready when it meets your needs.
Some artists prefer a thick very fast drying viscous oil, and others prefer a less viscous slower drying oil. Periodically take a few drops and mix it with a small amount of oil paint, then, smear it on a piece of glazed tile or a ceramic plate to see how fast it will dry. Do two tests. One with tube oil paint and one with dry pigment colors. Be aware that all colors dry at different rates. Umber dries within 6 to 10 hours, and white tube oil paint can dry very slow because many are manufactured with slow drying poppy oil.

FILTERING THE FINISHED OIL
The Old Master method requires a final filtering of the oil to remove bugs, dirt, dust and leaves. These are easily removed. Use a plastic funnel and place a wad of cheesecloth, loosely into the neck. Place the funnel over a clean jar and pour the oil into the funnel. Allow several hours for the oil to drain.

STORAGE OF THE OIL
Store your oil in tall thin clear glass jars. Tighten the lid tightly, then loosen the lid 1/4 turn to allow expansion air release. Keep the extra stored jars full of oil.
The oil in Half full jars will continue to thicken because of the air. Place the oil jars in a window to get light. It does not have to have direct sun rays.

CONCLUSION
BIBLIOGRAPHY
There is no separate bibliography for Volume 2
The Bibliography is the same as found in Volume 1

WHY I PAINT AND WHY I PUBLISHED THIS BOOK

My purpose and reason for making art ,
is to make the world a better place for others.

My goal as an artist, has been to know myself as a person,
as I evolved from childhood to old age.

Every time I see a fine work of art,
whether by a famous master or not, it stirs my soul.

Fine Art elevates my consciousness and fills my heart with goodness.
It makes me a happier person, with feelings of goodwill towards others.

Publishing my books is my way of sharing the lessons I have learned,
along the way, from all the artists I have known or written to.

I am a pioneer and a messenger,
sharing the CSO knowledge I have received
to artists around the globe.

IN GRATITUDE
I thank all the readers - many of which have become my good friends in our discussions on oil painting - for their support over the years.

Louis R. Velasquez [American artist , born 1943-]
San Diego, California , USA
Published 2017

POSTSCRIPT:
I have been asked if I am related to the great Spanish painter Diego Velazquez of the 17th century.
No I am not. My father was born in 1918, in Tampico Mexico with the birth name of Jose Fortunato DIAZ-CORDERO. In the Spanish tradition, his father's last name is DIAZ and his mother's last name is CORDERO. Mr. DIAZ died right after my father was born. His mother married Mr. Enrique Velasquez, who adopted my father. I was born in California, USA, with the name of Louis Richard Velasquez. My father was an amateur boxer and admired the great boxing champion Joe Louis. Hence, my first name of Louis.

CONTINUE
FOR A SPECIAL ADDITION TO THIS VOLUME

THE CSO WORKSHOP GUIDE BOOK :
Teaching and Learning
the Mastery of Oil Painting without Hazardous Materials

The CSO
WORKSHOP GUIDEBOOK
Teaching and Learning
the Mastery of Oil Painting
Without Hazardous Materials

By Louis R. Velasquez
2017

WELCOME,

**THIS BOOK IS FOR TEACHERS CONDUCTING A WORKSHOP
OR FOR ART STUDENTS WHO STUDY ALONE**

The purpose of a WORKSHOP is for an experienced teacher to demonstrate in real live time, how and why the materials are mixed and used.
Students who cannot attend a workshop can learn by reading the CSO BOOKS and by watching the CSO DVDS. Some of the videos are free on YouTube.

TABLE OF CONTENTS
Introduction p.183
PART ONE Materials, Mixtures, Tool p.184
Lesson 1 The grinding table p.184 , Lesson 2 The 3 ingredients of CSO p.185 ,
Lesson 3 The 5 CSO mixtures p.187 , Lesson 4 Painting with CSO p.191,
PART TWO Discussion of Topics p. 191
Topic #1 The support p.192 , Topic # 2 Safe colors p.193 , Topic # 3 Oil Paint Differences p.194 , Topic # 4 The hand palette p. 197 , Topic # 5 Slow drying paint p. 197,
Topic # 6 Varnishing without resins p. 198

TABLE OF CONTENTS [continued]
PART THREE Painting a picture with CSO p. 199
Step one - Discussing the procedures of the Old and Modern Masters p. 200
Step two – CSO Painting Demonstration p. 200

PART FOUR Historical Painting Methods p.202
Lesson 1 15th century Flemish p.202 , Lesson 2 16th century Italian p. 204,
Lesson 3 17th century , Rembrandt p.206 , Lesson 4 Mixed Media p. 206
CONCLUSION How Rembrandt's binder medium was recreated p. 207

INTRODUCTION: WE BEGIN BY DESCRIBING WHAT ' CSO' IS

'CSO' is the abbreviated name for ' Calcite Sun Oil'.

CSO is the name of Louis Velasquez' modern recreation of Rembrandt's oil painting binder.
A paint binder is a liquid or mixture that is mixed with a dry pigment to make paint.

The CSO 'binder" is a mixture of dry, powdered, calcium carbonate chalk that is mixed together
with a superior flaxseed-linseed oil to improve the quality of modern commercial tube oil paints

There is a second part to the CSO binder mixture. It is called an EMULSION.
An Emulsion is a liquid mixture made with oil and egg white glair.
There are 4 CSO Emulsions and they will be demonstrated in this workshop.

The Emulsions of oil and egg white are an important part of this method. Science proves
Emulsions were used by Rembrandt, Velazquez, Rubens, and others.

MODERN SCIENCE
There is no evidence that Rembrandt called HIS mixture 'CSO'.
Rembrandt only spoke Dutch, so he might have used other letters or a name.
My artist friends in Greece call CSO by the Greek name of 'LAKI'.

Modern science does prove the CSO "binder mixture" was used by Rembrandt. These paint
analysis studies were published by London's National Gallery in 1988. Other important
scientific studies show that Velazquez and Rubens, also used this binder mixture.

HOW IS CSO USED ?
CSO is mixed 50/50 with modern tube oil paints to create a sumptuous oil paint that allows
today's painters to achieve the masterful oil painting effects of the Old Masters.

CSO can also be used to mix with dry colored powders to make " hand ground" oil paint.

There is more information on this later.

With CSO, you can paint in oils with the finest ultra fine lines and minute details like Van Eyck, or, with the broad thick palette knife impasto seen in the late work of Rembrandt.

CSO is very simple to use, but it is very profound.
Once you understand it, you will laugh at its simplicity.

CSO is completely safe. It uses no solvents, resins, varnishes or driers. Artists do not have to follow the "Fat over Lean" principle. Artists must learn which of their paint colors are " fast" drying and which are " slow" drying.

THESE ARE THE BENEFITS OF USING CSO IN OIL PAINTING
DRYING is accelerated without driers
ADHESION, without drips and beading
BLENDING is facilitated
TRANSLUCENCY is increased
BODY of Impasto or Glazes
COLOR DEPTH and LUSTER is increased
MICRO-FINE LINES and DETAILS are allowed
THIXOTROPIC quality is promoted
SUEDE EFFECT of Tube Oil Paints is eliminated
WRINKLING of impasto is eliminated

PART ONE :
THE MATERIALS , MIXTURES, AND TOOLS FOR PAINTING WITH 'CSO'

LESSON ONE
THE TEACHER DEMONSTRATES THE GRINDING TABLE

THE GRINDING TABLE IS AN IMPORTANT TOOL FOR MAKING THE MIXTURES
To mix the ingredients, you must have a Grinding table.

- An effective grinding table is a low cost glazed floor tile bought at any home improvement center. Choose one that has a mid value. Do not buy a black one or a white one unless you wish to experiment with those colors.

- A mid value surface will register all your colors to advantage so you may accurately see the true values of light and dark. I prefer a brown sandy colored tile.

- Brown is neutral and is made by mixing the three primary oil paint colors.
The color Brown harmonizes with all colors.

- The grinding table is used in the preparation of CSO and paint mixtures. One can choose to paint directly from the grinding table, or one can transfer the CSO paint onto a hand palette.

- Make certain that the grinding table is cleansed each day. One should also cleanse the hand palette each day.

- One can save all the excess oil paint and CSO each day. Place it in a jar and stir in some non-thickened oil. The mixture will become a mud brown or gray. This paint can be used later to prime a canvas or wood panel.

LESSON TWO
THE TEACHER SHOWS THE THREE INGREDIENTS OF CSO

Aside from the normal oil paints, brushes, easels, canvas and other supports, the CSO method uses three ancient archival materials that have been used by artists for centuries

(1) SUPERIOR OIL (mucilage free raw linseed/flaxseed oil)
(2) CHALK (calcium carbonate powdered stone)
(3) GLAIR (frothed and distilled egg white)

THE TEACHER. DISCUSSES AND DEMONSTRATES THE THREE INGREDIENTS

INGREDIENT # 1: THE OIL
- The "Superior oil of the Old Masters" is easy to prepare in the home studio..
- The oil cleansing procedures will be demonstrated at the appropriate time in the workshop

- To produce the Superior oil, the raw Flaxseed-Linseed oil must first be cleansed of its mucilage.

- Once the oil is cleansed, it is then prepared as " thickened" oil...or " non thickened" oil... or "co-poly" oil. Each oil has a different viscosity and each dries at a different rate of time.

- For those not in a workshop, the CSO mucilage removal cleansing methods, with complete instructions, are included in the CSO books and CSO DVDS.

INGREDIENT # 2   THE CHALK (Calcium Carbonate)
- Calcium Carbonate is powdered stone with the chemical designation of $CACO_3$.

- Calcium Carbonate has several forms: These are ; Chalk, Calcite, Aragonite, Marble, and Limestone. The workshop will use only the Chalk.

- CSO uses the Chalk form, because it is soft. The other forms are gritty or sandy.

- Rembrandt only used chalk. Velazquez used both, chalk and calcite. The CSO made of oil and chalk is a light beige color. The CSO made of oil and calcite is white in color.

- Any of the Calcium Carbonate forms can be used in oil painting and each will behave differently when used in painting.

- Calcium Carbonate is one of two stabilizer (the other is Egg Glair) so the oil paint does not drip or spread.

- Calcium Carbonate has no tint strength and it will not alter the colors, because it is 98% transparent when mixed with oil. (Only white and yellow are slightly altered). This is easily corrected by adding a slight amount of dry pigment powder.

INGREDIENT # 3. THE EGG GLAIR

- Simply described, GLAIR is egg white that has been frothed and distilled.

- It takes 5 minutes to froth the egg white, and 10 minutes to distill it.

- Glair is 85% water and 15% Albumen. The Albumen is a sticky ingredient that helps control the flow of the oil. One drop will stop the flow, more drops allow the flow.

- Glair is used in making the CSO Emulsions. Testing of the Emulsions indicates they are one half of the Van Eyck's Secret Medium. The second half is the unique application method which will be explained.

- Egg glair is an ancient pigment binder that has been used by artists for centuries to make archival paint .

- Studies show the ancient Greeks in 500 BC mixed glair with powdered marble stone, to create a smooth layer of white plaster that was then painted on.

- Glair can be used as a final varnish on a dried oil painting.

LESSON THREE
THE TEACHER DEMONSTRATES MIXING THE FIVE CSO MIXTURES
THESE ARE MADE FROM THE THREE INGREDIENTS OF CHALK, OIL AND GLAIR

CSO mixtures are completely safe and non hazardous.
CSO uses no hazardous solvents, resins, varnishes, or driers.

- Each mixture is easy to make, taking only a few minutes.

MIXTURE. # 1: THE 'CSO' MIXTURE :
The teacher demonstrates making the CSO mixture.

- CSO can be made in 3 minutes

- CSO is a mixture of the "superior oil of the Old Masters" and Calcium Carbonate dry powder. This mixture is called 'CSO'. CSO is the abbreviation for Calcite Sun Oil.

- To make CSO, the ratio mixture is 3 parts chalk and 1 part thickened oil. For alternate oil - chalk mixtures, please read Chapter 12, on page 107, of my book, Vol. 1. Oil painting lessons with Rembrandt and Calcite Sun Oil.

- It is best to make CSO fresh daily. If you do wish to make enough for a week, place it in an air tight jar, and when not in use, store the jar on its lid. This way, the CSO will not skin over, causing waste. Next day, sit it right side up and slowly open the lid and allow it to settle before extracting the CSO.

- CSO is thick, viscous and opaque, however it is 98% transparent when used thinly.

- CSO has no tinting color and does not change colors it is mixed with, except slightly when mixed with white and yellow.

- CSO is essentially a pigment binder that is used to make oil paint.

- CSO can be mixed with dry powdered pigments to make 'hand made' oil paint
or , it can be mixed (50-50) in equal parts with art store tube oil paints to improve their effectiveness. The teacher will demonstrate both methods at the appropriate time.

- CSO makes an oil paint that is sumptuous with deep color, and a degree of translucency that gives the oil paint liveliness and depth.

- CSO , when used with the Emulsions, offers 10 benefits. These have been mentioned.

MIXTURE # 2: THE 'VE' MIXTURE (Viscous Emulsion)
'VE' stands for ' VISCOUS EMULSION' .

The teacher demonstrate making the VE mixture.

-The Emulsion is made in 2 minutes, if..the glair is at hand.

- It takes about 15 minutes to froth and distill the egg white, to make the glair.
The teacher can demonstrate the making of glair.

- The VE is a mixture of 3 parts of 'thickened" flax-linseed oil and 2 parts of Egg Glair. There must always be a larger quantity of oil than glair. The CSO book gives other ratio variations. Please read Chapter 6, on page 61, of Vol. 1. Oil painting lessons with Rembrandt and Calcite Sun Oil.

- Tests indicate this simple Emulsion is Part One of the Van Eyck Secret Medium. Tests also indicate the important, very unique APPLICATION rubbing method is the crucial second part of the Van Eyck Secret medium.

- An ultra thin application of the Emulsion is called an ' oil out'.
The teacher can demonstrate a proper ' oil out' application.

- An ' oil out' is a lubricant of a dry paint layer to allow easy application and adhesion of subsequent paint layers.

- **VERY IMPORTANT:** when an Emulsion, is used as an ' oil out' it must ONLY be rubbed in by hand. Only the bare hand must be used to rub in the Emulsion. Do not rub with brushes, towels or rags. This procedure must be accurately followed or it will result in failure.

- The VE is a white opaque mixture, BUT when properly applied as an 'oil out' , it is 100% transparent and crystal clear as glass.
The teacher will demonstrate this fact by rubbing a drop on a newspaper.

- Rubbing a drop on dry oil paint, brings out the true color of sunken in, matte areas .

- Rubbing in an ultra thin film, 'oil out', allows the painting of micro-fine lines and details as seen in the Van Eyck paintings.

- Rubbing in an emulsion, can allow thixotropic paint application. Thixotropic means, wet paint can be painted on top of wet paint. Please read the information on Thixoptropic painting in my books. Both Rubens and Rembrandt used Thixotropic paint methods.

- An emulsion can be used as a 'thinner' for oil paints. One drop will cause the oil paint to " sieze up and stiffen', while adding more drops will cause the oil paint to loosen and flow.

- An emulsion can be used as a final ' resin free 'varnish on a completed painting. This leaves a silky shiny surface, but not a harsh glossy surface like a resin varnish .

- Museum studies indicate Rubens never varnished his oil paintings with a resin varnish. After studying in Italy for 9 years, he must have observed that all resin varnishes will eventually become yellow. Modern scientific studies indicate he varnished his paintings with an ultra thin layer of thickened sun oil - with or without a mixture of glair.

- A final coat of the VE , or, of the sun oil, takes several days or weeks - to dry hard.

- Hot , dry , moving air , is the best condition for drying.

- Emulsions can be placed in an air tight jar, and refrigerated when not in use, or, one can place the capped jar in a cool place.

- When the egg begins to spoil, you will notice the mixture turns brownish. It is best to discard and make a fresh batch.

MIXTURE # 3: THE 'NVE' MIXTURE (non- viscous emulsion)

- NVE stands for "NON VISCOUS" Emulsion .

- The NVE is a mixture of 3 parts of ' NON-thickened" flax-linseed oil and 2 parts of Egg Glair. It is made in 2 minutes if the Glair is at hand. In ALL emulsion mixtures, there MUST always be more oil than Glair.

- Tests indicate this simple Emulsion is part one of the Van Eyck Secret medium.
Tests indicate the unique hand rubbing application method is the crucial second part of the Van Eyck Secret medium.

- The NVE has many important uses. Although many are similar to the VE, there are some differences. IMPORTANT: The NVE will dry slower than the VE.

- The NVE is a lubricant for dry paint , to allow easy application of new paint layers. This application is called an ' oil out'. The 'oil out' procedure is an important old master procedure.

- When used as an ' oil out' it must be rubbed in only by hand. ONLY the bare hand must be used to rub. Do not apply with a brush, nor rub with towels or rags.

- although it is a white opaque liquid mixture, when properly applied as an ' oil out' ,it is 100% transparent and crystal clear like glass. This fact was demonstrated with the VE.

- an 'oil out 'with NVE insures the adhesion of new paint layers and enlivens sunken matte areas.

- an 'oil out' with NVE stops drips, spreading and the loss of brush mark definition.

- The NVE 'oil out' allows the painting of micro-fine lines and ultra fine details as seen in the Van Eyck paintings. One can argue that the very finest micro fine lines and details can be painted with the NVE instead of with the VE. The skill of the artist can determine the results.

- The NVE can be used as a thinner for oil paints. One drop will cause the oil paint to " sieze up', while adding more drops will cause the oil paint to flow.

- if one wishes to thin the CSO oil paint to a more liquid condition, it is best to use the NVE instead of the VE . It is a stabilizer and will help prevent drips.

- The NVE is not recommended as a final ' resin free' varnish because it dries much too slow. It is best to use the VE for this.

MIXTURE # 4: THE 'AGUADO' MIXTURE

-The name ' aguado' is a Spanish word meaning ' a loose and soupy' liquid .

- This mixture is made in a minute. The teacher demonstrates making the Aguado

-Aguado is not an Emulsion because it does not contain Egg Glair. It is a simple thin soupy mixture of oil and chalk.

- Aguado is easy to apply with a brush, and requires NO rubbing by hand , and is a perfect 'oil out' for large oil paintings.

- like with the Emulsions, all excess must be removed by wiping away the excess. A straight blade palette knife is an efficient tool to scrape and remove excess oil. This can be followed by a lint free paper towel.

- the recipe is varied. One can use 1 part oil and 2 parts chalk , or even less chalk.

- it can be used as a final 'resin free varnish'. This leaves a slight shiney surface. This mixture dries faster than the VE or the THICKENED OIL.
The teacher can show examples of different final films on finished paintings

----

MIXTURE # 5: THE 'ESPESO' MIXTURE
The teacher demonstrates making the Espeso mixture

- the word Espeso, is a Spanish word that means a mixture is thick, like a thick soup.

- The CSO Espeso mixture was created after an academic research study of Rubens' methods and materials of Thixotropic oil painting. As previously stated, THIXOTROPIC oil painting, is the ability to apply wet oil paint layers on top of wet oil paint layers, without blurring or disturbing the wet under layer. This allows a painter to continue painting without waiting for the first layer of wet paint to dry.

- The CSO DVD on Rubens' methods, mixtures and materials is free on YouTube.
WARNING: Rubens used hazardous materials with hazardous solvent fumes that are dangerous to human health. Use Rubens' materials at your own risk.

- The CSO Espeso mixture is a safe non-hazardous substitute to Rubens' materials.

- Espeso is a mixture of the VE and dry chalk, which is then added to the CSO oil paint.

- There is no set ratio, and one must experiment. The result is a unique oil paint mixture that allows some degree of Thixotropy.

- Although Espeso mixture is an Emulsion, there is no need to hand rub this. It is applied either thinly or thickly with a brush or rag.
The excess must be removed before painting on it.

THE ESPESO ALTERNATE MIXTURE
Please read about the ' Thickened Emulsion Oil Paint' in this volume, Vol. 2. Page 110.
It differs from Espeso in that the GLAIR is allowed to FIRST thicken naturally by exposure to air. This thick glair is then mixed with thickened oil to create a ' thickened Emulsion' Then the dry chalk is added and then, this is added to the tube oil paint.

LESSON FOUR : PAINTING A PICTURE WITH CSO
The past Lessons taught the 3 materials we will use, and how to make the 5 mixtures .
We are now ALMOST ready to paint a picture with CSO OIL PAINT.
Before beginning to paint, several important Topics must be discussed.

PART TWO
DISCUSSIONS WITH LIMITED DEMONSTRATIONS OR EXAMPLES

DISCUSSION TOPIC NUMBER ONE
THE CANVAS OR WOOD SUPPORT THAT ARTISTS PAINT ON

This discussion will be brief. An entire workshop could be presented on the preparation of the supports that artists paint on.

Only wood or canvas will be discussed here. Some Old Master artists painted on thin copper metal sheets, but it will not be discussed here.

THE MOST IMPORTANT REQUIREMENT ABOUT THE SUPPORT
: The raw wood AND the canvas surface must be fully 100% sealed to prevent oil and moisture from entering the support.

- The 700 year old, time tested and proven archival material for sealing (sealing is called sizing) wood or canvas is 2 or more coats of animal hide glue with no additives.

- If any additive or powder is added to the glue, the glue becomes absorbent, and immediately fails to seal the surface.

- ALL GESSOS, either Old Master gesso or modern acrylic gesso...are highly absorbent

- All gessos must be sealed before applying oil paint.

-A recurrent argument is whether the backside and sides must also be sealed, and the answer is YES.

THE WOOD PANEL
Hardwood such as Birch or Oak are best. Birch is smooth, but Oak has numerous pock marks in the grain and these must be filled in and covered by scraping a gesso into them. Todays flat modern plywood is superior to the Old Masters wood planks, that have bent into curves over the centuries. The raw wood must first be made non absorbent and sealed 100 % before any gesso is applied.

THE CANVAS
There are many types of canvas sold at art stores.

Some canvases are pre- primed, usually with acrylic gesso, others are not primed.
I repeat that all forms of gesso are absorbent and must be sealed before applying oil paint, or, the absorbent gesso will absorb the oil out of the oil paint.

If the canvas is pre- primed with acrylic gesso, seal it with one thin layer of Acrylic varnish (gloss or matte) mixed with 25% water.

The old master gesso made of hide glue and chalk, should be sealed with a coat of hide glue.

An alternative liquid for sealing either acrylic gesso or hide glue gesso, is to apply a liberal coat of non fat milk. Place the canvas or panel in a vertical position to avoid puddles of milk. Use a wide low cost flat brush to apply even strokes.
Do not use low fat or regular milk, it must be NON-FAT milk.

DISCUSSION TOPIC NUMBER TWO:
CHOOSING SAFE OIL COLORS / AVOIDING DANGEROUS COLORS

CAUTION: HAZARDOUS AND NON HAZARDOUS COLORS
Many of the beautiful oil paints on the market such as the Cadmiums, are highly toxic, carcinogenic, dangerous or hazardous, causing severe human illnesses.

- To choose safe colors, you must read the labels and make inquiries.

- My website has a long list of safe and hazardous colors..

- I recommend artists use a limited palette of a few safe colors.

RECOMMENDED: A LIMITED COLOR PALETTE OF SAFE COLORS

BLACK AND WHITE
Titanium white (avoid Lead white, Cremnitz white, Flake white, all are poisonous), and avoid zinc white because it is unstable.
Ivory black - a cool black with blue overtones

MUTED - NEUTRAL COLORS
Burnt umber (a warm brown)
Raw umber (a cold brown)
Burnt sienna (a warm brown)
Raw Sienna (a cold brown)
Yellow ochre - a dull muted yellow
Venetian red - a dull warm muted red

BRIGHT COLORS (choose only safe colors)
Any bright red color - if it is safe (read the health label)
Any bright yellow color - if it is safe
Ultramarine blue - a very bright blue color

DISCUSSION TOPIC NUMBER THREE:
THE DIFFERENCE BETWEEN TRADITIONAL AND MODERN OIL PAINT

Today's colored pigments are normally made of synthetic materials.
High quality mineral pigments as used by the Old Masters, can still be purchased at a higher cost. Contact sources on the Internet, such as. Kremer- Pigmente, a German company with offices world wide.

HAND GRINDING DRY PIGMENTS LIKE THE OLD MASTERS
MAKING YOUR OWN OIL PAINT

- The Old Masters made their oil paint by mixing a dry pigment with oil. This procedure is called ' grinding' or ' hand grinding'. It is different from " mixing" in that to grind oil and dry pigment, one must apply steady pressure.

- There are important benefits for grinding your own paint. One is that the artist can choose which OIL to use. There are three oil choices:

(1) A fast drying thickened oil
(2) a slow drying non thickened oil
(3) A medium fast drying oil made by mixing a thickened and a non thickened oil. This oil is called a ' co-poly' oil, meaning : an oil made of mixed polymerization . By changing the ratios, one can customize it to one's needs.

- Hand grinding oil paint is easy and simple. One does not need a muller. A simple palette knife can do this well. The teacher can choose...make a brief demonstration on how to hand grind oil paint with a simple palette knife.

- If the chosen pigment resists the oil and beads up, the artist can premix the dry pigment with a tiny amount of alcoholic spirit liquor such as wine, vodka or whisky. Once wetted, the oil is added for easy mixing and grinding.

- If hand made paint is made, It is best to grind the dry pigment with a NON- thickened oil. This creates a buttery paste that does not flow. Do not use excess oil. Make the paste stiff.

- Once the dry pigment is mixed with oil, an equal amount of the CSO mixture is added to it (50-50) to create CSO OIL PAINT.

- The dry pigment can be ground with a thickened oil, but the disadvantage is that the result will be an oil paint that is much too thick and flowing to paint with.

- If one chooses use of thickened oil for the grinding, one must add several drops of the NVE (non viscous emulsion) to avoid excessive flowing and dripping and wrinkling.

- Artists can advance the drying of an oil painting, by following this procedure:
Hand Grind only a few colors for the under painting stage because these paints will dry faster. Then, for the over painting stage, mix and grind CSO with art store tube oil paints. To prevent cracking, the under layers of oil paint should dry faster than the upper layers.

- CSO is not concerned with ' Fat over Lean' because CSO uses no solvents. However, artist must paint slower drying paints on top of faster drying paints. Artists must learn which of their colors dry faster than others.

PROBLEMS WITH MODERN TUBE OIL PAINT

- It is important to know that tube oil paints are ground with a very slow drying oil ,
and sometimes with excessive amounts of oil.

- If you notice an excessive amount of oil, place the glob on absorbent cardboard or paper towel, and allow the excess oil to be absorbed. Once the excessive oil is removed, scrape up the paint and place it on the grinding table and add CSO 50/50.

- Another problem with tube oil paints is that they are ground up with additives of aluminum stearate. This transparent powder additive is designed to make a paint having a firm buttery condition. Unfortunately, this additive causes what is known as the ' suede' effect, meaning, all the brush strokes stand out when the painting is seen in a certain light, this effect is objectionable, disturbing and distorting.

- Once the CSO mixture is added in a 50/50 ratio to tube oil paints, the suede effect disappears. The old masters oil paint was exactly like our CSO oil paint. It can be described as viscous and flowing, with easy blending and absolutely no suede effect.

- The CSO mixture is mixed with the tube oil paint in equal amounts (50/50). There is no need to measure exactly. Some oil paints require a bit more CSO than other colors.

- a flexible straight blade palette knife is all that is needed for the mixing and grinding. You do not need a muller.

- Modern tube oil paints offer us convenience. These are sold in various grades, from beginner to professional. Choose a brand you like or can afford. I do not recommend any particular brand and I use many different brands.

- Unfortunately, the white tube oil paints are frequently mixed with extremely slow drying oils such as walnut or poppy or safflower. This is done because some believe linseed oil will cause the white oil paint color to become yellow. Once you use the Superior oil of the Old Masters, you will not have to worry about this, because yellowing is eliminated.

- If you buy oil paint in tubes, make sure they are ground only in linseed oil. Some manufacturers tout that they use "non- yellowing" walnut oil. I have made tests and walnut oil, will yellow, if used excessively.

- Walnut oil has the severe defect of extremely slow drying. I have made tests of hand ground walnut oil paint and compared it to art store tube walnut oil paint.
The hand made walnut oil paint took over a week to dry. The ready made art store walnut oil paint dried at the same rate as linseed oil paint in tubes. This indicates that driers are added to the walnut tube oil paint.

- if you want to hand grind walnut oil and dry pigments, be sure you buy RAW unrefined walnut oil that has no vitamin E additives , nor other anti-oxidant additives.

- Walnut oil has the same amount of mucilage as Flaxseed- Linseed oil, and it must be cleansed before using . Follow the same procedures as for Flaxseed-Linseed oil.

DISCUSSION TOPIC NUMBER FOUR
THE HAND PALETTE

Once you have prepared your oil paint mixtures on the GRINDING TABLE, you can choose to paint directly from the Grinding Table....or transfer the paint to a hand palette. Use of a hand palette is useful, because you can place it alongside near the painting for better comparison of values and colors.

When we see Old Master paintings showing self portraits at work, we see use of small hand palettes. We also see they have small amounts of few colors on them. Choice of few colors make oil painting fun, effective and simple.

- Most old master hand palettes were of wood and were a brown color.

- Brown is a neutral color that allows the artist to " see" the relationships of the hues, the values and the chroma.

TOPIC OF DISCUSSION FIVE: SLOW DRYING OIL PAINTS

- One of the concerns of artists has been that art bought, tube oil paints dry too slowly. CSO uses the ' superior oil of the Old Masters' that dries much faster.

- Metallic driers can be added to flaxseed-linseed oil to accelerate the drying.
These driers are hazardous to human health, and cause the oil paint to darken and crack over time. They are not recommended for archival fine art oil painting

- Correct processing and thickening of unrefined flaxseed- linseed oil, as explained by the CSO books and dvds, will create a naturally fast drying oil that does not require metallic driers.

- oil paints, Hand ground with fast drying oil, will dry in under 24 hours when the paint layer is thin. Tube oil paints purchased at the art store dry much slower, depending on the color used.

- The environment will either accelerate or slow down the drying rate of even the best oil paints. The Humidity in the air - whether hot summer or cold winter weather - slows down the drying of oil paints.

- Hot, dry, moving air will accelerate the drying of an oil painting. Artists can place a fan near the wet painting.

- Artists can work on several paintings at once. This allows time for wet paintings to dry while one works on another.

- underpainting with Tempera paints that dry within minutes, allows an artist to finish an oil painting faster.

TOPIC OF DISCUSSION SIX
VARNISHING WITHOUT RESINS

It is remarkable that the world's great masterpieces painted by our great artists, are made of very simple materials. These organic oils, eggs, glues, powders and colored pigments coexist and are compatible with each other.

Many Old paintings are now over 700 years old and remain in good condition.
These paintings must be kept in safe conditions to protect them from moisture, humidity, and excessive heat.

Traditionally, oil paintings have been given a varnish after the painting has dried for about 6 months. History shows that natural resin varnishes will crack and become yellow in under 100 years.

I believe there are better choices than the traditional natural resin varnishes.
Modern technology offers synthetic varnishes.

HERE ARE SOME CHOICES
Once an oil painting is finished and is dry to the touch, any of the following can be applied as a final film. These are not removable and become a part of the painting.
All should be ultra thin films.

AGUADO : This film will dry with the least amount of gloss than the others.
THICKENED OIL: this film will be shiny but not glossy like a resin varnish and needs weeks to dry hard.

VISCOUS EMULSION: this gives a satin shiny finish but needs weeks to dry hard
GLAIR: glair will dry in a minute, and protects the sticky surface of an oil painting.

PART THREE
PAINTING A PICTURE WITH CSO

STEP ONE
DISCUSSING THE PAINTING PROCEDURES USED BY THE OLD MASTERS AND THE MODERN MASTERS

FIVE DIFFERENT HISTORICAL OIL PAINTING METHODS
DISCUSSION AND EXAMPLES

The Old Masters lived in different European counties and spanned the centuries from the 1300's to the 1700's. They painted in many different styles using various different procedures. The Modern Masters followed in the 1800's, to the present. They too, use various different methods of painting.
The following list has the dominant historical methods of oil painting.
The art teacher shows reproduction examples of the various historical styles.

1500's VAN EYCK FLEMISH..draw first, and then apply thin color glazes
1600's TITIAN AND THE VENETIANS- use of a grisaille and glazes
1700's RUBENS, REMBRANDT, VELAZQUEZ - monotones and combined methods
1800's IMPRESSIONISTS, VAN GOGH, PICASSO - The direct modern Alla prima method
1900's 21ST CENTURY MODERN MASTERS. This development in creative painting is the freedom to explore use of anything. The methods are limitless. One can throw dirt or other items into the paint, or one can paint with spray cans, or sticks or other tools.
CSO can be manipulated to accommodate various styles, to include modern methods of splash, drip, and splatter.

STEP TWO
THE ART TEACHER DEMONSTRATES PAINTING A PICTURE WITH CSO

The Work Shop teacher will demonstrate how the CSO mixtures are used as well as procedures used by master artists.

Each teacher is different. Some may want the students to watch only.
Others may want students to paint along and duplicate what the teacher is doing.

The art teacher will only demonstrate painting a picture with the modern DIRECT METHOD. A separate workshop would be required to teach each of the historical styles and painting methods Students must realize that the shortage time of the workshop will allow only one painting demonstration.
It would take several workshops to teach ALL of the historical painting methods

THE TEACHER DEMONSTRATES PAINTING A CSO PICTURE WITH THE MODERN DIRECT METHOD

- THE TRADITIONAL DIRECT METHOD: Many Old Masters painted in a 'direct' method, called ' Alla prima'. However, a monotone or an underdrawing was ALWAYS FIRST placed on the canvas or wood panel.

- THE MODERN DIRECT METHOD:,The French Impressionists of the mid 1800's began to paint directly on the white canvas WITHOUT a careful drawing. They drew and painted at the same time with their oil paint.

- Van Gogh was known to begin by making a drawing with bright blue oil paint. Then he applied his thick oil paint into the figures that were outlined while the blue outlines were still wet.

- The modern direct method of oil painting is enjoyable and fun.
Artists today can experiment with the Old Master methods and the Modern methods.

- The teacher will decide whether students should watch first and then paint, or whether they should paint along.

PAINTING AN ALLA PRIMA DIRECT OIL PAINTING WITH CSO
Follow the teachers demonstration.
The MODERN DIRECT method frequently uses the white canvas to show through the oil paint. The Old Master method does not.

RECALL I SAID that CSO is so simple you will laugh at its simplicity. Here is the proof.
1. Choose and make a simple or detailed drawing. Use fixative if needed. Or no drawing at all.
2. Apply the "oil out". The easiest is the Aguado, and it allows great freedom of broad painterly effects like Rembrandt or VElazquez. Experiment with the Viscous Emulsion, especially if you want very fine detailed work effects like Van Eyck.
3. Begin to apply the CSO paint. Use any creative method you would like to explore.
4. ONCE finished for the day, wait until the paint is dry to the touch. Then, apply a new "oil out". Begin to paint a new layer on top of the dried layer.
5. You can repeat this over and over until the painting is completed to your creative and aesthetic satisfaction. The HARDEST PART OF PAINTING A PICTURE , IS IN FINISHING IT.

There is an old saying: "Anyone can start a painting, but only a master can finish one," Please do not take that too literally. All artists – including Rembrandt - had to have a beginning. We grow as artists as we gain experience in painting.

CSO gives today's artists the power to achieve the wonderous effects we see in the great masterpieces, and does so with 100% safety.
Enjoy the adventure of safe Old Master oil painting!!

PART FOUR:
VARIOUS HISTORICAL PAINTING PROCEDURES

LESSON ONE
INSTRUCTIONS ON THE 15th CENTURY FLEMISH OIL PAINTING METHOD
For centuries, Egg Tempera was the medium of choice in European painting.
Then late in the late 1300's, oil painting became the medium of choice. The Flemish painters like the Van Eyck brothers, and others, perfected the oil painting medium.
These instructions allow a painter today, to duplicate the Flemish method.

THE 15TH CENTURY FLEMISH METHOD, STEP BY STEP

1. Prepare a wood panel about 12 x 9 inches in size.

FIRST STEP: You must first seal the raw wood panel with hide glue, so it is 100% non absorbent.
This is how to prepare the hide glue the easy way. Heat 10 to 12 fluid ounces of water in a metal pot.
When it begins to boil, turn the heat off.
SLOWLY pour one volume ounce of hide glue granules into the water ... pour this slowly as you stir the water with a wooden spoon, or you will get lumps.
Continue stirring the water until the granules are fully dissolved.
While the glue is hot, apply two coats of the hide glue to the wood panel.
Allow the first application to dry to the touch. Use a wide, low cost flat brush.

NEXT STEP: We must make a gesso of the hide glue mixed with dry calcium carbonate chalk.
You can add some Titanium Dioxide White pigment if you wish.
Reheat the glue but do not let it boil.
Slowly mix this into the warm hide glue, stirring as you do, to avoid lumps.

You can apply as many layers as you wish. Allow each layer to dry to the touch.
You can use sandpaper to sand in between layers, or wait until the final layer.

REMINDER: All gessos are very absorbent, and more so if numerous layers are applied.
However, we do not want to seal the gesso just yet. We need to leave the gesso absorbent for the under drawing.

TRANSFERRING THE UNDERDRAWING:
There are many ways to make the design of the painting.
One way is to first make a finished freehand pencil drawing on white paper.
Another way is to use a photograph.
The one you choose to use is taped to the wood panel, face up.

On a separate white paper, cover the surface with vine charcoal or any powdered color pigment.
This is called a Transfer paper.
Place the transfer paper under the taped drawing, with the charcoal facing the wood. Use a ball point pen to press firmly on the outline to transfer the pencil drawing.

If you do not want to ruin the pencil drawing, first make a Xerox copy of it.
You can also make Xerox copies of a photograph, and transfer that.

FIXATIVE: You can choose to use a fixative so the transfer will not blur.
A safe fixative is to use a fine spray atomizer of non- fat milk.
Begin by placing the wood panel, face up, horizontal on the floor.
With the fine mist atomizer, spray over and across the panel, allowing the fine mist to fall and land on the charcoal drawing.
Use only a minimum of liquid spray. Let this dry before moving.

NEXT STEP : THE UNDERDRAWING:
The Flemish painters drew extremely careful drawings, usually on a pure white gesso ground.
They used different materials to draw the outlines of the design.
Try several methods to see which one suits you best.

METHOD ONE: INK UNDERDRAWING:
Use waterproof pigmented black (or brown) India Ink.
On a small porcelain dish used by water color artists, mix three values of ink.
One light, a medium and a dark. Save the pure black for later details.

Use any brush you like to paint the transferred image, so it has a realistic three dimensional appearance. Once the ink is dry, you can use an X-acto knife to scrape away parts you do not want. You can also choose to use sand paper to remove unwanted areas.
Apply pure dark ink in areas that will be left exposed to show that dark ink as a finishing part of the painting.

METHOD TWO : NON FAT MILK UNDERDRAWING:
Mix several small amounts of dry colored pigments- usually a brown or a black- with non fat milk. Three values, from light to dark are sufficient to create a realistic image.
As with the ink method, use tools to scrape or sand away unwanted areas.

NEXT STEP: SEAL THE GESSO.
Because the sealant liquid (of milk, egg, or glue) might blur the drawing, the safest method is to apply a liberal layer of ' thickened' fast drying flaxseed-linseed oil.
This oil layer will also serve to render the gesso nonabsorbent.
Place the wood panel horizontally, and apply the oil liberally, allowing it to soak into the gesso, then wipe off all excess oil.
Allow this to dry ...to the touch.

NEXT STEP: THE 'OIL OUT'
Before we begin to apply our oil paints, it is important to apply an ULTRA-THIN " oil out" film of Aguado.
The Aguado needs no rubbing, but it should be only ultra-thin.
All excess oil must be removed with a dry paper or lint free cloth towel.

NEXT STEP : THE COLORFUL OVER PAINTING

After the Oil Out is correctly applied, begin to paint in full colors.
The Flemish artists applied thin layers of transparent oil paint.
The paint was applied thinly to allow under layers to be seen through it.

There are many ways to over paint in full colors.
Some artists paint the images carefully and blend everything.
Others apply the oil paint in a rough manner to create the impression of life and movement.

FINISHING THE PAINTING
After the painting dries, artists frequently review it and make changes .
Apply an "oil out" before applying new layers of oil paint.
Finishing a painting may take several days or weeks , of changes.
Feel free to apply several corrective OVER PAINT LAYERS, until you get what suits you.

LESSON TWO:
INSTRUCTIONS ON THE ITALIAN RENAISSANCE METHOD OF THE 1500'S.
THE PAINTINGS OF TITIAN AND OTHER MASTERS

The 16th century Italian Renaissance masters expanded the Flemish method.
They painted larger paintings and used stretched canvas to lessen the weight.
Master painters like Titian and other Venetian painters used thicker oil paint than the Flemish painters did, and purposefully used visible brushstrokes , to express their ideas of aesthetic beauty.

- The Italian Renaissance artists of the 1500's divided the labor of painting a picture and called it : DISEGNO y COLORE ......Translated as DESIGN and COLOR.

PART ONE OF THE LABOR: THE COMPOSITIONAL ABSTRACT DESIGN:
This beginning stage allows the artist to ignore the color ....and to focus on the composition design and the placement of darks and lights as an abstract design.
Although the design was well thought out ahead of time, many times, the masters would alter the original design as they painted.

PART TWO OF THE LABOR: THE COLORING

THE FIRST STEP: DULL COLORS ARE USED IN THE UNDER PAINTING
Dull, muted colors, plus black and white, can be used in the beginning under painting stage of the painting. Once dried, the next layer uses all the bright beautiful lively colors. By overlaying bright colors on top of dull colors, one achieves a sensitive depth of coloristic beauty.

THE MONOTONE (one color) : Many Old Masters would begin their paintings with one color, such as brown , that when applied to a lighter base color , can show a variety of values, depending on how thin or thick the paint is applied, or by wiping away some paint with a rag. These value are called " optical grays", because you do not mix them, you only allow them to be seen by how thin or thick the over-layer of color is.
Once the monotone has dried, the full palette of brighter colors are applied on top.

THE GRISAILLE : A grisaille is similar to a monotone, but the focus is to use only grays plus black and white. With this method, the artist does mix the various values of grays and aims to paint a realistic image in grays. This method allows the artist to create layers of paint of different thicknesses. Many times, pure white is painted because colorful glazes of thin oil painting are placed on top when dried.

THE SECOND STEP : BRIGHT COLORS ARE USED IN THE OVER PAINTING
Once the under painting layer is dried, artists first begin with the application of an ' oil out". One can choose either of the emulsion mixtures , or the Aguado or the Espeso, as the " oil out" medium. While the " oil out" is damp, the full palette of brighter colors are applied.

There are many ways to over paint in full colors.
Some artists apply color within the images carefully as they blend everything.
Others apply the oil paint in a rough spotty manner to create the impression of life and movement.

Artists sometimes scrub , or rub, the top layer of oil paint on the dried under layer. This method creates " optical" mixtures that are very beautiful.

LESSON THREE
INSTRUCTIONS ON THE 17th CENTURY PAINTERS:
RUBENS, VELAZQUEZ, REMBRANDT

100 years after the Italian Renaissance, master painters like Rubens, Velasquez and Rembrandt used the Italian and Flemish methods in their own way.
Rubens brilliantly combined the Flemish and the Italian methods and developed methods that allowed him to quickly finish a painting in a matter of hours.

LESSON FOUR
TECHNICAL MATTERS IN MIXED MEDIA PAINTING

Artists can mix the various mediums when creating their paintings.
Modern artists sometimes begin with acrylic paint and finish with oil paints.
Acrylic paints will not adhere to oil paints, but oil paints will adhere to acrylic paints.
Tempera paints will not adhere to oil paints.
If Acrylics or Temperas are used, use them in the lower layers only.

WATER SOLUBLE PAINTS,
OLD MASTER TEMPERA PAINT, AND MODERN ACRYLIC PAINT

- Acrylic paints were invented on the early 20th century. These are water based and dry quickly by evaporation. Similarly, the Old Masters used water based fast drying paints that we call TEMPERA PAINT. Either one can be used as fast drying underpainting for oil paints....or....paintings can be completed without oil paints.

- Botticelli's famous masterpieces of the 1500's are painted with tempera paints and sometimes over painted with oil paints.

- There are three fast drying Tempera paints used by the Old Masters. (1) Egg Tempera (2) Milk Tempera, called Casein (3) Glue Tempera, called ' Distemper' .
Each Tempera paint offered different reasons for use. The CSO books and DVDS cover these topics fully.

- Glue Tempera would congeal when cold, making it difficult to brush on, but some wine could be added to liquefy it.

-Egg Tempera was used for easel painting in European art for hundreds of years prior to oil painting.

- Oil Painting was used by the Flemish in the late 1300's and later in the Italian Renaissance of the 1500's.

- Realism was difficult to achieve with tempera paints.

- Oil painting allowed blending , and achieving almost photographic effects.

- The master artist recognized for writing down the ancient method of Egg Tempera in the 1300's is Cennino Cennini.

- Cennini's manuscript was translated in. English and In the 1800's there was a revived interest in Tempera paints. Many modern masters continue to use tempera paint.

- In the early 21st century, I created two new paints.
(1) CSO Egg Tempera which allows impasto applications.
(2) Milk Oil Paint which is an Emulsified oil paint.
I have published DVDS on both methods. They are available on the Internet.

THE OLD MASTERS ALSO MIXED OIL AND TEMPERA TO CREATE A PAINT CALLED "TEMPERA GRASSA"

- When oil and a water based medium (Tempera) are mixed together, an Emulsion is formed. This is called a " Tempera Grassa" , loosely meaning an 'Oil-Tempera'.

- This binder offered the benefits of the aqueous tempera which dried fast, and the oleaginous linseed oil that allowed blending.

- Tempera Grassa paint was used by many great Masters, such as Botticelli, Rubens and others. It continues to be in use today by modern masters.

OIL PAINT PAINTED ON TOP OF TEMPERA PAINT (Or on top of acrylic)
- Many artists would underpaint in a Tempera. This paint dried within minutes. They then immediately overpainted with traditional straight oil paints on top, to allow the blending of colors.

- Oil paints have a lustrous depth of color that Tempera paints lack.

- It is possible to apply fine details of a tempera paint - into a wet oil paint or oil glaze. Frederic Taubes' book " The Mastery of Oil Painting" published in the mid 20th century
has photographs demonstrating this.

CONCLUSION - POSTSCRIPT

I began the recreation of Rembrandt's Oil Paint Binder in 1988. I named it 'CALCITE SUN OIL", abbreviated to CSO. Over the years, I have received letters from Art teachers who are teaching CSO in Australia, Spain, Greece, England, Puerto Rico, and other states of the USA.

This Book was made to help those who wish to teach the CSO Method in a WORKSHOP setting. The CSO METHOD is very simple, but because it is new, it seems to be very complicated. CSO is certainly profound, and is the reason why a large book and several DVDS help explain this extraordinarily simple method.

THESE ARE THE TRUE FACTS ON HOW I RECREATED REMBRANDT'S BINDER MEDIUM, WHICH I NAMED ' CSO'

In 1988, I began my research to recreate Rembrandt's 'binder medium', resulting in the
'CalciteSun Oil/Emulsions' (CSO) binder and method of Oil Painting.
Here is the proof of my discovery: In 2004 I submitted a Patent application with the US Government.
My Patent, US 7141109 B1, was granted in 2006 (see details at conclusion).

In 1988, I bought THE book, that inspired me to recreate mixtures of 'calcium carbonate powder with a superior Flaxseed-Linseed oil', as used by Rembrandt. THAT book was the first edition titled: " ART IN THE MAKING:REMBRANDT", published in 1988 by the National Gallery Museum in London.
In that book I learned that 'calcium carbonate chalk' powder was found in Rembrandt's oil paint.

The problem was that Rembrandt's use of Calcium carbonate chalk was found in microscopic paint samples. The book gave no answers such as ratio mixtures. I had many questions, but there were also no other books with answers . Over the next several years, I unraveled Rembrandt's secret of HOW and WHY he added Calcium carbonate chalk powder to his oil paint.

1992: The next crucial research step was when I bought THE book published in 1992, titled " VELÁZQUEZ: Técnica y Evolución ", authored by Carmen Garrido-Perez, head of the Conservation Department of the Prado Museum in Madrid, Spain . As with Rembrandt, the Prado scientists
found that Velazquez also added Calcium carbonate Chalk, as well as Calcium Carbonate Calcite, to his oil paint. Velazquez additional use of 'calcite' opened up more avenues of inquiries and research.

1992: The final push to my research was THE very important book titled, " REMBRANDT: The painter at work ", written by the leading Rembrandt scholar of The Netherlands, Ernst Van De Wettering, who was also the head of the Rembrandt Research Project. Years later I met him in person at the Los Angeles Getty Museum on October 27, 2011. I introduced myself with my name only. He instantly smiled and his face lit up as he said, " OHHH ...THE MAN OF THE BINDING MEDIUM!"

AN ABUNDANCE OF SCIENTIFIC INFORMATION ... BUT NO ANSWERS

It is important to note that neither of these three very scholarly books, gave any ratio mixtures of the powdered 'Calcium Carbonate mixed with the oil'. Neither did they inform how it was mixed with pigments.
Additionally, they provided some evidence of Rembrandt and Velazquez using non-solvent Emulsions, but this added to the complexity of the mystery. There were many questions and no answers as to how
Rembrandt and Velazquez mixed and applied all of these various mixtures, to achieve the wondrous effects seen in their oil paintings.

It took me many years of actual 'hands on' testing to understand all the facts, to dispel all the myths, and to recreate the Calcite Sun Oil (CSO) oil paint binder, as well as the Emulsions, as were used by Rembrandt and Velazquez.

I published my research and in 2004, I sent copies of my book to several internet artists.
Now, one of those persons wishes to claim making mixtures of Calcium Carbonate chalk and oil
before receiving my book.

Here are the details of the proof of my discovery:
THE FOLLOWING FACTS ARE FROM THE RECORDS OF THE US GOVERNMENT:
To locate my patent on the internet, type in my name and my patent number.

Paint medium and method of production US 7141109 B1 ,
This application claims the benefit of U.S. Provisional Application No.
60/576,563 filed on Jun. 3, 2004, and U.S. Provisional Application No.
60/582,775 filed on Jun. 25, 2004, and U.S. Provisional Application No.
60/582,776 filed on Jun. 25, 2004,
and U.S. Provisional Application No. 60/588,925 filed on Jul. 19, 2004.
US7141109 B1

Application number.	US 11/127,335
Publication date.	Nov 28, 2006
Filing date	May 11, 2005
Inventors.	Louis R. Velasquez
Original Assignee.	Velasquez Louis

Thank you sincerely
Louis R. Velasquez
San Diego, California, USA, August 2017

www.ingramcontent.com/pod-product-compliance
Lightning Source LLC
Chambersburg PA
CBHW082326220526
45470CB00008B/2419